LIGHTS ON,
RATS OUT

LIGHTS ON, RATS OUT

A MEMOIR

CREE LEFAVOUR

Grove Press
New York

For Nicole LeFavour

So meshed in nerves and hesitation, it could not be a thing to be afraid of; yet it was a real beast, and this book its mangy skin, dried, stuffed and set up squarely for men to stare at.
                        —T.E. Lawrence, *Seven Pillars of Wisdom*

Prologue

I'm somewhere in the sprawling mess of suburban New Jersey, sitting on damp earth. Shielded from the road by a gravestone, I put a flame to my Camel Light. Whatever irony or black humor my location offers, the graveyard is the only privacy I can find in this ugly matrix of unknowable highways, roundabouts, turn lanes, and exits. No more than one hundred yards away my thirteen-year-old daughter moves pointlessly up and down the soccer field in her cheery yellow-and-blue uniform, long brown hair pulled back in a slick ponytail, trying her best to get to the ball.

It's been twenty years. Would it be as good as ever? Taking a drag to fire up the ember. Choosing my spot. Holding the burning cigarette to my skin. Feeling my brain bleed out in a state of perfect concentration. I'd go inside the sensation, will it into pleasure until it became just that. Bliss. Time at rest. The world stopped in a pinprick of pain-pleasure. I might stay, light and use a second cigarette on the spot, then rest on the interior of my mind where that inky calm holds.

I guess I never finished the task of knowing my own mind well enough to see this day coming. What misshapen root bears the strange urge that makes holding a cigarette to my skin seem not just a good idea, but necessary? There's only one person who knows this particular kind of crazy because he's been through it with me before, my former psychiatrist, Dr. Kohl. It's been more than two decades since I left Burlington, Vermont, for New York City after three years in treatment with him. What had this fetish meant to me then and how did I stop only to feel it quicken now? The answer flaps about somewhere in the past, snapping now and again like a flag in a strong wind.

I wouldn't care so much about solving the riddle of my desire but for the pain of reconciling it with the reality of my beautiful daughter just over there. I can't match the impulse with what I am to her and how I want her to know me: strong, reliable, with ample belief in this wonderful, strange life. I'm pulled outside myself by the ref's whistle mixing with the claps and yells of doting, vaguely bored parents positioned, as I should be, in a row of folding chairs on the sideline. I long for Dr. Kohl as I crush out my cigarette on the wet grass.

The whistle is my cue to dodge the busy traffic, step onto the field, find my daughter, and envelop her with whatever it is she needs. I can do this and whatever's necessary to maintain normalcy and I will. But I need to reclaim the self I once was, the one I left with Dr. Kohl, if I'm going to avoid the 3rd degree burn I suddenly want so badly to imprint on myself.

At home, untouched in the attic all these years, is the fat file Dr. Kohl kept during my treatment—each of our sessions written out in dialogue along with his notes to himself. He copied the documents and handed them to me when I departed. I've left the radioactive pages untouched all these years. Now I need them to take me back to my younger self, the one who would make her mark and cover it with transparent Band-Aids, long sleeves, and anything she could find to keep her secrets.

11/11/2012

A NOTE ON THE TEXT

I have written this memoir using all evidence at hand including files of physicians' notes, hospital records, and my own journals. I've quoted from these documents verbatim. Some include grammatical and spelling errors that I have retained for accuracy. I have changed the name of my psychiatrist and several identifying details to preserve his anonymity.

PART I

POTTER: *Oooo. It damn well 'urts.*
LAWRENCE: *Certainly it hurts.*
POTTER: *What's the trick, then?*
LAWRENCE: *The trick, William Potter, is not minding . . .*
    —Harry Fowler as William Potter and Peter O'Toole
        as T.E. Lawrence in *Lawrence of Arabia*

To cease utterly, to give it all up and not know anything
more—this idea was as sweet as the vision of a cool bath in a
marble tank, in a darkened chamber, in a hot land.
                    —Henry James, *The Portrait of a Lady*

Pain has an element of blank;
It cannot recollect
When it began, or if there were
A day when it was not.
                    —Emily Dickinson, "The Mystery of Pain"

CHAPTER 1

Kid Gloves

1st degree: a superficial burn of the epidermis. Grazing the bare forearm against a hot baking sheet loaded with sugar cookies might cause such a minor infliction. 1sts heal in days and leave no scar. Baby stuff. At the other extreme, the most severe 4th degree extends through the epidermis and dermis, damaging the subcutaneous tissue, including muscle and bone. House-on-fire-and-no-way-out bad. This meanie requires "excision," a word as hideous as the procedure: cutting away and removing dead flesh and damaged bone only to repair the gap with grafts of healthy skin harvested from elsewhere on the body.

At the upper middle of the order settles the fetching moderation of the 3rd. It destroys the epidermis and much or all of the dermis beneath but no muscle or bone. Yep. Three is my number, although I do flirt with upper 2nds in weaker moments or when rushed. I've done a lousy job before and the proof of it is no end of pain—2nd-degree burns hurt—it's a problem creating its own reward as I go back in to fix things up.

3rds and 4ths can be done with a lit cigarette if you try. It's all about "the prolonged action of any intense form of heat." That cherry glow produced by a puff on most factory-made cigarettes produces roughly 900°F heat; a smoldering cigarette hovers around 400°F. The royal tell is not just a loss of sensation but an unmistakable leathery, hard yellow-brown surface. Snakeskin boots. Alligator hide belt. Kid gloves. Getting there takes holding the cigarette in place until the pleasure's spent. No less than one cigarette will do, with plenty of puffs in between to keep it lit, but two work better, allowing moments of leisure to enjoy the experience between drags. In a severe 2nd or 3rd the blister takes hours, not minutes, to appear. When it does, there's no change at the center, although the spot may be circled by a delicate golden pus-engorged halo. 4ths are entirely above such mess.

I know I shouldn't get hung up on the numbers. Guillaume Dupuytren's original 1832 classification of burns orders a lax spectrum even if its weak logic crushes the chaos of the modern bible of psychiatric disorders, the *Diagnostic and Statistical Manual*, or DSM. Then again, the deranged Richter scale, with its base-10 logarithmic formula, in which an earthquake registering 6 on the Richter scale is ten times stronger than a 5, makes the other two seem simple. All three models muster their sorry best to grade extremities of damage only to confound what might have been made tangible. Dupuytren's fixation on a burn's depth starts to appear positively sensible next to the seismographic measure of earthquakes or the numerically crazed symptomology of mental illness.

Whatever the number, eventually the skin sloughs off in one round piece. What grows back a month later or more is not new skin—neither dermis nor epidermis—but scar tissue, pink at first, later white. It will never disappear, only flatten and fade over the years from pink to silver to white. It's all collagen like the miraculously perfect surrounding skin, but the fibers arrange themselves not in a neat basket weave but in a unidirectional mess. Fibrosis.

I hate to leave a spot lightly touched. There's no going halfway—1sts are a joke and minor 2nds aren't my element. For one thing they hurt—later, when I don't want them to. It's curious not minding intense pain. It means, among other things, that I can go back over burns done feebly, old or new, partially healed but still pink, wet, as if they're done. But they're not. They're in play, ready for more. Ready for service.

Right now I need skin and my options are limited. I've been busy. Not only am I running out of time, but the sorry facsimile of a cast—gauze masquerading as plaster—blocks access to the choicest spots. Amounting to little more than two and a half yards, 2.2 meters wide, it is evidence of what I experienced as porn-level excitement when at my last appointment Dr. Kohl revisited his dormant medical skills: disinfecting, dabbing, placing pads, layering gauze, securing all with two lengths of medical tape. The bandage is tangible proof of my psychiatrist's attention and through it I track a juicy snatch of time. I know my attachment to it is no more logical than a lusty squirrel's persistence in guarding a cache of empty, broken walnut shells.

Johns Hopkins's proud. *Go Blue Jays!* Enough talk therapy. Let's practice *real* medicine. Leaning close, my psychiatrist, Dr. Kohl, cradled my arm as he tenderly dabbed ointment and then meticulously wove the sterile gauze from wrist to midbiceps. There's no escaping it—without the dignity of a blank slate of plaster awaiting fond words and doodles the appearance of this unwieldy thing I'm so assertively attached to must disappoint. It'll have to do. I know that what the shell conceals isn't all bad: A heavy coat of white silver sulfadiazine ointment cools the flesh beneath squares of Telfa nonstick pads. The pads guard roughly one hundred wounds—in various stages of recovery—from the grab of the gauze that, other than being spectacularly showy, is there to hold the pads in place and absorb pus. The skin at the bottom of the assemblage is not so much skin as an oozy landscape of red, pink, white, and yellow flesh speckled with fresh scars. Inexplicably, I adore the whole gruesome mess.

I home in on the palm rather than destroying a shred of his sacred evidence. It's definitely available. Naked, fleshy, and thick, abductor pollicis brevis, flexor pollicis brevis, and adductor pollicis—the three muscles control the thumb.

I pause, focusing on the torn foil frame where seven circular butt ends compete for attention, their claim to distinction driven by no logic other than a conspiracy of confusion in which one or the other tries to stand out as *it*. The admittedly illogical project is to see beyond the trick, to divine the real, right one—sorting through the decoys occupies the greater part of the work. Thirty seconds pass before I recognize the one I'm meant to choose at the edge, half obscured by a wafer of shiny silver paper.

With a gentle pinch it's between my lips. One practiced motion: wrists in a huddle, hands cupped to protect against a nonexistent wind, head down, thumb grinding the ridged metal wheel, flame popping cheerfully into view as it meets the cigarette's raw end. A pull of breath completes my business as the precisely cut and glued paper sacrifices a few filaments of dry, broken tobacco leaf, fragile and ready for destruction as finely grated chocolate. The confident flame coaxes the dormant object to life, a lambent coal its proof. The first drag—now this is what lungs are for.

It can take a few seconds but once I muster the determination to land the burning end on the pristine skin I've chosen for the purpose, once I make initial contact, my mind and body blossom into exhilaration. The sensation reads as pain—hot and fresh. But when its animal simplicity surges landing on whatever part of my brain, whatever section of that flaccid organ occupies the space just behind my forehead, I own it. Like nothing else, I am here. I am positioned. I am.

Holding the cigarette down, I focus on the intensity, its deep center, its hyper-sensory wake. Drawing on the cigarette, bringing it back to life, going back in. Holding. Holding. Holding it down. Focusing on the pain, willing it into something else entirely. Clarity. Filter nearing, part of me relieved it's almost over. Fading. I hold it there as it makes its way deeper but I've already nailed the forbidden flush of transcendence; it lingers. And again because it's not over yet.

Sucking the cigarette a few more times to use the last of it, I hold it down, edging it wider for a jolt here and there as it finds a fresh nerve beyond the neat circumference I've created. The burned edge of the paper, barely alight, is the destroyed ground the camel on the rubbery filter appears to cross; it never fails to evoke the film image of T. E. Lawrence's exhausted animal Jedha crossing the Sinai Peninsula. I crush it right on the spot, hitting hard skin that sheds the gray-black ash, leaving behind a few flecks of cinder and enough ash to obscure a yellow center now the color of a fifty-pack-years smoker's index finger.

Then I do another. And another. One for my cheek. Three on the top of my foot. Two for the back of my hand. I have all night.

Every postburn cigarette is as good as the one after an egg sandwich with ham and American cheese on a toasted, buttered English muffin. Good as the one you light up after masturbating. Consummate. The first-of-the-day-sip-of-fresh-hot-milky-coffee right. One in a pack of twenty. Resplendent.

CHAPTER 2

Medical Emergency

The plane ticket tells me nothing more than the dull geography of my future: BTV–BWI. One way, 9:00 A.M., Wednesday, 9/10/91. It's a cryptic string signifying my flight from Burlington International Airport to Baltimore Washington International Airport on what will turn out to be a practically tropical September day. On the 11th—the day after tomorrow, at which point there will be precisely 111 days left in the year—I will be admitted to the locked ward of the Sheppard and Enoch Pratt Hospital as soon as it opens for business. It's happening. Dr. Kohl's letter reads:

September 10, 1991

To Whom It May Concern:

This letter is to substantiate that Cree LeFavour is undergoing a severe medical emergency necessitating immediate hospitalization.

Sincerely,

Adam N. Kohl, M.D.

LIGHTS ON, RATS OUT

Dr. Kohl laid my options before me like richly patterned carpets I might wish to go home with—or not. That was the day I blew the contract I'd signed a month or so prior: my promise to stop burning. In writing, in my file, was an impossible-to-dispute paper. I'd agreed that if I did burn myself even one more time I would go to a psychiatric hospital. Or never see him again. It's not even a close contest. My profound attachment to Dr. Kohl makes my choice simple. I've agreed to check myself in.

If I don't sign the voluntary admittance papers once I arrive at the hospital in Baltimore, if I prefer not to board the plane, Bartleby style, just one glance at the mess I've made of the skin on my arm will be enough for Dr. Kohl to rally any two psychiatrists and a judge in either Vermont or Maryland to agree to an involuntary commitment, otherwise known as a civil commitment. This, he argued, will happen whether I decline to admit myself or sign myself out once I'm in. A stay there is the only way to return to Dr. Kohl for treatment. He won't see me again unless I stay as long as I need to and earn honorable discharge. Then, and only then, can I come back to him at 112 Church Street to sit in my favorite chair. That was his play anyway; I'll go if I can have him.

This mess I'm in, sitting up through the night waiting for morning, playing with fire while I still can, began with ruthless scientific clarity a bit over a year ago. That was the day of my first appointment with Dr. Kohl. I went to him because I was a bulimic, unhappy, confused twenty-four-year-old. What I wanted, though I couldn't admit it to myself when I walked into his office for the first time, was for someone to recognize I needed help. The bulimia was just an excuse to get myself in the door; what I yearned for without expecting to find it in Dr. Kohl was an inchoate balm to soothe the lack I felt. I never once believed it was a thing that could be made, found, or bought.

For too long, as long as I can remember, I've been uncertain whether the effort to keep going day after day is worthwhile. Although there have been many times when I've felt alive and happy to be so, the older I've gotten the more exhausting it has become to don an acceptable disguise to present, one convincing enough to keep people from recognizing the odious, unworthy, deeply unhappy person beneath.

In going to a psychiatrist I feared seeking attention, asking for what I didn't need or deserve. Part of me still believes there's nothing wrong with me, or nothing self-discipline can't fix. The cycle of self-loathing goes on and on, part of what Freud called the "compulsion to repeat," in which the drive toward the inevitable end takes on a dark, unruly pattern. I'm more confused than ever about who I am and what I want, and yet in some form this feeling has been with me as long as I can remember. Maybe there's something fundamentally off and unfixable about who I am that makes me want to escape. What's worse is that some part of me likes it—a familiar masochism deep within relishes how special this shitty core makes me feel, how different I am from everyone else because of it.

My mind was less right than it ever had been when I asked for that first appointment with Dr. Kohl. My dreams were blurring the line between sleeping and waking, and the scary hallucinatory essence that followed me out of slumber was closing in on the day. Reality was slipping, nudged out by the presence of an ungainly force pressing against me.

Maybe that's why, when Dr. Kohl asked me on that first day, "What's your greatest fear?" the answer formed like a memorized line delivered slightly off cue, a beat too fast.

"Losing my mind."

Taller than me—and I'm six feet—he's trim, well proportioned, and wears what most upper-class East Coast males wear at leisure: soft earth-tone sweaters, button-down shirts in subdued blues, khaki pants, and plain leather lace-up dress shoes. My father dresses much the same way. Dr. Kohl is precisely put together and comfortable in his body, never fidgeting or shifting his penetrating gaze to escape mine. His brown eyes communicate a dangerous intelligence and sensational warmth. His plain brown straight hair is cut short. He has no scent—or maybe I've never gotten close enough to discern any. Being in his presence is to be recognized. From the moment he called me in from the waiting room and closed the door behind us that day I wanted what he had—a centered self.

His corner office occupies the ground floor of a two-story white-painted brick building in downtown Burlington. Three other psychiatrists share the building with him. The efficient receptionist answers the phone and writes out names, times, and dates on the doll-size appointment cards she hands to patients. She is master of the blocks of minutes that are transmuted into sessions she types out as billable hours on a humming dusty-blue Smith-Corona. The receptionist's handling of the grubby business of dispensing bills and collecting checks made out to Dr. Kohl confirms Freud's observation that "money matters are treated by civilized people in the same way as sexual matters—with the same inconsistency, prudishness, and hypocrisy."

Where we sat that first day and in the year and two months since, the space I'll find tomorrow before I leave for the airport, is tasteful and understated with a worn couch upholstered in Bing cherry velvet positioned under a wide horizontal window. I sit on the leather swivel chair facing him. His broad desk angles away from the wall, its position blocking any view of the framed photographs there. A side table with a clock and a box of tissues separates the couch and my beloved chair—the one I've collapsed into session upon session right from the beginning.

After the first time, I remember sliding the magic token of an appointment card into my back pocket with only one of the six lines completed: 7/19/90, just like the one I have now marked for tomorrow—9/10/91. Dr. Kohl's name is printed on top, immediately beneath the line for my name, M _____ HAS AN APPOINTMENT WITH, and then DR. ADAM N. KOHL. Six blank lines skip down the length of the card with space for the date punctuated by AT followed by a smaller blank for the time.

As I drifted down the sidewalk in the garish light reflecting off Lake Champlain that first day, I imagined a completed card, even a full deck, the ink expanding accordion-like down linked rectangles representing future time in his presence.

CHAPTER 3

IPE

Initial Psychiatric Evaluation (IPE)—Date of Evaluation:
6/26/90; **Referred by:** Self; **Patient's Name:** Cree LeFavour;
Sex: ♀; **Age:** 24; **Birth Date:** 9/20/65.

1. PRESENTING PROBLEMS:

"I'd like to pinpoint why I'm unhappy. (Though I've felt
a lot worse.) I've been really depressed."

Rxs [symptoms] of her depression:
1. "I hide completely, shut self off, don't speak, isolation
   is really key. Need. I find a lot of freedom in that."
2. "Feel a need to escape and not contact anyone."
3. "Abstain from everything, including food."
4. "Sleep as reaction to depression."

Relationship: 1. "'I feel like Matthew's mother.' This
has brought something out in her. 'I used to be more
independent, more myself.'"

As a psychiatrist with an M.D. from Johns Hopkins might do, he probed my mind during the first appointment as if he meant to take a scalpel to it, his purposeful manner failing to suppress the attar of sympathy that memorably bathed every one of my senses. Emboldened by my instinct that it was my only chance to show him everything—"What you say here is confidential"—I told the truth, blushing when he asked me how often I had sex and if I had orgasms. His directness and interest in the minutiae of my biography tempted my starving narcissist to deliver monologues I didn't know I'd been waiting to perform.

The IPE proceeds:

2. **RECENT STRESSORS:** He checks **Pregnancy** and notes "abortion" in the column **EXPLANATIONS.** He also checks **Marriage, Divorce, Separation, Argument,** adding, "Relationship with Matthew Agnew." He checks **Change in Residence** but not **Sexual Difficulties.** I miss out on **Sudden Increase in Wealth, Extended Vacation.** If only.

3. **PAST PSYCHIATRIC HISTORY:** All questions beginning with **When last felt well** on through **Prior psychiatric treatment with** _____ and **Drug, Individual and Group Therapy, ECT, Hospitalizations, Longest period without psychiatric care, Diagnosis, Successful medications, Medication problems** are blank or show a 0.

4. **PAST PSYCHOLOGICAL HISTORY—CHILDHOOD:** He checks **Yes** for **Math difficulty, Falls or accidents, Left handed, Nightmares, Fear of dark, Death or separation in**

family, and **Frequent moves.** I've happily escaped a check
in the **Yes** column for **Cruelty to Animals, Fire Setting,**
and the ominous **Promiscuity, deviation, incest.**

5. **PRESENT PSYCHOSOCIAL AND
NEUROPSYCHOLOGICAL HISTORY:** He checks **Yes**
for **Phobias, Obsessions, Rituals,** and **Excessive Eating,
Vomiting** ("None for 3 months; used to do it more"),
Speeding ("Likes to go 85 mph"), **High Fever** ("When
younger"), and **Dizziness** ("Fainted once"). He adds and
underlines, "Severe Nightmares." Even if bulimia was my
ticket in the door, my up-front reason for going, it was a
symptom that paled next to my scary obsessions. I wasn't
going to go into this private madness straight off; I just
said yes when he asked if I had "obsessions."

6. **MEDICAL HISTORY:** He notes, "Broke limbs falling
off horses" and circles the words **Alcohol, Cigarettes,**
and **Street Drugs.** I tell him I've smoked, swallowed, or
chewed "marijuana, cocaine, hallucinogenic mushrooms,
ecstasy (MDMA), and speed." But I don't do any drugs
now nor have I done any for at least three years. I drink
very little these days—a beer now and again.

7. **FAMILY HISTORY:** "Father (56) and mother (52)
divorced in 1981. Father is a chef and lives in St.
Helena, California. Throughout her childhood he
owned restaurants in Aspen, Idaho, and California.
Mother lives with her partner in Eureka, CA. Sister,
Nicole, good health, close, lives in Idaho." He then asks

me for maternal and paternal history of various mental
disorders. He marks **Yes** for a history of **Depression;
Mental Illness, Alcohol,** and **Drug Use; Eccentricity,
Creativity; Aggression, Mood Swings,** and **Financial
Problems.** As a whole we LeFavours managed to escape
Yes to **Attempted/Committed Suicide** along with various
physical disorders like **Cancer, Stroke,** and **Color
Blindness.** We seem to have the remainder covered.

8. **MARITAL AND SEXUAL HISTORY:** Under **If Female**
in the column **Most of Life** he checks **Difficulty Getting
Excited, Disinterest in Sex,** and **Masturbation,** noting
after the last, "Don't now, in this relationship." All but
one of the remaining questions have checks under **Never,**
including **H/O Fetishes, Cross-Dressing; Reaching
Orgasm Too Quickly;** and **Sexuality with Females.**
Contraception: "Diaphragm." **Frequency of Intercourse:**
"3 x/week." Under the remaining **Different Sexual Habits**
he writes "???"

9. **EDUCATION:** "Middlebury, B.A. 1988"

10. **WORK AND FINANCIAL HISTORY:** "Chittenden
Community Action. Helps people with welfare
problems." He notes to himself, "Emotionally
really dangerous."

11. **HOBBIES, SPORTS HISTORY:** "Read a lot—no
favorite. Used to compete x country skiing (high school).
Now I don't exercise."

12. RELIGIOUS AND SOCIAL HISTORY: "Parents both atheists, me too."

13. MILITARY HISTORY: 0.

The final part of the form has a separate title: **MENTAL STATUS EXAMINATION (IPE).** He skips all but two of the unnumbered sections, including categories for **BEHAVIOR, BEHAVIORAL EXPRESSION OF AFFECT,** and **DISORDERS OF SPEECH.** Under **COGNITIVE FUNCTIONING** he completes only **Estimated Intelligence:** "Above average." He then skips all but the last part of the longest category, **APPERCEPTUAL FUNCTIONING,** including **Hallucinations, Thought Disorder,** and **Delusions,** to focus on **Proverbs and Similarities: Stitch in Time, Bird in Hand,** and **Glass Houses.** I pass, completing the phrases with the correct proverbs and explaining the meaning of each. It was a fairly simple, not particularly accurate test of abstract reasoning—proverbs are, after all, culturally specific. I came up cold on **Burnt Child.** (The answer is, "A burned child dreads the fire," meaning we learn to avoid harm through painful experience. At the time, having never burned myself with a cigarette, I didn't recognize the uncanny significance of my failure to complete the phrase.) My reply to the final partial proverb, **Tongue Is Enemy,** was apparently worth note: "Talk too much get head cut off." What an odd proverb to include on a questionnaire to launch a course of psychotherapy. **Similarities** are: **Orange—Apple:** "Fruit," **Airplane—Bird:** "Fly," and **Man—Squirrel:** "animals."

ASSESSMENT

1. Symptoms (DSM-II)
> Axis I: "<u>Bulimia</u>"
> Axis II: "Bulimia with vomiting long history
> History of depression
> History of severe drug abuse (alcohol, cocaine,
> amphetamines)"

2. Circumstances Associated with Symptoms
> **a. Environment:** "F/H [family history] alcoholism."
> **b. Physical Illness:** "Ⓛ handed, Ⓡ eyed."
> **c. Drug Abuse:** "Alcohol abuse in college; heavy
> use of amphetamines, 1987 (6 weeks); periods of
> regularly using cocaine but not for long (2 weeks)."
> **d. Other:** "Severe family deprivation (left totally alone
> at age 13). Learned to survive alone so she equates
> surviving with aloneness." I tell him, "My mom not a
> mom, just not mothering type." He writes, "Aloneness
> is source of depression." I report that my sister and I
> had lived alone since I was in 9th grade. "It's just the
> way it was." "LITTLE BUDDY = small child who was
> totally unattended." That was my mother's favorite
> nickname for me. Rosy Rotten Crotch was another.

PLAN:
> "1. Discussed alcohol, speed, cocaine with her." What he
> said was if I was doing drugs or drinking there was no
> point to being in therapy.

> There is no number two. Time was up.

The IPE interview was not my first encounter with Dr. Kohl. I'd been to his office once before as a favor to my then boyfriend, Matt, who asked me to come along to one of his weekly appointments with Dr. Kohl. These sessions were mandatory—whether by agreement with his parents or by court order. Matt told me only that there was an incident in high school. Despite our living together for more than a year the explanation remains a void I fill with the worst possibilities: gruesome suicide attempt, child molestation, unspeakable violence. Those are the worst causes I can think of—the only answers to explain why he refuses to tell me what happened and why he is required to see Dr. Kohl once a week. I'd agreed to go along to one of Matt's sessions to describe his lack of motivation and offer my insight into the bad choices he made. Matt thought me quite eloquent on these points.

Curious as I was about meeting a psychiatrist—would he see through me and if so what would he see?—I had no idea how significant the request would be in determining who I would become and where I'd end up. After meeting Dr. Kohl for the first time, I asked for an appointment of my own. Without that introduction I would not have had the courage or audacity to see a psychiatrist, no matter how I felt. It simply wasn't in my WASP-atheist-hippie repertoire.

I remember the throat-tightening embarrassment of asking if he had time or would be willing to see me. In part I was ashamed because of my very secret bulimia. Even more shaming was admitting I wanted his help, imagining I might be worthy of seeing a psychiatrist. Begging for money from him would have been easier than requesting 55 minutes of his amply compensated time.

At the end of our third session he gave me a suggestion and two homework assignments.

First, Overeaters Anonymous. I scoff. As a devout atheist and someone who loathes group anything, I wasn't going near a VFW hall or church basement. I'm not sure how rude about this I was at the time. Likely, very.

Second, write down how often and what foods I ate. A "Vomiting Diary." The name alone was enough to make me want to stop. I agreed to comply, as sobering as it was to see the pattern of failure on paper. Showing him the diary was the rebar cementing my humiliation.

Third, read Alice Miller's *The Drama of the Gifted Child*. I devoured every word. "Gifted" in the context of Miller's theory refers to certain children's heightened sensitivity to the dynamics of the adults around them. Her point is if these adults are self-involved or neglectful the hyper-attuned—"gifted"—child exhausts herself to please her parents. The price she pays is the negation of her individuality and all the needs, desires, and emotions that belong to it. It all sounded terribly familiar.

* * *

Dr. Kohl and I quickly covered the facts of my past over the next several months while I fell more and more in thrall to him and the process. I was born in Aspen, Colorado. I have one sister, Nicole, sixteen months older. She is a teacher and political activist living in Boise, Idaho. Different as we are in character, body, and intellect, you'd know we're sisters at a glance even if only from the jaw we share and the sound of our voices. On the phone nobody can tell us apart. Having shared a childhood we carry a collective knowledge nobody else is privy to. It makes a powerful bond.

My father the chef—gentle, brilliant, and emotionally withdrawn. Little as he knows—or has wanted to know—of my inner life, my father's warmth and generosity are rich compensation for his flaws. Always financially supportive given his income from the trusts that held the family newspapers in upstate New York, he agreed to pay the roughly $40 per psychiatry session my insurance doesn't cover. He is remarried and retired, having sold his well-regarded restaurant, Rose et LeFavour, in the Napa Valley, where he lives.

My mother, who doesn't do much, lives in the far reaches of Northern California. She once played at being an artist—she painted, made sculptures, worked stained glass—but lacked discipline and drinks too much. She's tough, cool, and one of the boys—a flirt who kept up with the men hunting deer, ducks, grouse, and elk as easily as she keeps pace with them at the bar. It has been a long time since she was pleasant to be around until she has imbibed her necessary dose of vodka, gin, tequila, whiskey, beer, or wine. Until my teens I failed to connect drinking to why she was brittle and snappy until midday only to unfold, growing voluble and funny as the day unraveled into night. As I told Dr. Kohl, "The mother I liked was drunk. Bitch mother was sober."

In 1965, the year I was born, my parents opened the Paragon, a restaurant in Aspen. Occupied with the new business, they left my sister and me in the care of a string of live-in babysitters, including an eighteen-year-old girl and her 55-year-old boyfriend. Our community in Aspen was tight and lively. Gonzo journalist Hunter S. Thompson was a neighbor and friend. The levels of drugs, booze, and guns during the first decade of my life in Aspen, between 1965 and 1974, were abundant. I was nine when we moved to Robinson Bar Ranch, a hybrid hot springs–dude ranch in central Idaho. OshKosh B'gosh overalls, turtleneck, Keds sneakers, and long braids, Laura Ingalls Wilder style, were my look back then. For a year Nicole and I attended Stanley School, a two-room Quonset hut at the base of the Sawtooth Mountains. I was ten years old and the only student in fifth grade. The next year we were homeschooled by a hired teacher who taught a gaggle of kids whose parents lived and worked on the Ranch.

After three years running Robinson Bar as a restaurant and inn my family left to spend the dark winter months traveling in the South Pacific. We returned to Idaho on Christmas Eve 1978 from what was billed as a "round the world" trip four months and half the globe shy of our April goal. Given the limited options for high school in rural central Idaho we first rented and then bought a small second house in Sun Valley. Cutting the trip short meant I spent half of seventh grade, Nicole half of eighth grade, at the public middle school in Hailey. The following September we enrolled in the private Ketchum–Sun Valley Community School for the remainder of high school.

Unsettled, my parents shuttled that first year and a half between the Ranch and the house in Sun Valley as they did their best to ignore the drab marriage they'd tried to escape by traveling halfway around the world. By the end of my first year at the Ketchum–Sun Valley Community School my mother had left my father and they divorced. I was thirteen years old when my father left Idaho for the Bay Area. I lived pretty much parent-free in Sun Valley for the next four years, my sister with me for all but my final year of high school. My mother, having fallen in love with my best friend's mother, had disappeared to enjoy her second adolescence. She spent the years between 1979 and 1983 living with various girlfriends or at the Tunnel Rock Café, a funky place she bought one hundred miles north of Sun Valley with the proceeds of the sale of the Ranch.

Before college I took a year off to live in Norway while pursuing the last gasp of my career as a cross-country skiing prodigy. I then spent four years at Middlebury College in Vermont, graduating in spring 1988. That first postcollege summer I lived in Taos, New Mexico, working in a bakery, as far away as I could get from anyone I knew. I returned east that autumn to work for the newspapers that had been held in trust for my father for nearly two decades, the same newspapers that had supplied the money to support the family in the absence of any truly profitable business. In January 1989 I escaped back up to Vermont, leaving the grim rust belt landscape west of Albany along with my humiliating newspaper apprenticeship as the boss's daughter. In Burlington I rented an apartment and found a waitressing job. I left my apartment the following August to move in with Matt. A year later, right around the time I quit my waitressing job and started working at Chittenden Community Action (CCA) as a low-income advocate, I left Matt. I was used to living alone; having my own apartment again was like returning home after a long, unsuccessful trip.

*   *   *

Working for CCA didn't require calculated charm the way my former waitressing job did, although I soon discovered it stuck to me in the same way, only this time accumulating over the months to form a critical mass of human misery and hopelessness. The people who sat in the chair by my desk now needed real help—not just coffee, eggs, and toast on the double. I got to know many of them: a different sort of regular from what I was used to.

Dr. Kohl noted on his intake that CCA was "emotionally very dangerous" work. He was right. The parade of suffering and especially the kids with their vacant looks and flat affects pulled me down. Happy endings were rare. A little salve here, a Band-Aid there; nothing much ever changed. I was perpetually ashamed: how fucking spoiled I was, how devoid of the simple grace to be content in the material paradise that has long been mine.

Most nights I got lost in a novel—*The Master and Margarita*, *The River Why*, *A Confederacy of Dunces*, *The Adventures of Augie March*. When books failed me or I needed a break from the relentless quiet of the room that seemed to turn up the volume of my thoughts, I took breaks by bingeing and purging. Frosted Flakes afloat in cold milk. A pint of Mint-Oreo Ben & Jerry's. Buttery, salty fusilli. Avoiding the obligations answering the phone might impose, I cringe at its sound, rarely answering. The cycle was unstoppable. I soaked in the scalding, soapy water of the bathtub, hoping some part of me might dissolve.

Dr. Kohl argued from the start that surviving by isolating myself had worn out its usefulness. What had once been a necessary adaptation to protect me from rejection was cutting off any real chance at happiness. He has prodded me to form relationships outside his office and spend more time in contact with my sister and the few friends I have. But rather than getting better as I continued therapy over the summer and fall of 1990—socializing more, throwing up less often, feeling happier, sleeping better—I got worse.

Maybe Dr. Kohl's wrong and I am a natural loner. It feels that way. But he calls me an "unlikely misanthrope," meaning that although I cultivate being alone it's unlikely I'm incapable of emotional connection. He theorizes that I avoid people out of fear, insecurity, arrogance, and sheer habit. I'm not so sure. Being alone feels real.

In November, four months in, it seems, however, he wasn't sure.

"Can she not feel real contact?" he wrote in a note to himself. "I feel contact with her here or has it not been there?"

CHAPTER 4

Fabulous Patient

The ritual. An hour before every 8:00 A.M. appointment I sit down on the leatherette banquette of Henry's Diner for pre-session prep. I sort myself out on paper the best I can. There, at 55 Bank Street in the same booth by the window under the fluorescent lights, I've been an irregular regular: Mondays and Thursdays. I don't chat. I don't know anyone's name. No one knows mine. Once, a waitress called me "Honey" or maybe "Hon," but it must have felt as wrong to her as it did to me. She never tried it again.

They take my order and write it down every time even though it never changes: Cinnamon toast, $2. Regular coffee, $1.25. Total $3.25 + 9 percent meals tax of 29 cents = $3.54 + tip. Somebody delivers a clean glass ashtray, Green Wave cup and saucer, coffee, Dairlyland creamers, and a set of silverware swaddled in a white paper napkin. I always leave $6 on the red-flecked Formica table next to the scalloped edge of the paper placemat. The tip ensures the occasional swapping out of the dirty ashtray and a steady flow of timely refills.

At 7:55 A.M. I walk the two blocks to Dr. Kohl's office, where his black Lamborghini reliably presents itself, slick as a wet snake, the engine still hot from the 22-minute drive from Charlotte. Fresh off the road, it exudes heat steady as fresh blacktop into the usually chill Vermont mornings. Metal clicking, contracting, expanding; the engine does its expensive thing quite alone in its special parking place in front of the tidy white-painted brick building. Dr. Kohl is an understated, modest man; the car appears to be his one indulgence.

By the time I arrive he's inside, but there's no point in trying the door before 7:58 A.M., when he unlocks it. Once in a while when he's late his car is there but, having gone inside to do whatever he does before his day begins, he finds me trying the door as he comes to turn the latch.

The embarrassment and excitement of his proximity outside the formality of his office thrill and sicken me. The experience is surpassed only by weigh-ins on the doctor's scale in the bathroom located just off his office. It seems I'm not the only one with an eating disorder. Once we're inside the tiny bathroom together, the intimacy of the space, his presence so close I can hear his breath, his arm reaching close to slide the weight up or down the metal arm of the scale until it finds my equal, prompts a frisson of sexually charged humility I can live off for days. When he marvels at my anticipation of the number to the half pound I smile; I don't own a scale but this is no great feat for anyone worth her Axis I eating disorder.

You might call my refusal of all pleasantries at the beginning of each session a tic: he nods me in from the waiting room, and inside there's never so much as a "Hello," no chatting about the weather or the weekend or any other polite throat clearing. Once we're settled I go. You might think this would be awkward. It always is. Maybe I like the awkwardness because it collapses the distance between the public space out there and the private one with just us inside behind the double soundproof doors.

Fabulous patient that I am, I launch right into whatever I've planned to say in that loaded moment a second after the bag and coat are heaped on the floor to the side of the leather chair. By then Dr. Kohl faces me, clipboard in lap, chair pulled out from behind the desk for an unobstructed line of contact. A fresh page for the day with my name and the date at the top waits to be covered in the ink of his pen—then it's time—55 minutes to go.

I feel liberated with him. Usually an expert with pleasantries—they lubricate and diffuse virtually every interaction to a repulsive degree, shorting out real contact—I refuse them in his office. It's the only place I've ever been where I'm free to not pretend to be something I'm not without fear of judgment. He never makes me feel like a freak. I decided early on that if I don't tell the truth, if I'm a coward, the delicate process would be a fraud and I'm far too reverential of what goes on between us to compromise it.

The practice of free association, the act of speaking without censoring what surfaces in the mind, was invented by Josef Breuer in the 1881 case history of Anna O., the ur-patient of psychotherapy. It was Anna O. who invented the term "talking cure" to describe what Freud referred to as the "cathartic method." It was also Freud who developed the rich significance of this kind of speech over the course of his seminal career. Anna O. called the process of unearthing unconscious thoughts "chimney sweeping." Smart girl. How apt that the material just beneath conscious thought figures in Anna's phrase as a wasteland, burned through, messy cinders the residue of memory.

That's what it feels like to me. And yet I'm still surprised when my feelings and desires get lost in the sooty mix Dr. Kohl and I generate together. The marvels of the subconscious and the devilry of the process: snatching that first "free" association before it's covered up by the mind's censors, bringing my unconscious mind's scary detritus to the surface. The process demands disturbing honesty—direct, unfiltered speech so far buried I don't even realize it's mine. But in the context of Dr. Kohl's office, with him as my confessor, I forgot I'd been trained to monitor thought before speech.

If I'd known the first thing about psychotherapy when I began maybe all of this disruption wouldn't have been such a surprise. As I've learned, treatment would be a failure if no mess were made; it's practically the point. Given the workings of transference and countertransference—the baggage the patient and doctor bring to their relationship from past experience and how it mingles in treatment between the two—it's impossible to predict what will evolve between doctor and patient.

Once the patient is invested there are, as Freud noted, "two alternatives: either she must relinquish psychoanalytic treatment or she must accept falling in love with her doctor as an inescapable fate." As dated as this view may be, I'm with the poet Anne Sexton, who called this imbalance the "big cheat."

Why did it have to be that way? Maybe because the falling in love, what Freud calls the "erotic transference" brings out an extraordinary opportunity, even a central opportunity, for analysis. "To urge the patient to suppress, renounce or sublimate her instincts in the moment she has admitted her erotic transference would be not an analytic way of dealing with them, but a senseless one." I was drawn in by Dr. Kohl himself but also by the artificial premise of two people sitting in a room facing one another with nothing more on the agenda but forming a relationship.

Even if I had understood the usefulness of my emotions when I began to see Dr. Kohl the knowledge wouldn't have done me any good. Reason had no chance. I fell in love with Dr. Kohl fast, quickly experiencing an entirely novel depth of affection and longing. I failed to calmly accept my feelings for him and the implied rejection—his inability to reciprocate my love—that was a condition of the analytic situation. I learned by hard experience what Freud meant when he wrote that whether the doctor's rejection is verbalized or not, "the patient will feel only humiliation, and she will not fail to take her revenge for it."

If I was ever afraid of what Dr. Kohl might have thought of me and consciously tailored my words to please or manipulate him, I would have squandered the conspicuously precious time I had with him. However brave I felt speaking "truth," our exchanges still felt like mind games played out in gestures, facial expressions, and our choice of words. The mistakes we made were as telling as the successes. No matter the results, I delighted in every moment of it.

CHAPTER 5

Hard to Fake

I'd long believed my childhood was privileged and, if not ordinary, not a significant factor in my uneven mental state; I liked to give myself full credit for that. I experienced what Dr. Kohl called depression as a sort of miasma I passed through in high school and college; as therapy progressed it settled for good, a thick fog I can't find the edge of.

"I'm alienated and separate," I told him a month or so after my first session; it's a feeling that "creates a distance from other people. I'm more authentic, not being fake, when I feel depressed. My ability to withdraw avoids compromising" myself.

"How old is the depression?" Dr. Kohl asked.

"Last year of high school," I replied, not quite certain how far back my desire to withdraw and hide could be called "depression." What I can date to high school is the all-consuming self-loathing and hopelessness. The self-sufficient, calm person I present to the world, the one I see as an act, has long drained me. Pleasing and polite, this competent persona is so at the ready I confuse her with the real me.

I'm a chameleon, able to adapt to please almost anyone. Of course this leaves me questioning everyone else's authenticity.

Because I'm so changeable it's difficult to trust who I am unless I'm alone, not pretending. When alone I look back and feel tainted by contact as my smooth performance jars against a hypersensitive core. Curt tones, scents of exclusion, subtle hints I'm intruding, mild criticisms, even compliments—none of it shows but all of it penetrates. I respond to most requests and invitations as traps, future obligations to put on a show. When I do talk about myself truthfully my internal self deflates the moment—what I should have kept private hits the air.

I can be cold or even mean without realizing it. As adept as I am at reading others, I have a limited sense of my own affect. Anyone who puts on a polished or calculated performance repels me—maybe because I know too well how to play that game myself. With the exception of a tiny handful of people, I don't care what people think of me—I'm far too busy most of the time managing my own thoughts. I'm almost too good at being around others but I always pay the price for my own show later, when I realize I've lost track of what I think, of who I am or want to be. Time alone or with Dr. Kohl is the only cure.

I've survived the time between therapy appointments these fourteen months by filling it with the only contact I can tolerate: a smoke with my only real friend in town, Jess, a skinny, sweet butch lesbian I could talk to all day; a long-distance call with my sister replete with a blood-quickening fight that's as rich and unfiltered as my exchanges with Dr. Kohl; attending my two graduate classes at the University of Vermont, where, as I was in the last two years of college, I'm the A+ student who never talks to anyone but the professor; and of course, performing sad duties forty hours a week at Community Action. In the gaps of this life I fit in familiar, comforting sex with my old boyfriend,

Matt. These messy exchanges are mostly driven by some animal need for human contact—I mean touch, not even sex.

I broke up with Matt last September for many reasons— he'd cheated on me for one. His body is skinny as a Chinese long bean; he has fair wavy hair halfway down his back and kind lucent blue eyes compassed by wire frames holding thick lenses. I felt lonelier when I was with him than alone—at once used and unwanted. The way I experienced my time with him echoed the way I felt growing up: I was handy, often quite useful, but never the priority.

When I discovered Matt had cheated on me for a second time I told Dr. Kohl how I had refused to so much as open, never mind read or respond to, the letter of apology the woman Matt had slept with slipped under my door. I put the unopened letter back under her door. But then it felt wrong.

"I don't know if I should have done that."

"I know you don't."

"I'm going to make everyone feel bad about it" was followed by but then I need "to fix everything up."

"Like you did with your parents."

"Yes . . . but I don't want to be gratuitously mean." This is one of my fears—a thing my sister accused me of when we fought. I hate mean people and I didn't want to be one of them.

"Overwhelming betrayal that takes the breath away," he said then, almost to himself. He applied mercy where I'd installed a raft of doubt and shame.

"If sadness and despair is present after November trip then consider Prozac," he wrote in mid-November, prior to Thanksgiving break.

*   *   *

I'd been seeing Dr. Kohl for four months at a low point in November. The frost had wiped out every trace of green but no snow had yet fallen to camouflage the ugliness of the landscape. I felt myself winding down, going soft, giving up. I'd invited Matt for dinner, desperate for a connection of any kind beyond 112 Church Street. Returning from work, I showered and then, to fill up the emptiness, gratified my self-loathing by gorging myself on ugly carbs and throwing up before he arrived. The action of bingeing and purging mirrored, as Dr. Kohl pointed out, my deep ambivalence about sex with Matt, "Something I try to say no to but can't." I guess I was warming up.

At these moments of abandon hatred eats me as if I'm the dessert; the demolition of my will to resist followed by gulps of ice cream's frozen cream and sugar, the crunch and give of frosted cookies, bowls of crispy, milky cereal and other dainties ending in the final sad, sweet thrill of denial.

Numbly eating whatever the fuck I want in whatever quantity I desire is relaxing, but it's the feeling I have after I throw up that I return for.

"Haven't you realized how calm you feel?" Dr. Kohl asked during one of our seemingly unending discussions of why I did it, what I got out of it.

"Calm . . .yes," I said, acknowledging the post-purge euphoria, the afterglow that is the bewitching reward. My uneasiness soothed for at least an hour.

I've long detested my physical self. I'm tall but just plain big when I'm overweight, well proportioned, but ungainly. Changing my body, manipulating it, was all I could come up with as a focus; to be thin had long masked itself as a prerequisite to change, as if rapture waited if I could shed the burdensome twenty pounds of flesh that weighed me down. To be thinner has always represented a tiny triumph over chaos, although I'm not sure it represented the desire to disappear or return to a prepubescent state as is so often said of girls who want to waste away.

As the inability to master the desire to eat for sport failed, my mind contracted into a taut loop of disgust. I'm ashamed of my vanity, of caring about how fat I am and eating too much anyway. What kind of feminist am I? But I wasn't able to stop. I'd increased the frequency of bingeing and purging, often throwing up two to three times every day and as many as six times in one day. If only food were like air—necessary to life but never chosen, impossible to overindulge in. I thought I was truly hungry once but desire has gobbled up too much of me. Now I can't tell the difference between filling up and eating. The familiar raw, scraped feeling I know so well as the aftermath left me wondering that day, waiting for Matt, what to do next.

I remember that chilly, late autumn day so well. I felt light enough to float into the cool austerity around me. A Camel Light was all I needed to pull myself together before Matt arrived. I sat outside on the stair, the porch boards' shiny gray splinters clinging to my wool socks, the arctic air getting the better of the angled sun.

Before my cigarette had burned through Matt appeared, calling to me, his stride energetic and playful. As he leaned for a kiss, his cold nose grazed my cheek. He's a VW mechanic. That day he was fresh from his cars and men, clothes stinking of engine oil and exhaust, breath heavy with cigarettes and beer. As usual he'd spent the day on his back, floating around on a mechanic's creeper looking at the undersides of antique Volkswagens, making small talk about the dynamics of metal, rubber, grease, gasoline, and sparks. He'd no doubt finished the day by passing a pipe or jay with his boss and the other mechanic. Rarely have I seen him not at least slightly stoned.

I went inside with him that day and observed him take a chair and yank open the broadsheet *Burlington Free Press*, turning the pages slowly, taking time to read each headline, lingering on the comics' splashy colors. I was in the kitchen cooking when he caught me watching. From experience he knew he was expected to speak—as if I was always eager for him to ask me about my day, how busy I'd been, and to talk about his day. I remember catching his weary consciousness of duty snap-to. Afraid to be caught out by letting too much time pass, he deliberately folded the paper and set it aside. I then watched the machinations of his lips and eyes as he clumsily attempted to pay attention to me.

"You have a good day?"

"Fine," I said. "Not too bad. Slow. How's yours?"

"Good, good. Worked on that blue '67 bus. You know the one, big white roof rack? Needed brakes, shocks, muffler. Darla, she used to work with me at Blondin's. I don't know, it was good to see her again, you know. Nice bus. You know the one? Blue, new paint."

"No, I don't know. It doesn't matter. So your day went okay? That's good." It's always been easy to be chilly when he was oblivious, trying to make conversation and failing. I was playing nice. That day I was barely pulling it off, with an inchoate rage building that had little to do with him. I was better off without him but I needed more reason than my own estrangement to give up and shut him out for good. So there I was, making him dinner.

He picked up the paper, unfolding it. Released, he was soon engrossed. I thought, fuck him and fuck everyone. Not worth the bother. The surface of the pasta water rose and broke, the edge green with olive oil. My lenses captured and held the steam, rendering the scene's clean lines a milky distance.

I had nine minutes remaining on the timer when I heard a flourish of rustling as Matt neatly folded the newspaper to move on to the glossy pages of *Popular Mechanics*—or maybe it was *Car and Driver*.

As if it's before me now, I see the sauce sputter, bubbles exploding with force enough to blot the white enamel surface of the stove with red circles. It's caught the pox and what a little wife I was and I knew I'd probably fuck him later, half willing, almost present. Later, tasting him, I'd wonder why. Occupying the role—daughter, friend, sister, employee. I still can't tell why I need to pretend that I'm okay. I hated Matt for failing to notice how not okay I was that night.

I was hardly there as I poured tomato sauce over the pasta, scattered cheese, rolled and tore basil. The bruised herb focused me for a flash, flooding the present with a woozy pleasure; I remember recognizing the smell as the best thing that had happened to me all day.

I studied my plate as Matt ate, his chewing too loud. Distracting myself in an effort to hold back any display of weakness, I remembered Goethe's line "You don't know what life tastes like" unless you've cried and eaten at the same time. No way. Explaining the tears was work I didn't want; Matt has never known how to respond to my inarticulate misery or understood how cooking and eating dinner could be a lie concealed by a performance. I keep many secrets.

I waited for words. Not giving up hope of hearing a whisper to catch me, to draw me in and hold me. Instead, the quiet snuggled right up close until I was adrift, easily far enough away that words could no longer find me. I then observed the scene from outside: vertigo did me in at that insufficient supper.

In the bedroom I lay facedown on the mattress, suffocation position. I could have drowned in the sheets and blankets, warm and quiet. Just me.

Why did I ask him over that night? He never demanded much more than sex from me and that he has expertly exacted with flattery and a palpable desire that even I find worth a response. Until I don't.

What happened to me? Didn't I once yearn for more than pure sex, for the feeling of skin on skin, arms and legs entangled with another body? I simply wanted to be left alone. Human contact could never quite hold me in place.

CHAPTER 6

Chiclets or Razzles?

How did I go from being a mildly depressed bulimic with a history of abandonment and neglect to pressing cigarettes on my skin until the pain is used up? How did I go from a highly functional, responsible twenty-five-year-old to a patient heading for a locked psychiatric ward? I'd say there were two reasons: the 11s and Dr. Kohl.

The number 11 represents my own, entirely personal dark magic. Appearing with unnerving frequency, it is the icon of my nutty religion or maybe, less generously, the sign of my private cult.

The way a Jesus fanatic sees an outline of the Virgin Mary burned into a slice of toast once in a lifetime I repeatedly see 11s. On the clock when I walk into my bedroom at 11:11 P.M. and again when I wake right at 2:11 and again at 3:11. Important things happen on the 11th of the month. Too often the total for my morning bagel, coffee, and newspaper is $5 and 11 cents on the same night my change at the grocery is 11 cents and when I leave the store I'm greeted by an 11 in neon red blinking at the crosswalk. It's as if the entity the number represents is communicating with me.

When the 11s appear I read them as a reminder directed
at me from an unknowable, vaguely menacing power that must
be placated. The power behind the 11s—but not the number—
dates to memories of myself at five or six years old, growing up
in Aspen. I remember thinking about this abstract, scary power
as I methodically tied an inexpert bow to secure my blue Keds
or while pondering my tenuous place in the world as I pulled a
turtleneck over my big head, painfully yanking my straight brown
bob down with it. Back then, in a corner of my messy young-girl
mind, I was loosely aware that a misplaced move might end it
all—with me as the primary object of this ruination. I suspected
and sometimes firmly believed my world was a play put on just
for me. At any moment the curtain might come swooping down
to cover me in darkness. Looking back at this self I'm reminded
of James's observation of Maisie, "Her little world was phantas-
magoric—strange shadows dancing on a sheet. It was as if the
whole performance had been given for her—a mite of a half-
scared infant in a great dim theatre."

Constantly mindful of this arbitrary universal design that
chose to keep me—for the time being—as a kid, I believed all the
world was in on it, watching me, waiting for the right moment
to trip me up. Was my dog complicit? My sister? Now I wait for
the whim of the machine to smite me but with the perspective
twenty-five years confers. I can examine and question the utter
lunacy of a belief system I've hung on to way past the glorious
peak of natural childhood narcissism. And yet, even though I
know this, the menace of the 11s fills me with inchoate dread,
the evil behind it spilled ink spreading through my brain.

Before Dr. Kohl I'd never told anyone about what I had at
times understood as a relatively harmless if strange and illogical

thought pattern mixed with rituals wound up in divining and then selecting the right object—a cigarette, a carton of milk in the dairy section, a coffee filter from a box of thirty, the left or right door.

When I was with my sister, my dog, or both I was shy and quiet but not preoccupied with this particular danger. We ranged over the whole of Little Woody Creek valley from our house at the end of the dirt road: past or into the houses of our friends and neighbors, through groves of scrub oak and aspens; among the horses and cattle in the pastures beside the road. It felt idyllic in so many respects, while in others my mind was in contention with its authenticity, making my world a confused mix, at once strange and wonderful but ultimately unreliable. I did not believe the world was real.

On allowance day we'd trek to the Woody Creek Store with a fortune of $5 to fill brown paper bags with candy. Throughout I heard the dim background hum of the lethal organizing principle that later came to be represented by the 11s patiently directing me. Candy wasn't just candy. Which candy—both which flavor and which particular piece from a box of ten or twenty? I must divine the correct choice even if I feel a little sorry for the ones left behind. It was a vaguely crazy-making test, the echo of it there even now like a poorly written, nonsensical song . . . *Teaberry, Beemans, Clove, Black Jack, Fruit Stripe, or Juicy Fruit? Chiclets or Razzles? Hot Tamales, Cinnamon Bears, Red Hots, or Atomic Fireballs? 3 Musketeers or Milky Way? Candy Buttons, Pez, Bottlecaps, or Jaw Breakers? Mary Jane or Squirrel Nut Zipper? Grape, Orange, Raspberry, or Cherry Pixy Stix? Bonomo's Banana Turkish Taffy, Banana Laffy Taffy, Kits Taffy, Banana BB Bats, or Banana Split? Candy Cigarettes or Necco*

Wafers? Whoppers or Mallo Cup? Junior Mints or U-No? Saf-T-Pop, Unicorn Pop, or Charms? Caramel Cube or Ice Cube? Jolly Ranchers, Life Savers, Root Beer Barrels, or Brach's Butterscotch Discs? Milk Maid Royals or Hershey Kisses? Cherry Mash, Big Cherry, or Cherry Bomb? Heath, Krackel, or Crunch? Almond Joy, Mounds, or Coconut Slices? Red Vines or Twizzler? Mike & Ike, Chuckles, Jujubes, Jujyfruits, or Dots? Cracker Jack? Abba-Zaba or Reese's Peanut Butter Cup? Milk Duds or Raisinets? Good & Plenty or Licorice Pipe? Bubble Gum Cigar, Double Bubble, or Super Bubble? Wax Fang, Bottle, or Lips? Butterfinger or Kit-Kat? Candy Corns or Pumpkins? Rocky Road Chunky or Pecan Chunky? Lemonheads, Lemon Drops, or SweeTARTS? Goo Goo Clusters, Charleston Chew, or Zero? Sixlets or M&Ms? Hershey's or Nestlé's Milk? Mr. Goodbar or Snickers? Caramel Creams or Bit-O-Honey? Tootsie Pop or Blow Pop? Candy Bracelet, Necklace, or Watch? Rock Candy or Candy Crystals? Pop Rocks or Zotz? Tootsie Roll, Slo Poke, or Black Cow? Sugar Daddy, Mama, or Baby?—Precisely which pack? The one in the back? No. Front left? That's it. I'm safe for now. Once the trial was over I ate my candy, as I now smoke the cigarette I've selected, without a qualm.

These beliefs, choices, and the elaborate superstitions about the magic qualities of objects I owned were manageable. The order had long been best left undisturbed. I played along as the presence waxed and waned through adolescence and young adulthood, never much questioning the rules or logic or considering the possibility that my behavior is strange.

Although it was monstrously dangerous to say it out loud to Dr. Kohl—an unambiguous violation of the rules of the 11s' power—I conceded minor obsessions when he first interviewed me and then, once I couldn't keep it quiet any longer, I fully explained the 11s and their history to him. Dr. Kohl framed my pact of silence with the 11s in the context of my propensity to protect the sanctity of my thoughts, fears, ambitions, and emotions by keeping secrets. As Dr. Kohl noted, my credo has long been "Keep your mouth shut to survive."

As I understand it, in psychiatric terms this fixation on 11s and the mildly paranoid structure that predated it fall between an obsession and a delusion, the difference between the two being one of degree. My preoccupation with 11s causes anxiety and compulsions—choosing objects, seeking signs of the number, attributing extra power and significance to various objects like mugs, sweaters, my copy of *The Magic Mountain*. What makes the 11s border on a delusion is how insidious, incorrigible, preoccupying, and idiosyncratic they are. A well-seated delusion carries the danger of blurring reality's edges, which my 11s have been doing a lot more of lately. As often as I've tried to talk myself out of them since I first explained them to Dr. Kohl, there's a strong, important part of me that isn't conceding the argument. I can't shake my belief in their external reality.

"There's something about being here that makes me feel really good, like I never expected it would." But "I have to create, justify, make myself useful to be paid attention to, listened to. I don't feel like I have a place. . . ."

"In anyone's life," he finished for me. Yes. But now he's linked to the 11s, possibly their foe, maybe my friend.

"I feel my attachment to you is scary, very risky," I said.

My infatuation had corroded my defenses and it was vacation time for him (the first and least significant I'd encounter while in treatment). I confessed my dependency.

"It seems really scary but is it a good thing to progress in a relationship with you so I trust you more? It's a good thing to rely on you more—right?" I was stuck because, as I pointed out, "You know more about me than anyone else but me." From that point on he's been dangerously on the inside.

By admitting he's the idealized center of my existence, I risked rejection from both him and the caprice of the 11s. They haven't quite settled on where he stands. But it's worth the gamble or, as Hans Castorp in *The Magic Mountain* calls it, "the whims of the card-goblins, ensnared by the fitful and fickle favour of fortune, which sometimes let the face-cards and elevens pile up."

I envy Dr. Kohl's purpose, his ability to escape the devastating relativism that makes so much of what I do pointless. The best I have is the 11s, a malignant structure that engages me in rules within a larger, incomprehensible system. I fear their wrath. I've never read even the most essential religious texts. I fall on the most extreme end of the nonbeliever spectrum. Bearded gods, fairies, sprites, and prophets have never had any appeal for me. The novels I read with reckless urgency have been my moral and intellectual guides—Hemingway's crisp purpose; Fitzgerald's idealized beauty; Dostoyevsky's grubby existentialism; Harrison's western landscapes and manly men; Tolstoy's flabby effulgence; Thomas Wolfe's gorgeous musings; Wharton's class-conscious brittleness; Cather's lovely rustic longing; Flaubert's stylized dreams; Mann's intricacies of time and death; Morrison's racial rage and mourning; Bellow's sexy male bravado; Rushdie's mind-bending brilliance; V. S. Naipaul's seductive, sleepy elegance; Melville's broad informational scope; Faulkner's self-indulgent stylizing; James's layered interior complexities. Those and the fairy tales I read and reread.

As I told Dr. Kohl at one point, "When I feel like I'm really losing it I read fairy tales." Unlike the 11s, they never fail me. Like the orderly world Dr. Kohl embodies, a fairy tale's transparent logic of good, bad, just and unjust, strong and weak, wise and dumb, greedy and generous never falters. In "The Goose Girl," a Brothers Grimm tale, a maid (who is, of course, a princess) confesses to an iron stove the secret of her identity that she's "sworn before the face of heaven on pain of losing my life" to keep. Finding such a confessor to relieve her of the lethal secret in the form of an inanimate, utterly trustworthy object marks one of the form's most pleasurable tropes: that objects, beasts, and even nature speak truth. In "The Goose Girl" the wise voice comes from what remains of the horse Falada, who has been decapitated by the knacker, her (talking) head nailed to a dark gateway. The all-knowing magic of the advice Falada offers up saves the Goose Girl from destruction and restores her rightful identity.

I encounter a similarly transformative magic in Dr. Kohl. He's wiser than I am, much wiser than anyone else I've met. It doesn't matter what we talk about; being in the same room with him enlightens, animates, and liberates me. Letting him take me in, listening as he slowly makes something sensible of my words and reported actions, intoxicates me more than booze, sex, ecstasy, sex on ecstasy, coke, or speed. "'Seven and four,' said Hans Castorp. 'Eight and three. Knave, queen, king. It is coming out.'"

*   *   *

I never imagined that going to talk to this kind man, this wise doctor, would precipitate a crisis. We built what Freud called a "special affective relationship." Preoccupied as I was with Dr. Kohl, I failed to anticipate how thoroughly my weary consciousness could dissipate, grinding into low gear, slowing, and coming to a halt as something new crawled in beneath.

"Are you getting more depressed?" he asked in February.

"I can't tell how I feel," I said. "I gave up old ways of defending myself, my life's philosophy, structures are gone. I have hints of what to move toward but they're not strong enough. Leaves me with very few ways of living."

"Coming here makes you feel more vulnerable."

"Yes," I said, more vulnerable as the desire for him chiseled away at my equilibrium. In my family, I told him, "There was always something wrong with wanting."

"As if you didn't feel badly enough already," he said sympathetically.

His presence and the knowledge he's listening to and looking at me have been among the great pleasures of my limited life. I leave the better parts of myself in his office.

"You haven't learned how to take 'here' outside of here and not feel vulnerable," he told me. I feel kind, smart, funny, and charming when I'm with him but none of it travels well.

"Alone I feel ugly and strange," I confessed. But each time I returned I knew I'd find a better self tucked away somewhere in his office, ready to animate.

I need him and, as evidenced by the bed waiting for me at Sheppard Pratt Hospital in Baltimore, I'd rather commit myself than lose him. Although I haven't sorted it out with the 11s, I know I'm unwilling to give up the terrifying mix of sexual excitement, longing, and anxiety that nearly asphyxiates me in his presence.

As distressed as I've been and as earnest as my efforts to feel better have been, I'm sure the symptoms are keeping Dr. Kohl close, listening to me, thinking about me, working on me. I vowed not to be simple and easy. I wouldn't let him grow bored or frustrated, sending me on my way, all fixed up or possibly hopeless, but as ready as I'd ever be for the world. No, not a simple case: DSM-IV 309.28 "Adjustment Disorder with Mixed Anxiety and Depressed Mood." Not so fast. I'm not nearly done.

CHAPTER 7

An Unnatural Teenage Fantasy

My mother had often told me I'd make a good shrink because I had long acted as hers. Never having had one of her own, she wasn't particularly qualified to judge. I was it.

One night when I was thirteen I lay reading in bed when my mother's voice came to me distinctly—happy, very, very happy! Inflections of love and togetherness filtered upward from the kitchen like so much helium. Laughter cut her words apart, turning them into rambunctious pops, the way she sounded when drunk and still drinking. I knew she wasn't talking to my father, who was probably already in bed. My mind capered to a guess. The sole possibility—she was on the phone with Dick Millington.

She'd been passing unnatural intervals of time with the Millington family—sleeping over at their ranch house in Picabo, riding, trading livestock, traveling. She had even acquired a pet that was their doing—a raven she'd named Edgar. He was her take of three hatchlings plucked from the nest with the benefit of Dick's piloting license and a rented helicopter.

Was my mother unfaithful? Cheating on my father? Betraying us all for this slip of a man, a nothing? That conversation ended in whispers and then the screen door banged and the door clicked closed. Gone. We lived at least ten miles from anywhere with a light on. It was as obstinately cold and black outside as winter far into the Northern Hemisphere can be. The ground white, with hard-packed snow cemented at 5°F.

I grabbed a towel, tripping after my mother through the icy, bobsled-worthy chute that formed the path through the snow to the Ranch's high-volume natural hot springs pools. I spotted her white skin glowing in the dark, her nude body crouched as she inched into the scalding water. Peeling off my clothes, I followed her through the sting of the frosted air into the keen luxury of the sulfured heat. Passing her on the broad slippery wooden steps, I headed to the center. I would have a confession; never mind that part of me must have not wanted to know. I would fix the mess between my parents.

"Are you in love with Dick Millington?" I demanded. Happily unable to see her expression in the dark, I anticipated her answer, expecting a scene. The undeniable answer—simple—would soon be in the air between us. Obvious. Stupidly apparent as I thought back on all the time she spent there with him, how often she was on the phone, how many excuses she made to leave the ranch to go to Picabo, where their hundred-acre property sprawled—the latest crippled excuse for leaving falling flat even before she'd unpacked her bag and washed her clothes from the prior liaison.

"I'm in love with Pat Millington."

I had no words as the absurdity of her words dented my consciousness. Pat? Dick's wife and the mother of my best friend, Poppy? The woman in the large plaid shirt and Levi's, the big drinker, the attentive, warm parent of my friend? I couldn't imagine this woman sexually connected to my mother. It seemed strange and unnatural.

Speechless, I buckled my knees to submerge my head beneath the surface. The black water closed over me, hot on my dry, cold scalp, as liquid slowly displaced the air bubbles clinging to each follicle; my eyes closed, and the abrupt absence of sound, the obliteration of my mother's voice and form, secured me. I stayed under until breath propelled me to the surface. As F. Scott Fitzgerald writes in *Tender Is the Night*, "Fifteen minutes ago they had been a family."

Eventually the ranch was sold to Carole King, the earthy singer-songwriter still flush from her first big album, *Tapestry*. She played a few songs for my mother the first time she came to look at the place and then showed up with her white goats and trailer once the papers were signed. By then we'd dismantled our life as a family and dispersed the possessions that had given us definition—art, sculptures, books, photographs, linen, china, silver, furniture.

Sun Valley, Idaho, 1979: My mother left Nicole and me to live together, popping in now and again to pick up some clothes from her unoccupied bedroom or to complain that the place was dirty. I was about to turn fourteen, going into ninth grade. For the first time in my life there was a television in the house. Other than that there was nothing on the walls of the Sun Valley house, hardly any furniture, and none of the residue of our previous lives. It was as soulless as the cement slab it rested on, as unattractive as the bulldozer tracks that served as a yard.

Living without adults around throughout high school was an unnatural teenage fantasy. Without knowing it, my sister and I had been practicing to live this way since we were born. A steady regimen of casual parenting combined with an extremely high value placed on independence did the trick.

My father, far away in California, reinvented his life. Making what he could of his abruptly child-, wife-, and pet-free condition, he lived alone for the first time in seventeen years while the rest of us adjusted to our own versions of a strangely unfettered existence.

My father had to know my mother lived with Pat at her house in Picabo and later at Tunnel Rock. We called my father frequently to referee our arguments or just to hear his voice. For the longest time I blamed my mother while letting my father off as the victim of her infidelity. Given how I maintained his innocence all those years, I must have desperately needed to believe he'd been magically released, making it okay for him to save himself even if that meant leaving my sister and me in the nearly nonexistent care of our alcoholic mother.

It wasn't until Dr. Kohl questioned the arrangement during the early days of therapy that I began to recognize and believe that living alone all those years was out of the ordinary. It was just as he'd written in the IPE on day one: "Severe family deprivation (left totally alone at age 13.)" When I pointed out this oddity to my sister it took her a minute to realize how right I was. Her astonishment at our blind acceptance of this level of neglect equaled mine.

That was living. Teenagers never want a parent around—until they do. What teenagers desire is simple: food, money, and freedom. We had all three. With this bounty in hand I closed the door to my room, listened to the radio, made faces in the mirror, painted my nails every other day, shopped for clothes, read, and studied the novelty of my budding breasts while trying to resolve if

I was pretty or ugly, smart or dumb, weak or strong, good or bad, worthless or important. I told nobody when I first got my period; I just sneaked a few of my sister's tampons. The general absence of adults in my life other than my cross-country skiing coach, Kevin, left me free to draw my own conclusions about who I was while eating a pint of Rum Raisin Häagen-Dazs for dinner. Or nothing.

Thanks to Idaho's farm laws, my sister had her agricultural license. It was meant for teens in rural areas living on ranches and farms. Whatever its restrictions, she didn't follow them. There were no tractors or mowers within sight. She drove the beat-up blue Datsun 510 over the hill from our tract house in Elkhorn to the Ketchum–Sun Valley Community School, snuggled down along Trail Creek, not two miles away. When I was stuck at school I rambled home over the blunt, freshly cut grass of the golf course, hitchhiked, or begged my sister to come pick me up.

Nicole and I were free to stay out all night, drink, have sex, do drugs, or sleep all day. We generally didn't. A curfew or rules might have made rebellion more appealing—as it was, we did our homework and muddled through our teen years more steadily than many. I'd never wanted anything to do with the marijuana, cocaine, and, when we had guests back in Aspen, hallucinogenic mushrooms set out like Chex Party Mix. As I learned without knowing it long ago, it's almost impossible to rebel against indifference. I went to a few parties in high school, got a little drunk, and found my way home. I wasn't comfortable with boys or the party scene where the guys lurked, intent on getting their hands up my shirt and down my pants.

As always, but perhaps even more during that period, my mother drank a lot. There were two DWIs. Aside from the weed she smoked, she took up snorting coke again, having more or less left off the habit in Aspen. Dieting or not, she effortlessly peeled off forty pounds of accumulated marital sludge. When I was fifteen she offered me a line as we sat together in the cab of her red-and-white 1972 GM truck. Manipulating a razor to arrange three slender stripes of white powder on a compact mirror kept for the purpose, she held it out to me. "Want a hit?" She was taking me to dinner while she was in Sun Valley for the day; we were about to join her new girlfriend, Polly, at the restaurant. I remember thinking what a stupid child she was. I didn't want her drugs. I didn't want anything to do with her.

Our family had collapsed in on itself, unable to bear the weight of its competing parts.

I can't imagine what my life would have been like without Nicole. What she and I were to each other then, what we've always been to each other, was much bigger, more inscrutable than the honeyed word "sisters" suggests. There was no sharing clothes or make-up, no boy talk; there were no friends in common. We're too unalike for any of that. But for all that she has always been the one person who knew me. We were stuck with each other—nobody else in the house, no other consistent presence in our lives. Like prisoners sharing a cell, we've long had an unspoken solidarity.

In spite of our differences we had a hell of a time signing our names to the standing account at the local grocery store, Atkinson's, for milk, cereal, ice cream, cookies, peanut butter, and the occasional whole chicken that one of us would stuff with thyme and parsley, slather with butter, salt, and roast on high. The most formal meals my sister and I shared were taken standing at the kitchen counter, eating these crispy birds with our hands, paper towels serving as an imperfect bone dish, glistening fat shiny as lip gloss on our mouths.

My loneliest, unhappiest year of high school was when
Nicole left for Berkeley and I was farmed out to live with Mrs.
Thorson. She boarded kids who moved to the area to join Sun
Valley's world-class Alpine and Nordic ski teams. I couldn't live
alone—even I knew that. I was afraid of noises in the night and
of the dreams that followed me into sleep. So I moved my books
and clothes into a room in the Thorsons' big house with two
other boarders. They all ate dinner together at night, soaked in
the hot tub, watched movies, and sat in awe before the novelty of
MTV. I tucked myself away in my room to avoid them, grazing
from the refrigerator when nobody was looking.

CHAPTER 8

Catch Me

Time, quick and stingy when I'm in session, slows to the pace of cold honey every other minute of the day. Waiting. Always, it seems, anticipating the next appointment.

My frustration with Dr. Kohl arises out of the inherent tension between the formality of the office setting and the emotional intimacy I experience within it. The tension I feel is no mistake; it's highly productive—an emotional and intellectual hot zone generated by the friction between form and content. I was caught in this heat as an unambiguous rage built in me. Its object was Dr. Kohl. The bastard.

As Freud would have it, Dr. Kohl's "excessively warm interest" in me amounted to no more than expert professionalism, "evinced only as a means of psychic treatment." Session after session, the thought bore in on my fidelity to this perfect man, sullying his take on my past and present.

C. G. Jung thought the doctor should "catch" a patient the way one "catches a cold"—becoming entangled with, perhaps even possessed by, the patient. I hoped I'd provoked such a "psychic contagion." The patient of a lifetime. But did I pay him to pretend he cared so much? I wanted to allow myself to care without doubting, but it was as though a window tax had me bricking over his access. I could be satisfied only if I knew I'd infiltrated his professional shell, getting far more than money could ever buy. All I needed was a hairline fracture to slide past what he practiced professionally to a private region where I could mark him. I wanted him to be mine as much as I was his; never mind that he never asked me to give myself over to him.

He cared—it was not a complete sham. I believed that much after a single session. Soon afterward he made me feel exceptional with offers to call him at home. But wasn't that simply his job, taken perhaps one step beyond the norm? It was a role he performed with grace for hordes of patients who sat in the same leather chair where I sat. Never cooling, the chair carried the heat of their flesh like a toilet seat in a busy bus terminal. My greatest fear was that it wasn't just me calling but all of them. I imagined his home phone ringing throughout the evening like an insistent bell for service, patients on the other end of the line desperate as I was for him to impart calm with that voice of his. Picking up the phone, I often wondered how much his wife hated me for inserting myself—even invited—into his domestic life.

Freud knew all about patients like me, even deploying the feeble word "love" when he warned doctors against reciprocating the patient's feelings. "He must recognize that the patient's falling in love is induced by the analytic situation and is not to be attributed to the charms of his own person." He adds, "It is always well to be reminded of this."

In early winter I asked him if there was "One thing I can do to feel better—just one."

He wrote to himself that day, "This is an indication of analytic despair or totally giving up."

Sagging through the solo nights unnerved me; the excess hours were plastered to me, indelible as my own skin. After a long argument about how it messed with my authenticity, I agreed to take 20 mg of Prozac. When I felt like it I drugged myself to sleep for twenty-four hours with the Trazodone he prescribed around the same time. Relentless insomnia peeled away at the contours of whatever normality I was clinging to.

He observed I was using the Trazodone "to sustain aloneness. (Sleeps during day to survive.)" I took it when I couldn't sleep at night and on weekends I took it during the day to melt the long hours of waiting until I'd see him again.

"I'm afraid I'll die," I told him in February.

"Unusual response to dependency," he wrote in my chart. In April he wrote, "Atypical Depression/Compulsive Urges," and around the same time, "Doubt Bipolar." He suggested hospitalization as an option if I felt dangerously suicidal. I didn't think he was serious.

"I feel like running away," I said.

"I will try to find you," he said. This felt impossibly good until he said, "I will not stop until I do." That's when I thought I might have cracked his professional shell by somehow eroding an invisible line of protection. He couldn't promise all his patients he'd try to find them if they disappeared—forever after. This was an impetus to push further.

Session after session through the winter and spring I tested his resolve by challenging his commitment to me and to the professional rules.

"What do you have to lose here? Your professional integrity . . . if you felt that you didn't do a good job?" At this he locked those strong eyes of his on mine and answered with what seemed like a non sequitur but wasn't.

"You can be lonely," he said. "Who would lose in the intimacy war?" he asked rhetorically. My nose had been rubbed in the rejection.

In his notes for that day Dr. Kohl wrote, "Pouring out her annoyance with Dr. Kohl." It was the title of a list that included interrupting, feeling more depressed, having unprotected sex with Matt and then feeling sorry and filthy, biting my cuticles and fingernails until I tasted blood, bingeing, vomiting, and starving myself in between. I'd lost thirty pounds since therapy began.

Despising the remaining edges of my former softness, I slipped the rings from my fingers and put them in my dresser drawer along with my earrings and bracelets.

"I'm paring down" the "encumbrances," I explained.

"It's all magic," he said. And it was, but it was a magic I liked because it made me feel different, more in control. I made and gave Dr. Kohl a papier-mâché collage with a baby figure at the center to represent the abortion I had on 11/11/88. The 11s liked it. I woke up five times in the night on May 5, 1991: 1:11, 3:11, 4:11. They were closing in.

"Freeing though, they're pretenses," was my way of dismissing the frippery.

"That's a big word for a little girl," he said with a laugh, meaning the magical logic I was wrapped up in came from what he referred to as my controlling, punishing three-year-old.

On me, weighing me down, the jewelry I removed was transferable, lies of prettiness I was sick of passing off as part of me. Long straight hair no longer complicates me either. No. Each strand was cut an inch or less from my scalp—you could generously call it a pixie. Raw. Think less Audrey Hepburn and more the kind of haircut you give your doll when you're six.

On my monster-worthy six feet, my big head, newly shorn, looked unbalanced—I felt fragile and exposed. I was shy and embarrassed when Dr. Kohl saw me without my hair, smiling too much as if I knew I'd been naughty. His gaze calmly met mine, communicating that he knew precisely what I was up to. He argued that people don't just cut off all their hair without talking about it first.

I was exhausted by a ridiculous life lived through the scraps of time I spent with him. The 11s were "bugging me" with their insistent presence and yet, as I explained to him, "I have to defy" this force because "I can't control it." I accused him of confusing me into a state of dependent unhappiness.

"Feeling more here is not me confusing you, it means something is happening here," he said. But it wasn't good enough.

"I thought a lot about leaving, freed me to make a decision, assessment, commitment," I said to begin one late-spring session. "I felt a lot of important things happening. Forced myself into being more involved with what I could see happening: a strengthening process. I felt I was cementing myself."

"You've been working hard already," Dr. Kohl said.

"I felt pretty good over the weekend, pretty happy. Had an idea I could sustain that sense. Elation that I should stay on but wanted to <u>wean off.</u>" I meant wean myself off my attachment to him. "I don't think I'll leave."

"Could you tell me?" he asked.

"Yeah, I could leave . . . " I said evasively. I paused, smiling. "But I won't do it in the next month or so."

"I know this game," he said. He meant what he calls my obsession with the game of "Catch Me," when a toddler runs away as the adult pretends to try to catch the child, letting just enough time pass before grabbing the giggling child, scooping her off her feet, and enclosing her firmly. The child feels a thrilling joy in the terror of escape but only because she knows she'll be caught and embraced safe and secure as a baby in arms.

"That you would follow me makes it feel more serious."

"It is a serious 'game,'" he said.

"Yes, I sense it is very serious, very deathlike, to leave like that. I'd be picking up pieces for so long."

"Like your parents, who upped and left important 'things' behind," he suggested.

"IT'S MY VERSION OF SUICIDE I THINK. I've thought about actual suicide. Never came close to doing that, it didn't attract me that much."

"That much," he echoed. "The only person you could make a commitment to was yourself," he said. "I'm Cree," he gently mocked, "I'll get my shit together so I can make a promise I'll never leave." But "It's just the old you trying to give me presents. It doesn't work that way."

I wasn't sure what to say but as always it felt good to have him see through my posturing, my brazen attempt to please him—even if I didn't realize that was what I was trying to do. What he meant by giving him "presents" is the work I do to entertain him, amuse him, please him, be a good—no, a perfect—patient.

"It doesn't work that way . . . " echoes in my head. I understand why it doesn't work that way but I don't know exactly how it does work.

Cutting my hair, making threats to leave, biting my nails as I did all through my childhood—I regressed physically, practically begging to be taken care of.

Hell, at that moment I figured if I could strip myself so easily, why not slip right out of the light?

CHAPTER 9

Unholy Pleasure

It was mid-May, just two weeks before I burned myself for the first time, when I told him, "I feel exposed."

He said, "That's what happens to a 3-year-old when an adult walks in the room while she's walking around self-centered and secure in her fantasy." He was right, of course, his answer a surprise and a revelation. I do feel shocked and a tad embarrassed, as if I've been caught pretending, talking to myself. But the biggest problem I have to overcome is that the 11s don't like Dr. Kohl, resent him for tricking me into spilling our secret magic.

Awakened into immediate, lively omnipresence, the 11s threaten, calling me out with the aggressive appearance of the number and its multiples, its special signal present everywhere, demanding my attention with constant noise. The power looms, patiently waiting to finish the job. Perhaps they intentionally relaxed their vigilance all those years just to catch me out now? Maybe long ago the timer was set to end here—it's all part of the larger plan. Now the magic whispers in my ear while betraying me fully, knowing I'm off guard, a disposable decoy, easy for the taking. Or worse, far worse, maybe Dr. Kohl is theirs. An obedient soldier carefully planted, groomed, in on the plot. A test of my fidelity to the secret. If so, I've failed and this is their masterpiece, the final score soon to be tallied. They play to win. It might be over soon, as they knew it would be, the victory all theirs in a twinkling.

"I've exposed too much. I've revealed the magic. YOU'VE WRECKED IT," I told him.

"What enables the other system is connected here," he said.

"NO. The other system is a rejection of this. A new magic."

And the "involuntary thoughts of jamming obscene things in your vagina. You must feel violated," he said.

This is a recurring compulsion. Horrible thoughts that spring like fleas, alighting on my consciousness uninvited when a truly disgusting object appears on the street or sidewalk—dog shit, roadkill, phlegm. It's a long-standing annoyance. When these revolting images arrive I'm briefly humiliated and disgusted with myself even though I haven't done anything but look down.

"Those thoughts come out of nowhere. They control me more than I control them."

At this he observed again, this time to himself, I'm feeling "SUPER VIOLATED." At that moment, stuck in the chaos of this primitive terror, I needed to resist him.

"Oh, I don't mind this shit anymore," I told him.

"Therapy?"

"Yes, I have a sense of being shown something here I can't have, an evenness, a world where things make sense, are manageable, understandable."

"Love, caring, security," he said. "Being connected in a normal way."

"I don't know if I buy that."

"From yourself?"

And then I laughed, because what else was there to do? I wasn't buying it from myself. It sounded too sweet to be true and it's not even close to how I experience the world when I'm outside his office.

"I'm anxious all the time, self-conscious, exhausted. And the way I feel changes so much hour to hour."

In his notes to himself for the day he wrote, "What's precarious is how she feels about herself." I burned myself for the first time on June 2, 1991. It was somewhere past midnight. I was reading while the space right behind my forehead seemed to expand, the pressure building until concentration was impossible. It was a feeling I'd been growing more familiar with: as if all the thoughts in my frontal cortex were combusting, neurons wildly firing as on the 4th of July.

I set aside *The Idiot* and as I did I noticed an old scar on the tender, white skin of my right, inner forearm, maybe two inches long, with tiny dots to either side where the stitches left their trace. It was the remnant of an incision to remove a benign fatty lump years ago. Unremarkable, the scar was almost pretty in its delicacy, but it bothered me.

A careless, unsympathetic doctor had left his mark on me when he removed that lump and I suddenly didn't want evidence of him there, on my body. The scar was foreign, like the jewelry, fingernails, and long hair I'd already rid myself of. Destroying it was not destructive; it was a way of wiping away the taint, of purifying myself. The realization that I could erase the faint white line by burning it away with a lit cigarette appealed to me the moment it came to mind. That was the first time I felt the unholy pleasure.

In my Thursday session with Dr. Kohl the following day I swept in and told him what he already knew.

"When I'm not here I feel really angry with you and it disappears when I come here," I told him. "It's a real battle; I guess I don't trust being here, yet on another level I trust it more than I've ever trusted."

"I can't see any of your negative qualities, it's so one-sided." I was seething with resentment at the peace of mind I'd given up; the interior logic of the 11s telling me enough was enough. Part of me believed in his ability to make me right if he only would—the way a child feels her parents are omnipotent.

Willing my allegiance to them, willing my difference from him, that was why I began to mark out my loyalty on my skin in a pattern that followed right rituals. Ever since, it's been logical and obedient—never mistaken. I've placed each one, listening and watching, getting into line. Stay right. Burn me please. Right here. Make a mark. Show your strength. Time to stop the dalliance with Dr. Kohl. The enemy. Burning is a sublime offering I'm more than a little proud of.

"I'm miserable all the time, self-destructive, exhausted." Seeing him twice a week wasn't enough. I wanted all of him—or none.

"2 hours is only part of what you're angry about," he said.

"Yes," I agreed, "it's what the 2 hours do to me."

He suggested that the limited time we had together, the smallness of his presence in my life, ended up feeling a lot like what my parents did to me: sparing too little time, leaving me alone and short on affection. As he'd noted in my chart three months prior, "Isolation perpetuates childhood."

I confessed to throwing up the previous week on Thursday but not over the weekend. The session wound down, ten minutes to go. And then I said it.

"I had this compulsion to burn my arm with my cigarette. I did it and it worked. I didn't vomit." I was hoping for an impassioned response. I wanted to jolt him, to get his full attention, and to have it I'd go as far as necessary. But the fantasy reply—whatever it involved—didn't arrive.

"You're furious with me," he stated calmly. "Maybe," he suggested, "I'm having difficulty dealing with your rage, like your father."

"True," I said. "My parents were the same as it is here. When challenged they smoothed it all over like you do. I say something, you comment on it . . . admit it . . . it's perverse and sick." This isn't true—as I explain later when he asks what's different about being with him; I say, "The way you've responded to things, you haven't ignored things, they get somewhere, I'm not left with them."

But at that moment, postburn number one, I was just mad.

"Chaos, Anger, Rage. Visit Suicide Observation," he wrote in a note to himself that day, adding, "Set limits on violence toward self." Beside it he drew a crude diagram of my arm to record the location of the relatively minor blister I'd created, the blister I would refinish within the week by reburning it properly. It took time to learn that 3rd-degree burns don't hurt at all once done properly.

It seems he did pay attention to the burn—very much so. But from my perspective that day the act made little impression.

So I tried it again. And again. My surprise at the pleasure of the process and its long aftermath as the burns healed took me by surprise. A plain Band-Aid concealed a rapidly expanding map of dreamy, powerful secrets I happily tended. "Oh, it's just a bug bite," or "It's nothing. Poison ivy," I'd say if anyone asked.

The initiation on June 2 was unworthy of my later skill—nothing more than a severe 1st-degree. As June passed I practiced, getting better and liking it a great deal. I'd found a lively new way to clear my head of the terrible pressure and all that alarming desire.

CHAPTER 10

Sympathy to Ingest

"Can I hold her?" Dr. Kohl wrote in my chart in March 1991. The answer was no: "Too sexual, too blurry of boundaries."

He considered this embrace long before the burning started, taking the idea seriously enough to write it down, his countertransference testing his training to the extent that he entertained satisfying the impulse.

The treatment well in process, I fused with Dr. Kohl as what Freud called the "analyst-parent-love object." I put immense demands on him. The level of my "acting out" both in session and outside would have put most therapists to the test—burning, vomiting, arguing, provoking, imagining, and talking about suicide. I regressed rapidly. As is often the case with bulimic self-harming patients, "aggression and aggression to the self," as the psychoanalyst Otto Kernberg writes, "are fused in the patient's efforts to destroy the analyst's capacity to help" her. Worse, "the therapeutic relationship easily replaces ordinary life, because its gratifying and sheltered nature further intensifies the temptation to gratify primitive pathological needs in the transference and acting out."

My whole world was 112 Church Street. I lived for my appointments.

Dr. Kohl couldn't stop me even if part of me wanted to stop, to bring the contest of wills to a close. That's not how the process works. The dance had to go on both because I couldn't stop it and because he was trying to follow through on treating me. Throughout June I burned myself frequently. He told me if I didn't stop by the end of August, then I would have to go to the hospital or end treatment. The distant deadline gave him time to argue with me about the burning. He wanted to work through it with me rather than giving up as my parents had done. I'd regressed in treatment so he attempted to parent me; abandoning me in the middle of my tantrum would have duplicated what my parents did—leaving me alone to fend for myself. He told me he didn't want to do that—he wanted to prove to me that people could be counted on but he also said there was a limit to the damage he could tolerate. August 31 felt so distant as not to be real.

I enjoy feeling soiled by taking pleasure in wanting him. I'm grateful for the way the tension and confusion fall away when I'm in his presence. Most sessions leave me feeling that I can recognize myself in the present for long enough to make missing him worthwhile. I can't pass up the desire, no matter how much it makes my hours outside his office unbearable.

With a body and a mind at odds with one another, post-orgasmic or postburn moments deliver a brief détente before the duality and the longing for what I can't have kick back in. The quiet a burn earns hangs on longest, a ghost of the act with me as I tend the wound. Burning serves too many purposes to account for—particularly since I don't even understand most of what it does for me. I do know it's better than any fix I've tried; soothing the knot in my gut, clearing my head, and evaporating my anxiety.

My ongoing desire to hold a cigarette to my skin reflects my detachment from my body, a tool at best, evidenced by the violence I do to myself when I make myself throw up or ski so hard I burst a lung, as I did during a cross-country race in high school. So I took to the unexpected appeal of burning my body that started by so tentatively erasing the line of that old scar as if it were written in pencil. Gratified enough to be rid of it, I replaced what had been alien with a self-fashioned circle and let myself go from there.

Dr. Kohl suggests that burning "cauterizes my desire" and "closes off sexual feelings." He's aware of my desire for him and how it repeats through satisfaction in session, renunciation when alone, shame at wanting what I can't have, regret at having revealed myself, and the punishment that follows. The cycle regenerates like the Hydra; containing the monster and its infinite regrowth requires branding its severed stumps.

Gaining mastery over myself, I kept at it. Position: chair, feet up on the heater, hot milky Earl Grey tea in The Mug by my side, the McGarrigle Sisters cooing "Kiss and Say Goodbye" or Leonard Cohen "Who by Fire." The latter feels like my theme song as I listen to him rasp "and who in her lonely slip, who by barbiturate." I'd discovered a source of purifying exultation gained through intense mental and physical concentration. The willful perseverance as I hold the cigarette down erases everything but sound, which only intensifies in the void of concentration I experience as a kind of rapture.

Habit. Ritual. The beauty of repetition. The music and I have a thing that goes together. There's a secret to this even if

I'm not entirely in on it. I'm chasing it. The 11s are in play. I'm placating them with every burn. Meanwhile, pain and I, we have a date. I am beautiful, clear, and uncomplicated inside the pain. If it didn't matter, if nobody were around to see or know, would I cover the right side of my body from ear to toe with marks, never stopping? I think I would.

As I draw near the next though the one finished a moment before still radiates heat, every location feels like the right and only choice—as with choosing a cigarette from a pack, it takes time to decide where to hit next. The spot, once chosen, isn't ever let off or forgotten. I connect the dots, thinking about where I will go all day—or I fight off the plan for days, the chosen spot begging to be had, hard as I try to ignore the inevitable.

I stayed on the inside of my right arm to begin; it was easier to hide the Band-Aids. The right–left split exists within the economy of my own internal logic, in which the devaluation of the right side's alienated flesh begs burning while the sanctity of the left side's innocence is never subject to damage. It's enough.

All I lack is remorse. I've never hated myself after creating a new hole in my skin—quite the opposite. I revel in my work. Admire it. Observe the progress of the developing scar as it morphs into what will be a permanent feature of my body. I suppose the failure to recognize that it matters that I do this—or not—is no small part of the pathology. Caring would entail balancing the damage I've been doing to my appearance with the immensity of the pleasure the act gives me. Maybe it's all those tasty opioids flooding my brain in response to the pain? No, my failure to stop, my ultimate inability to cease, exceeds the physical.

I'm actually scared by the power of the compulsion. I have an inkling of how a serial killer feels, the pressure to do the deed building until there's no stopping it because the momentum of inevitability beats down the part of the mind that doesn't want to repeat the offense.

"The pressure builds until I burn myself. It's 'a forgiveness,' 'a numbness.' Sometimes I can do it and it doesn't hurt and I can do it and do it," I told Dr. Kohl.

CHAPTER 11

Hide Better!

It was the vacation that did it. Isn't that always the way? August. In the weeks before Labor Day psychiatrists and other professionals who set their own schedules take their precious families to breathe the cool air, eat buttery lobster, and stain their teeth with wild blueberries in company with the rocky ocean pleasures of Kennebunkport, Camden, Mount Desert, Bar Harbor, Blue Harbor, Monhegan, or the sandy expanses of Goose Rocks. If not this, they remove for weeks to the fashionable pleasures of glittering Martha's Vineyard, Nantucket, Hyannis, Newport, Narragansett, Montauk, East Hampton, or Southampton. August: the dreaded annual shrink drought.

That year it wasn't August; it was July. Dr. Kohl, against precedent, went on vacation a month earlier than every other shrink in the Western Hemisphere.

"It feels like it cheats me out of any degree of sanity," I told him two sessions before he left. "It has to be funny to me. What will I do?"

"Kill yourself?" he asked.

"I am considering it carefully, or doing something else first. If you were staying it would be manageable. I kept burning myself this morning. It's like a chink in my brain, a slamming door. Something gives in. It didn't work today. I've created this incredible dependence and now it's almost killing me when it's going away . . . I am kind of daring you."

"You're going to kill yourself?"

"If I try I don't want to die. . . ." All the talk was bringing the fear closer. "You're daring me! I know you're going. Why is this different?"

"Who said it was?" he asked.

"Now I'm pissed."

"We all know what you can do to yourself. I am going to leave. I am going to Alaska no matter what." It sounded as if he was reassuring himself more than he was assuring me.

While he's with his family in Alaska he leaves me in the care of his colleague.

The notes she took when Dr. Kohl briefed her before leaving for vacation on July 8 were not optimistic. She hadn't even met me but, according to Dr. Kohl, she might be confronted with handling a psychiatric emergency. Her notes from Dr. Kohl's debriefing read:

> Parents abandoned. Now feeling this in relation
> Dr. Kohl vacation. Wealthy. Self burning R arm.
> Limits set with A.K. Not expecting competence—
> key. Can she stay alive: this would be key. May need
> to hospitalize.

I can't say he didn't prepare her. She was a blank to me other than the curious fact of her gender. I was nervous about meeting her.

We spent our session talking about what it meant for me to come to her office and how being there reminded me of Dr. Kohl. This made "missing him harder," I confessed.

"I have a tendency not to let anyone have a concept of my needs. But," I added, "you know my needs, so . . . " I didn't have to start from zero or pretend to be something I wasn't. Not only would this have been a waste of time; I didn't have the energy.

She bullet-pointed the basics of what I told her about burning and vomiting. "Seems to occur when I'm feeling 'usual' not at times of dissociation. Both seem like fuck-yous, but most common when feel most isolated," she wrote.

"The pain clicks me into another mode," I said.

"WAITING for Dr. Kohl to return," she wrote.

The next day she asked to see the burns. Nobody but Dr. Kohl had ever seen them. Scattered jumbo Band-Aids bunched in patches with generic nonstick pads covered the damage. I peeled them away to expose the flesh. Afterward, she drew a mini-illustration of my arm in her notes with a dotted line indicating the burned area.

"Looked at arm," she wrote. "Burns appear quite serious and now complicated by infection. Large area of scar, desquamated, red, swollen, with pus in places. Made arrangements for evaluation at Lakewood Health Center, Dr. Ahlers."

True, the loosely clustered matrix of mostly overlapping burns was the tiniest bit infected. But it would clear up soon enough. I was pleased because she took me seriously.

I suspect there are few cases a doctor likes less than a patient with a self-inflicted wound. In my experience, it fundamentally pisses doctors off. They work all day to heal and then some nut arrives on their examination table having hurt his or her body on purpose.

The doctor I saw that day, Dr. Gordon Ahlers, acted as if I'd set out to purposefully steal time and expertise from his other, more deserving patients. Cigarette burns are characteristic of child abuse. Maybe the hostility I perceived was associated with the treatment of the real burn *victims*, who make up roughly 10 percent of child abuse cases. The children are usually no more than ten years old but most of them are under the age of two. Doctors are trained to identify non-accidental burns caused by hot objects and to distinguish them from hot-liquid burns. The evidence of liquid is in the "sparing" or spots where the position of the body naturally protects the skin. Hot-object injuries, once identified as such, must be assessed as accidental or intentional. Minor burns from a hot object can, of course, occur if a child accidentally touches a hot iron, pot, sheet pan, or oven rack. Doctors are trained to recognize such accidental burns by their shallow irregularity. Most suspicious are perfectly circular blisters or scars on a child's back or buttocks. Such confined damage to the skin can't be caused by accidentally walking into a lit cigarette.

Silent for the most part, after a few minutes Dr. Ahlers shook his head and looked away.

He asked if I'd burned myself with cigarettes.

I wanted to say, "Yes, genius," but I kept my silence. He was about to debride the extensive open wound. I nodded, barely. He and his nurse then proceeded to wash the wound and brush away the dead and infected tissue on my inner forearm.

If treating self-inflicted injuries once makes a doctor angry, watching them expand enrages him. I covered a good bit of ground in the ten days that Dr. Kohl was on vacation. The repetition of the debriding when Dr. Kohl sent me back for more after he returned from vacation was more awful than the first round.

But before Dr. Kohl returned I had another appointment to fill while he enjoyed the beauty of Denali or trout fishing on the Kenai River with his wife and sons.

"It's a relief not to have to cover the burns," I told her at my next appointment. My new "cast" fully concealed the damage but it was difficult to miss. I asked about the picture of a child on her desk. She told me it was her daughter. We discussed mothers, because mine had called to tell me she was in Connecticut at her mother's house for five days and would I like to come down for the weekend? It was of so little significance to see me that she'd already arrived on the East Coast from California when she called to invite me.

I expressed my hesitation about going to see her.

"You need to stop having expectations that all of sudden they'll be perfect parents," she said.

Actually, far from expecting perfection, I expected almost nothing and readied myself to freeze my emotions. My mother didn't know I was in therapy; really, she doesn't know anything about my life. Asking questions is not a thing she does much of.

"I'm in a quandary," I told her. "I'd like to fill the weekend but it horrifies me to lie to them [my mother and grandmother], but having them accept the lie is all the more distancing." At this she made sympathetic noises and gestures.

"If I go I'll just end up taking care of her," I said.

I did go and when my mother noticed, despite my long sleeves, evidence of the thick gauze that encased my arm from just above my elbow to my wrist—or my grandmother noticed and asked—I lied.

"Poison ivy," I said. I spent the weekend concealing my unhappiness in the interest of everyone's comfort.

Driving home, I couldn't stop thinking how the feminine clothing, hair, and well-tended nails of Dr. Kohl's colleague contrasted with my mother's short-cropped hair, bitten cuticles, and personality—not to mention confidence—requiring the lubrication of liquor to operate at all. This substitute shrink took charge of my well-being by sending me to Dr. Ahlers. My mother never told me to do anything, advised, listened, or expressed much sympathy. I'm not sure she knows how. I suspect she exists deep inside her own anxiety, continually working to quell her own emptiness and fear.

I say this because I observed as a child how my mother dreaded being alone in the house, day or night. Maybe that was why she spent so much time trail-riding on her bay quarter horse Stonecrop when she wasn't clocking in hours at the Jerome Bar, my sister and I asleep on the sticky floor under the table blanketed by cigarette smoke and the mixed perfume of booze and beer. Resigned, we curled our little bodies around one another, entwined in the table's metal pedestal like French lapdogs.

My mom liked her guns as much as our neighbor Hunter S. Thompson loved being famous for his. I doubt he slept with one under his pillow as my mom did. Guns have always scared me; a loaded gun in the house invites destruction.

When I was growing up, we had a locked gun cabinet for half a dozen hunting rifles, but a gun in there did my mother no good if her imaginary bogeyman sashayed his way into her bedroom at night, so she kept her guns close. The serial killer Ted Bundy was making news in the Northwest—I knew I'd find a loaded pistol in the glove compartment of her truck and another in the drawer of her bedside table amid shiny green packets of slender, sugar-dusted wafers of Wrigley's Spearmint Gum, its bullets rattling up against the ceramic Carmex canister. The heavy cold metal barrel exuded the unmistakable scent of a freshly minted coin as my sister gingerly lifted it out to show off to a friend.

One of my mother's imperfectly spelled but chatty post-cards, sent from France while my aunt Sid stayed with us, mailed to "N. and C. LeFavour, P.O. Box 104, Aspen, CO 81611 U.S.A." on September 18, 1973, from Hostellerie La Demi-Lune, Propri-etor Madame Vve. Teuschel, Sundhouse, Bas-Rhin, France, read:

Hello! Crec, Nicole and Sid, First day of pedaling very sore fanny. This is a favorite spot and Madam recognized us. We went 25 miles today. Last night had a very piggy meal in Strassbourg. Thrush Paté, Trout ala Creme, Quail, Cheese, Desert, Rasberry Liqueur. Sunday tomorrow + a 3 Star. A friend from Aspen met us in Strassbourg and another very nice fellow joined the biking for a bit. We miss our bunnies.

xxxooo Mama + Papa.

Then, written up the side of the postcard:

Sid, take down pistol (loaded) from top of dresser. Hide Better.

This was mailed two days before my eighth birthday. I wonder where my aunt hid it.

*   *   *

While my mother never went so far as to make sure I brushed my teeth, Dr. Kohl's colleague didn't stop tending me by sending me to the doctor. She finished her three-session record with a note to herself: "Self burning needs direct address with Dr. Kohl. Will discuss with him Wed. July 24 (wished for earlier time)."

I sported that soft white gauze cast, courtesy of Dr. Ahlers, some form of which would remain with me for months, along with a prescription for the broad-spectrum oral antibiotic Keflex. The 3rd-degree burns I've been making take about six weeks to heal; infection slows the healing process. All I had to do was wait for Dr. Kohl's return.

With the exception of the weekend I spent at my grandmother's house in Connecticut, I burned myself daily while Dr. Kohl was on vacation. By turning the talionic impulse inside out, I punished Dr. Kohl for activating my desire for him; leaving for Alaska only underlined his priorities as far as I was concerned. A shrink might call this self-punishment introjection. Never mind "an eye for an eye"; I prefer the full Code of Hammurabi articulated in this translation of Exodus 21: 23–25: "Life for life, eye for eye, tooth for tooth, hand for hand, foot for foot, burn for burn, wound for wound, stripe for stripe."

CHAPTER 12

Appetite for Destruction

I was nervous when I arrived at the post-vacation appointment with Dr. Kohl on July 24. He was about to see my professionally bandaged arm. I'd betrayed him by showing others the burns; they were our secret. But I didn't notice any surprise or discomfort. Rather, he told me he had spoken with Dr. Ahlers about the burns and infection.

The denouement of that heady day was, after more than a year of sitting so frequently, so intimately together in that room, I felt his skin on my skin.

"Changed her dressings for her," he wrote at the bottom of the page. Did he. Patiently he helped me unwrap the bandages while I pulled at the gauze with brusque, nonchalant efficiency to cover my excitement. He cleaned and sterilized the wounds, and laid down the Tefla nonstick pads, overlapping them to cover the open wounds on the inside of my arm that extended by then from mid-biceps to halfway down my forearm. He then took a roll of gauze to secure it all in place, just as Dr. Ahlers and his nurse had done. As I said, it had all the trappings of a cast without the plaster. I don't remember where the gauze, antiseptic, tape, and pads came from. In my memory they just appeared.

I don't remember that detail, because the nimble feel of his fingers overwhelmed me; for so long he'd been over there, eyes on paper, pen in hand forming letters out of strokes of black ink to note, graph, number, and line me up. The wreckage of open wounds on my arm lured him in so close I could touch the wrinkles around his eyes, put my finger on his lip, run my hand over his nearly invisible stubble. I didn't dare do any of this. As he bandaged me I sat up straight and pretended not to notice the collapsed distance while his proximity dried my mouth and tightened my clenched left fist.

"Visibly shaking as I bandaged her," he wrote.

Dr. Kohl changed after he returned from paradise to three dozen or so new 2nd- and 3rd-degree cigarette burns. Perhaps the "direct address of the situation" with his colleague altered his engagement ever so subtly.

The limit he had set before leaving for vacation, that I must stop burning by August 31, became an ultimatum. I would cease to be his patient or be hospitalized if it happened again after that date. The idea of being hospitalized if I didn't stop burning myself scared the shit out of me. It also intrigued me.

"The burning is an angry message," he said to me. And then he wrote, "Time to fight."

"I'm scared," I told him at the next appointment.

"About?"

"Talking about all this stuff. I don't understand it."

"The burning relieves pressure to work on things," he said.

In answer to this I said, "Yesterday I burned and vomited and slept really well."

At the end of the session he wrote a note to himself: "I can't fight with her over life or death."

On Monday, August 5, I told him, "I threw up and burned myself again on Sunday." We talked about Aspen, childhood, parents, and being alone. Nothing new. I left my session and went to work at Community Action, where I spent the morning on the ramp at the back of the Commodity Credit Corporation's truck parked in front of a Grange Hall, handing down giant blocks of surplus government cheese from the Temporary Emergency Food Assistance Program.

Distracted, thinking about and smelling the earthy, sour cheese, I wondered what the people who came for their portion did with it. The cheese was expendable because the government paid farmers to keep the milk off the market. Rather than dumping the milk they decided to use it to help solve the problem of hunger and poverty in America. Brilliant!

As I passed out the cheese, block upon block, I felt my mind churning over the course of the morning, forming a litany of dishes that ran restless and slightly unhinged up and down my brain: *Macaroni and Cheese. Cheese Pizza. Cheese Sandwich. Cheese Cubes. Cheese Balls. Cheese Log. Cheese and Olive Loaf. Cheese and Crackers. Cheese Crackers. Cheese Dip. Ham and Cheese Sandwich. Cheese Panini. Cheese Fries. Cheese Casserole. Cheese Grits. Cheese Danish. Cheese Sticks. Cheese Fondue. Cheese Soufflé. Cheese Lasagna. Cheese Melt. Cheese Nachos. Cheese Dog. Chili-Cheese Dog. Cheeseburger. Cheesesteak. Cheese Quesadilla. Cheese Taco. Egg, Bacon, and Cheese Sandwich. Cheese Soup. Cheese Cauliflower. Cheese Toast. Cheese Scone. Cheese Biscuit. Apple and Cheese Pie. Cheese Quiche. Cheese Puffs. Cheesecake?* The sickening cheese and the stupidity of the system created greater and greater friction in my brain. I badly needed a shower.

Against the backdrop of doing a job that addressed poverty with the most cynical bureaucratic hypocrisy, Dr. Kohl and I continued to wrestle over the burns. He'd given me time to argue and burn, so I kept right on at it.

"Burning is <u>real</u>," I said. "Smoke, fire, odor: Pain is real. Not like the rest of the day. Maybe I'm burning myself for Dr. Kohl. So fine, I'll make it for him," I told him. "Then I'll say, 'This is for you. This is for you, Cree.'"

"Dr. Kohl is inside her. Not knowing what to do about this," he wrote in a note to himself after this comment. What he said to me was, "Burning is very confusing for you."

"It's you. It's not confusing. I'm trying to get it out."

"Proving to yourself that you'll get burned for trusting."

"Yes, going back to <u>betrayal</u> thing. People trick me into trusting. Once I do there will be a trick." This was the 11s talking.

"Will be?" he asked.

"You can't tell."

"Physical, sexual abuse?" he asked, speculating.

"No, this trick was an illusion. It will be gone and I've learned to rely on it," I said, missing the strength of my own magic.

"Is it worth killing yourself to preserve that?" he asked.

"Yes," I said. The whole exchange was enigmatic, with references to the trickery behind the 11s nestled against every word.

In his finishing notes for the day Dr. Kohl wrote, "Danger of therapy, caring, bonding: furious with Dr. Kohl for knowing what she wants and needs (to be held and comforted, parented) and not doing it."

*   *   *

Our argument over what I was doing and why crawled into the first week of August.

"Stop burning yourself," he said simply after I told him I'd finished off five in a row the night before.

"Does it matter?" I asked.

When I told him that I almost cried because I got shampoo in my eye the same night I burned myself five times, he wrote to himself, "Suffered child abuse, maybe there was torture." But this was all wrong and I think he knew that.

The next day, Tuesday, August 6, I arrived for my regular 8:00 A.M. appointment.

"I don't like the deadline," I told him. "I think I can stop doing it. The deadline feels like a dare—it's making the desire worse, more urgent."

I had burned myself three times the night before. As a kid, "I craved rules so I could break them. I can see that now." But I can also see, I said, "I am in fact losing, not winning" this game.

I watched him figuring out how to respond. He was uncharacteristically quiet. Changing the subject, filling the air with words, I told him I actually went out with my friend Jess the night before. I then told him, "I didn't take the Trazodone last night. But I slept. I didn't take the Prozac this morning either."

"Why not?" I was surprised at how irritated he sounded. I smiled.

"Eyes batting. Little Miss Innocent," he wrote. Whatever was going on in his mind felt risky. I usually knew where I stood; not that day.

"I need to convince you not to put me in the hospital."

"I accept the candor but not the lie," he cryptically replied.

"What lie?"

"Something else," he said.

I genuinely didn't know what he was talking about, but whatever it was he meant it. As it turned out, from my caution in not taking my medication he deduced that I had had a drink or two with Jess. He was right and, as he said at the beginning of treatment, he wouldn't see me if I was abusing alcohol or drugs. I didn't consider a drink or two abuse.

He's convinced I'm in danger of becoming an alcoholic like my mother. I don't have a problem with drinking—it's a form of social play I've rarely indulged in since college. I'm aware that getting drunk swallows sadness. I loosely agreed not to drink while in therapy but in my mind it wasn't a strict prohibition; it was more of a strong recommendation against excess. I'm pretty conservative—two drinks are hardly a bender.

"You are furious with me," he said. I couldn't believe he was accusing me of lying. I didn't think having a drink or two was a big deal and if I had I certainly wouldn't have omitted the information only to be accused of lying.

"Yes, I'm pissed off . . . there's no way out . . . I won't leave."

In his notes for the day he wrote, "This is a tantrum. If she can't tell the truth therapy isn't good for her? Clarification of line. Limit is Thursday. NO Alcohol."

The next day, sitting in the blazing light of day in the grave-yard a block from my desk and coworkers, I burned a deep hole on the bottom of my foot. Because the foot is difficult to burn effectively, the extra-thick skin richly crosshatched with layers of nerves, it took a full three cigarettes to get to the painless point.

My Converse on, laced up, with only a trace of sensation at the spot as a reminder of my work, I walked back to my desk. No need for a Band-Aid at this stage—the center of the burn was tough and dry as cured cowhide.

I called the receptionist after that to ask for an extra session. Leaving work an hour early, I told Dr. Kohl about the burn.

"I feel like I want to hurt myself"—and I didn't mean with cigarettes. As he had done since I began treatment, he tried to help me peel away the layers of how pointless and hateful I felt. By the end of the session I was no better.

"I'm afraid I might kill myself. I feel nasty. Burning myself isn't good enough."

It was then that he told me the jig was up. No more games. I had less than twenty-four hours to stop—the burning needed to end by my appointment on Thursday.

CHAPTER 13

Not Safe Enough

An original Daffy Duck hand-painted cel hangs neatly matted and framed to the right of Dr. Kohl's office door. I look at it every time I walk out of there. Arms akimbo, head at a jaunty angle, eyes fixed in a low, knowing gaze, the duck expresses an assertive, unrestrained bravado at odds with Dr. Kohl's placid demeanor. In the stillness of the morning session, backlit by dust particles floating demurely in the washed-out northern sunlight separating our two chairs, I dodged the echo of the duck's humor and the irony—if that's what it was. "Of course you realize, this means war."

I wouldn't be heading to some hellhole of a hospital, if it weren't for the foolish deal I made with Dr. Kohl the next day. The contract I signed that day laid me open to dismissal. Therapists can do that. They fire their patients for abusive language; threats; tardiness; being drunk, high, or asleep; or simply not showing up or not paying up. I've just discovered you can also be fired for holding too many lit cigarettes to your skin. Or for agreeing not to and then doing it anyway.

That Thursday, August 8, I began the session by telling him I'd dropped my German class at the University of Vermont. To put off what I knew would be the day's real conversation, I also told him I needed to sell my car to pay for my lit class because my dad, having paid for college, was done. Delay.

Finally, having spent half the session on nothing, I got to the real business at hand. "I did burn myself again yesterday." I figured Thursday was the deadline—it was Thursday, so I'd had one more fling right up to midnight the night before. But he was immediately stern, as if he was about to throw me out for breaking the rules. I genuinely didn't understand. He'd said I had until Thursday's session—of course I wasn't going to stop a second before I had to. Then the contest escalated. By filling the air of that session with the mundane mechanics of my life, by waiting until late in the hour to mention the burn, I didn't give us much time for discussion.

"Was I going to say that, tell me?" he asked.

"Yes."

"When?"

"I just told you," I said, adding, "I've done it the last time. That's the theory."

"The theory isn't safe enough," he said.

"I was trying to say . . . I'm unsure about what you're saying . . . " I was at a loss. In trouble. I'd snared myself with my own words.

"It's what you're saying that's scary," he said.

"I really don't intend to do it anymore." I thought from then on, I'd be done.

"Not safe enough."

"I have said it, I mean it." Oh God. I remember thinking how out of hand our conversation was getting.

"You don't have to say anything. You had your infection, you're on Keflex? Remember?" He was genuinely convinced that the infection was life-threatening; this seemed a bit of a stretch, but given the surface area maybe it was. I'm not a doctor. Keflex was the strongest, widest-spectrum antibiotic out there. My arm had been grossly infected; it was much improved by then.

"I went right away" to have it looked at when it got infected last time, I said, just so I could fill the air, however irrelevant my words. He didn't take the bait of my diversion.

"You're living on borrowed time."

"I hate this game," I said, scared I'd pushed it too far, blown it for good. He looked at me with that penetrating, caring, but authoritative gaze. Cut the shit was how I read it.

And then he said, "Okay," and he told me I had to agree to a contract. Then it was negotiation time—again.

As if we were at the altar, he said, "Repeat after me: 'I won't do it again, ever.'"

"I won't do it again, ever." As I spoke he wrote the words verbatim in my file.

"Are you a person of your word?"

"Well, I can't guarantee I won't do it again ever, but I will certainly try hard not to do it again. I'll probably call you." I was looking for space, instinctively trying to perforate the clarity he wanted. I thought it might work . . . maybe?

He looked at me as if he couldn't believe I was still trying to wiggle out of the deal, and rather obviously at that.

"Not good enough," he said. Time was running out. "No decision by 5 minutes to 5 P.M. is a decision." That meant out into the world alone or to a hospital.

I saw then that my slippery, equivocal promises weren't sliding by him. Stepping into line, I tried it again and he wrote my words down.

"I feel certain I can call or get myself somewhere if I feel I am going to burn myself. I'm not going to burn myself."

Again, he asked, "A person of your word?"

I replied dutifully, "I am a person of my word and I'm telling the truth."

He then took his eyes from the clipboard and stared me down, holding my gaze. "Are you fully telling the truth?"

"Yes," I said.

He then handed me the clipboard and his pen, still warm from his hand. I fixed my scrawl of a signature at the bottom, on the line he'd made by my name, and that finished it.

Although I'd promised and sworn and signed his document, he left nothing to chance. He asked me to unwrap the gauze from around my arm so he could see the burned area. In the bit of white space remaining on the left of the paper he drew two crude sketches of arms. He then marked the burn area with black ink, annotating the drawings to document the extent and exact placement of the damage. Indicating the specifics with arrows, he wrote, "Scary deep one, deep 3rd degree," "pus," "scarring."

After finishing the ill-fated evidence he bandaged me up oh so carefully—my favorite thing in the whole fucking world. That was when he ordered me back to Dr. Ahlers for another round of debriding.

In my file he noted, "Burn area has increased. Fresh burn on lateral arm."

We were moving forward. It was a deal. I thought I could do it. I thought I could stop.

*   *   *

Once the written contract kicked into effect stopping was an abstraction: a game more than an imperative. He prodded me to call when the urge came on, when I got close, or even when I felt lost or confused. Sitting by the phone at home, I'd stare at the device as if I was waiting for it to come to life. But I wasn't waiting for a ring. When I want to call him I'm a girl getting up my courage to ask for a kindness I can't believe he wants to give me; the thought of speaking to him on the phone makes my gums hurt and lards my stomach with unworldly weight, all the while shooting adrenaline through my cells, and with its arrival come nausea and the desire to spin, pace, walk, run. I know I can pick up the phone and have Dr. Kohl's voice there, all mine, for as long as I can talk to him. But most of the time I can't get close to calling because the process of thinking it through and deciding to do it is so excruciating it's better not to begin.

How many nights have I stared at the phone, lighting the next cigarette, holding the fresh one between my lips while the embers of the old one burn down between my fingers. When I press the two together, they mate perfectly—fire to fire. The shiny black clumsy lump of technology waiting by my side: pick up the receiver, bring the dial tone to life, punch the keypad in the pattern I know all too well; listen as each of the seven shrill beeps registers the sound of a self-fashioned purgatory.

On the third ring it's all up—are they just sitting down to dinner? In the middle of a movie? Watching their favorite TV show? In bed? Sleeping? Reading? Having sex? I always want to hang up. Why did I call? I imagine his wife's annoyance even though her voice barely betrays it when she says, "Hello." If her cool neutrality can be mistaken for a chill, I felt it. She's a pro.

But she never fails to hand him the receiver and then I'm his.

"It's nice you called," he purrs, as I swoon with guilty pleasure because the illusion of comfort is on me again, a cloying syrup I can't take in fast enough, and all I can do is hold him on the line without keeping him too long, because if he winds it down first I'll succumb to humiliation and remorse until I see him again and talk it away. So I speak, keeping the conversation brief while clinging to enough of what he says and what he makes me feel to get through the night intact—long enough not to expand the design, long enough not to stay up all night smoking, reading, writing. Long enough to find sleep.

Our contract was in effect, inked onto paper in my file in his office file cabinet: no more burning or I was out. I felt like a junkie with tracks all the way up my inner arm and a habit that wouldn't give. Dr. Kohl made it as clear as possible that if I slipped I'd have to go somewhere else. He claimed he couldn't be liable for more damage—he couldn't, in good conscience, let it go on, the wounds and the ordained scar traces expanding up the right arm to meet the torso, creeping from the feet up the calf to the thigh, only to meet in one massive raised cicatrix at the belly button, the disfigurement a dividing line between left and right body; one pristine, the other ravaged. Where he sees scarring I see strength and beauty. I deny myself a smooth, pure whole.

I remain bewitched by the ritual. I lack the signs of a penitent ready for reparation. I wake nearly every night to crusty sheets, the fabric of my pajamas glued to the oozing bandages. The raised florid pink halo around the newer burns itches. I scratch and rub as the healing process evolves but the epithelial cells migrate in from the circumference of the wound to the center, where the nodules rise up, raw and wart-like, eager to break and bleed at the lightest touch. The preoccupation with bandaging, washing, wrapping, and, if I only could, laying fresh tracks had taken up a roomy corner in my brain.

A flash of remorse when the mind clears is pure hypocrisy. Regret, if I have any, shows itself only briefly in the moment after the pressure to act is released. Then the cycle repeats. Burning myself is better than anything I can think of, except the feeling of sitting in that chair facing him. I'm so not sorry. But I had to try.

CHAPTER 14

Quackery

From August 8 until September 4 I didn't burn myself once. I was taking the Trazodone and Prozac. Going to work. Hanging on, I tried to forget the exquisite pain of a fresh burn.

I was distracted that month by going public—Dr. Kohl insisted I tell my family and friends what I'd been up to. Putting my dirty secret out there would make it worse if I backslid. Letting my family and friends know was supposed to make me connected. All telling did was defile the preciousness of the secret and the magical thinking that made the burns feel special—that made me special. I felt used and pathetic. Vulnerable.

I did agree to call my father from Dr. Kohl's office. I recited the number and he handed me the receiver.

"I generally lie to people," I said. "I don't want to lie to you, it's distancing . . . I've been burning my arm with cigarettes."

The idea of saying this to him was agony. Fortunately, I was hardly present when I spoke, my words forming automatically, devoid of emotion. My anxiety at what was happening had long since spun me into a nether zone. I handed Dr. Kohl the receiver after I spoke and he told my father I'd agreed to go to a psychiatric hospital if I continued burning myself. He also suggested my father might feel better if he met Dr. Kohl and saw me.

My mother didn't require any information. She had accepted the lie about "poison ivy" I'd offered in Connecticut during Dr. Kohl's July vacation. I have her at a distance as much as she's had herself at one with the help of pint glasses of Stolichnaya over lunches of Cobb salad. I didn't owe her the truth.

When I told my sister over the phone from my apartment she was horrified. We'd been thinking of doing a backpacking trip together in Idaho. Her response was, "You're not doing that *here*." Dr. Kohl thinks it's pretty healthy as responses go. The trip was canceled; I wasn't leaving Dr. Kohl.

I also told my friend Jess, and Matt. He got concerned and teary while Jess took it pretty well; she claimed she knew all along.

My father arrived a week later, defenses up. Suspicious. In his hybrid WASP-hippie world, seeing a shrink was a sign of weakness, subject to accusations of quackery. I suspect he associated talk therapy with a pseudoscientific worldview fixated on the sexual drives Freud believed to be "the strongest of all human impulses." That the modern version of the therapeutic process had evolved considerably since Freud's brilliant, frequently incorrect, wild theories probably didn't matter. My father wouldn't recognize the fact that the graffiti of memory Freud's theories depend upon, most notably the marks of developmental stress and trauma, anticipated important discoveries about how the brain shapes itself in response to various forms of deprivation. Stress matters. That's why Dr. Kohl suspected I was sexually abused. But not having responsive, invested caregivers at various developmental stages also leaves its mark—more on some than on others. I'm sure my father would have agreed humans are social beings. The social imprinting that occurs through the process of nurturing is critical to survival—in evolutionary, biological, and social terms. Neuroplasticity is not fiction.

No matter. My father didn't see the deprivation, even if he had trusted in any brand of psychoanalytic theory. Why, he might ask, would anyone buy into the limitations of half-assed, pseudomedical self-realization? If Freud's place in the popular imagination weren't enough, the rank subjectivity of the whole psychotherapeutic project would be enough for scientifically minded people like my father to dismiss it. Seen through this lens, its claims are no more viable than a belief in the almighty God—and it doesn't get much worse than that in my atheist family. This is the air I've long breathed.

I wasn't raised to concede weakness. I knew my father didn't approve of the indulgence of seeing a therapist. Why can't I be as self-contained as he is? I've nearly exhausted myself trying.

In the world I know best, deviance is valuable. Why squash it out of existence with a normalizing formula? Out with the old, in with the new. Don't just question authority. Fuck authority. The names of the rebels I've heard praised, the ones I've read or listened to, ring through my brain. These figures of the counterculture populated my crowded mind. If the goal of psychotherapy is misconstrued as a normalizing project, then what's it good for? If becoming ordinary is not the goal of therapy, what is? And why not simply fuck it all up if it's not working? If you need to know how just ask one of them . . . *Timothy Leary, Abbie Hoffman, Gloria Steinem, Edward Abbey, Herbert Marcuse, Kurt Vonnegut, Pete Seeger, Martin Luther King, Joni Mitchell, Joan Baez, Hunter S. Thompson, Patti Smith, Oscar Zeta Acosta, Rachel Carson, Carole King, Thomas Pynchon, John*

Lennon, Frank Lloyd Wright, Louis Kahn, Martha Graham, John Coltrane, Philip Glass, Ken Kesey, Anthony Burgess, Andy Warhol, Joseph Heller, Cormac McCarthy, Betty Freidan, Claude Lévi-Strauss, Alan Watts, Angela Davis, Diane Arbus, Janis Joplin, Keith Richards, Mick Jagger, Aldous Huxley, Tom Hayden, Bob Dylan . . . I've forgotten more than I've included, I'm sure. It doesn't matter. I've absorbed the idea that their collective legacies of disruption reflect a refusal of smallness. The very scent of the 1960s and 1970s provided my parents and their friends with what seems like a relatively effortless ride to identity.

Rejecting limitations as beneath you while living off the money someone else earned may be ungrateful and spoiled but it's far from unusual. I should know; I was raised on trust fund hedonism. Although we lacked the materialist gusto of good Americans—no expensive cars, jewelry, designer clothing, or immaculate lawns—the fact is that my parents didn't have to work for a living. Expenditures were made to reinvent the rules 1960s style and expressed through food, wine, grooming, clothes, travel, music, and books.

Family money on my father's side meant he grew up wealthy, with trips to Europe, prep school at Andover, and college at Dartmouth—until he decided to drive west to the then sleepy town of Aspen, grow his hair and beard, live in an unheated cabin, and write a novel. He left most of the traditional values of his East Coast upbringing behind—although his patrician manners never rubbed off. Nor did the cash.

Living large as my parents did required a robust faith in the rewards of going too far paired with a deep cynicism about living a purposeful life, one that went beyond cultivating pleasure. Unfortunately amid all this robust pleasure in living I haven't swallowed much optimism—I've swallowed only determination. My future feels formless and uncertain. I have nowhere spectacularly new to go—nothing grand to rebel against or reject. There are worse things than drowning in an aimless routine of work, reading, eating, and sleep. The superabundance of my life feels cheap and not entirely worthwhile. I've spent the past year examining who and what I am with Dr. Kohl through the lens of my words, behavior, failures, and shortcomings. Surely I've failed, but not in a way my father likely anticipated. Whatever my flaws, I'm certainly guilty of lacking the resilience to gracefully get on with it, whatever the world around me looks and feels like. It's the least I could do given all I have.

When they met, Dr. Kohl observed that my father is "Bewildered by parenting." This shouldn't be surprising considering his mother died when he was nine years old. Despite the steady presence of a kind father, he was essentially raised by nannies and boarding school. Fortunately, even if he never quite knew how to parent me, I adore him.

When he arrived to talk about the mess I was in we went out to dinner and talked books over chicken tikka, garlic naan, saag paneer, and saffron rice, all washed down with Kingfisher beer. The next morning we met for breakfast at the faux-French restaurant Leunig's, where we tore at croissants, smeared apricot jam, and nursed café au lait while trading sections of the *New York Times*. What could he say? He's never so much as pretended to know what's best for me except when he told me he didn't think it was a good idea for me to move to California to live with him while I was in high school. It's hard to forget that moment.

He also may not have wanted to delve deeper into my psyche—he and his second wife enjoy a rich, presumably fulfilling life together. At twenty-five, you might argue, I'm old enough not to be his problem. We have a warm, easy relationship but we're more like friends than father and daughter. We never fight or even disagree. I'd chosen to dig and question where he'd always chosen, as far as I could tell, to cover and duck. After all, "We LeFavours never complain." Why should we? Forward march. Open another bottle of wine. Salt and temper the meat. Warm the plates. Is the cheese out? Watch the reduction! Who wants to switch to the Romanée-Conti? Well, maybe just a sip.

So my father came and went and I had it my way. A session with Dr. Kohl and me—the three of us together. Dr. Kohl probes my father, wondering if there might have been any evidence of sexual abuse when I was a child. My father tries but comes up with nothing more than the grubby family at the end of Little Woody Creek Road and their teenage boys. But it's a dead end. That's all there is. So it's more therapy for me. Dad continues to pay what the insurance doesn't cover. He can afford it. Maybe there's something disrespectful about squandering someone else's hard-earned money even once removed. My father raised me to help him piss away the inherited money that arrived in his bank account quarterly. Compound interest? Yield on investment? Corporate dividend? Advertising revenue? Drinks all around!

CHAPTER 15

Said Spontaneously

The month dragged on—all I had to look forward to was figuring out how to sustain a life I didn't want.

"I feel like I'm going to die if I don't burn myself. The healthy shit," I told Dr. Kohl, "isn't going to work."

In my chart he unconsciously (or consciously) echoed Daffy Duck as he wrote to himself, "So it's war."

"What are you like when you get really angry?" he asked.

"I don't get angry. It infuriates my sister."

"Makes life easy for me." He's trying to get me to fight with him rather than self-destructing all alone. "You're charming, bright, funny, witty. I sit back and enjoy it." Of course he didn't, because he knew too much. Pills in pocket, cigarette to skin. I needed relief. As Churchill observed of the dangers of standing too close to a speeding train, in a second a single "action would end everything." All it takes are "a few drops of desperation."

I'm not big on razors, but since I couldn't burn myself I gave one a spin, carving a bloody triangle "straight around old burn on palm." When I confessed, I told him it was minor.

"I don't care how small it is, you're stretching our contract," he said, having a look for himself. I should have gone deeper . . .

"I felt terrible."

"I believe that," he said.

Again, I was toeing the line while trying to do what I could to keep my brain from detonating. He writes in my chart that I'm "like a 3-year-old preoccupied by the rules."

He asked, "Have you already decided to die?"

"I don't think so . . . " It was the best I could do. The cut was a warm-up, the preparatory mark of a death I hadn't committed to.

On September 4 I struck a deal with myself. It was the spawn of aberrant logic made comely by a feeling of inevitability. If I burned myself one more time, I could stop. I needed this last one to get through the night. I figured out a way to give the act legitimacy because, I told myself, this one time was different. Just one more. Again. My darling, back. The pleasure waited for me, however impatient.

But it was our deal, so ink-and-paper solid, that promiscuously spilled out into the expectant quiet of the next day's session. The 11s had taunted me—turning up to strut about in denominations ordering time, space, money, communication, mass, weight, and volume. I had no choice.

"I burned myself one time."

"Something about first degree, slight burn," he wrote to himself.

"Defiant is better than disengaged," I said.

"You're punishing me."

"I don't mean to."

"It's not me, it's your life."

"Couldn't believe I did that much. Took a shower and did it again. 11 minute thing going on again."

"You've pushed me too far," he said.

"I know the contract and I know I broke it. It seems like it just happened."

"That makes it worse."

I was angling to get off, but seeing that the degree of the burn and the supposed spontaneity of the action weren't getting me anywhere I tried honesty.

"I realize it's a game to argue that I didn't burn as deeply."

"Did you feel it?"

"It felt great and I wished I could have done more."

Long silence.

I'd gone too far, even wearing myself out. I wasn't sure I could keep going much longer and I certainly couldn't do it without him. Rather than leaving literally or figuratively—rather than being ingloriously thrown out—I said, "I want you to say 'Yes' to my going into an institution if you'll be willing to see me when I get out. If that's the only way, then I'll go in."

In his notes he wrote, "SAID SPONTANEOUSLY." I'd made him an offer.

"Long silence with her," he wrote. Then he said, "I'm trying to figure out what I'm going to do with your being unable to be responsible for your life."

"Continue contract discussions Monday," he noted at the bottom of the page. He didn't agree that day to my proposal to go to the hospital, but he did call me over the weekend to see how I was doing. (Wow! He'd never done that before.) Nonetheless, I felt the increasingly tenuous filaments holding my life in place breaking. There was no good solution. I didn't know what would happen once the impossibly slow hours of the weekend passed by.

On Monday, September 9, 1991, a month and a day after I signed the contract, I told him I wanted to die if he wouldn't see me again.

"I feel up in the air. I tried to fill the time between Thursday and now. I get angry, I have suicidal thoughts when I thought you wouldn't see me again. I did burn myself more this weekend. Saturday, late A.M."

"That brings us right back to Thursday," he said, observing in his notes my spontaneous offer to be hospitalized.

"Burning is getting close to self in a negative way. Only way to connect is through horrible feelings," he said.

Of course, having blown the contract the previous week justifying that "one time" as the last time, I burned again over the weekend. One last time is always a lie and I knew that even when I made the bargain, even if I pretended it could be different, that maybe for once when I promised the last it would take.

That Monday he noted in the chart, "Three 2nd degree burns on her right arm." He then told me if I agreed to go to the hospital he'd see me when and if I was released, but not "Against Doctor's Orders."

I had no choice but to agree.

He wrote at the bottom of the page, "I'm willing to argue with her about anything but she can't put her life on the line." He called my father during the session to tell him I was going into the hospital. Listening to the call, I cringed and blushed. My share of shame leaned in, bloated and oppressive. My father was, once again, on his way.

Dr. Kohl called the insurance company and wrote, "Rx $2,000,000." (The Rx stands for treatment. I have $2 million to spend at the psych ward. That must be good news . . .) He called around to various psychiatric hospitals. On a separate note he wrote:

Sheppard Pratt

Availability [circled "Yes" next to it]

Cost $19,000 per month

Proof of insurance (to call me tomorrow)

Book a flight. Board the plane. All of it was much too soon. My fate unfolded as inevitably as the bill the receptionist tallied as I walked out the door.

No surprise. Here I am, waiting. If I pack maybe I'll believe I'm going into a psychiatric unit. Gathering everything I think I'll need for a place I can't believe in, I pack as a naive honeymooner—the surprise destination to be sprung by my eager fiancé on arrival. Skiing in Zermatt? The white sands and azure water of Bali? A culinary tour of Rome? It doesn't really matter, does it? Honeymoons are for fucking.

CHAPTER 16

A Well-Conducted Hotel

Shopping and packing for a few days, ten at the most? Maybe no time at all. Maybe I won't go or maybe they won't have me, turning me away at the door with a breezy, "You're fine. Go home." Maybe I won't sign the legal document to commit myself, the one I haven't read. Most likely I will put my name to it blindly, as if I'm applying for a Visa card and all I want to know is where to put the pen down because I can't be bothered to decipher the irksome block of letters blossoming above it when I badly want all that free money.

When my father opens my American Express bill with the U.S. Postal Service's official yellow "Forward To" sticker plastered on its face he'll scan sheets enumerating clots of dollars spent. Delighted he will be to sign the check and send it on its way to the American Express Billing Center in Duluth, ND. How could he not be happy to pay another bill, this time one I've run up properly in my version of a hangman's meal?

Why not buy whatever I want? I'm post-consequence now. Credit card in hand, over the past twenty-four hours I've fulfilled needs that belong to another girl: Swiss-made cotton underpants, fine-grained Italian leather pumps with slippery soles, watery

Japanese silk cut into strappy camisoles, Scottish cashmere car-
digans in ghastly aquamarine, pearl pink, and babyish ice blue
fit for a blond. Over the counter I slid the magical mint-green
card with the embossed black letters: 3732-10459-2002 Exp 09/92
Cree LeFavour. "Sign here."

I've hoarded Camel Lights. What do I know about what
I'll need once I get there? Do they sell cigarettes off a cart making regular passes through the hall, lobotomized candy-striper
pedaling dated mysteries, cum-stained romances, Hershey bars
and Marlboros, concealed by a uniform of insipid cheer and red-
and-white-striped ruffles? Is there a squalid mini-mart where the
most functional depressive on the hall sells butts, condoms, girlie
mags, and candy? What about a vending machine, commissary,
boutique, or emporium?

Can I expect these or any other amenities or should I
dream bigger—a convenience store for depressives, schizo-
phrenics, anorexics, bulimics, and the generally indeterminate
psychotics. Pajamas de rigueur. This store, instead of offering
the standard array of Slurpees, burned coffee, Twinkies, and
potato chips, would sell only cigarettes, nylon ropes, matches,
straight razors, and strong sedatives in jumbo bottles. Check-
out time is 11.

Gigantic, the vaguely menacing black duffel bulges, sated with
new clothes, old clothes, shoes, cigarettes, toiletries, pens, pencils, and books. It's all inside, packed taut as a 22°F-below down
sleeping bag in a compression sack, expedition-ready. I set aside
my favorite pink Converse high-tops, black pants, and a trusty
white T-shirt to wear the next day.

One black dress—"Women's 10, J. Crew, 100 percent Silk, Made in China, $139.50, On Sale $99," with tax and shipping $115.47—has been spared. It hangs crisp, unworn, tag on, safely falling from the metal hanger like a mourning flag in the absence of so much as a puff of wind, black leather pumps set parallel beneath, sheer black stockings a step away snaking their randy passage through my drawer amid a tight tangle of solo socks and colored tights. There will be no passing off an appropriately expensive '88 Michel Redde et Fils Pouilly-Fumé to sip as an aperitif along with a long gabardine coat and cashmere scarf still warm with animal scent. No fumbling to secure kid gloves in the sleeve. No hostess waiting to make another coat disappear. Social lubrication followed by a tasteful if not tasty dinner at eight is not on the agenda. That much I do know. The dress stays.

Sheppard Pratt. It sounds like a cozy liberal arts college where students take two languages and volunteer in the organic garden. Not the looneybinpsychwardbughousemadhousenuthousefun-nyhousefunnyfarmlaughingacademycuckoonestrubberroompad-dedcellsanatorium. The asylum. Hooking the obvious cliché of the authentic-rebel-against-the-man, I conjure Milos Forman's Jack Nicholson as Randle Patrick McMurphy faking madness and wreaking havoc on the ward as the quietly sadistic Nurse Mildred Ratched and her accomplice Big Nurse draw the life out of every patient within reach, their sticky coercion effortless as the draw of a hypodermic needle. But Sheppard and Enoch Pratt Hospital is no Oregon State Hospital, nor is it a low-level mental health facility like the grave in Menlo Park, California, where Kesey volunteered. Noooooooo . . . I'm destined for a private, expensive institution. "One of the best." Dr. Kohl said so. Twice. Once to my father before he flew out from California and once to me when he discovered it had "a vacant bed." I don't like the sound of it.

Dr. Kohl had called McLean first, but it had no immediate openings so he decided on Sheppard Pratt. I wish I'd drawn McLean. At least it can boast literary cred—I'm not sure Sheppard Pratt has anything of the sort to offer. I'm certainly not putting its most famous inmate, Zelda Fitzgerald, up against the brilliance of McLean's infamous Sylvia Plath.

The best I can claim is F. Scott's pseudo proximity to Sheppard Pratt. He wrote *Tender Is the Night* right next door in Towson, Maryland, while managing Zelda's first institutionalization. He tentatively spelled out that grim time in the apology-cum-rationalization that is Dick Diver. Zelda tried to have her say with *Save Me the Waltz* but ended up crushed by horrendous reviews and poor sales. I hardly blame her for taking it so hard. Setting aside the reviews and sales, recovering from your famous writer husband publicly calling you "a third-rate writer" and a "plagiarist" would do in many robust writers, never mind a mentally fragile first-time novelist. Not everyone can be Günter Grass. The "first-rate writers" club admits new members reluctantly, and only when forced.

With a charter from the Maryland authorities, in 1853 Moses Sheppard supervised and funded the transformation of a 340-acre farm known locally as Mount Airy into his vision of a mental hospital. Sheppard and his money were likely marks for social reformer extraordinaire Dorothea Lynde Dix, whose distaste for the inhumane treatment of the insane was well established by then. Sheppard fell in step with Dix's long-standing crusade to call, as she put it in her 1843 "Memorial to the Massachusetts Legislature," "attention to the present state of Insane

Persons confined in the commonwealth in cages, stalls, pens! Chained, naked, beaten with rods and lashed into obedience."

As compassionate and ambitious as Sheppard was, he was also a fiscal conservative. Like any WASP worth his dry martini, he refused to touch the principal of his generous endowment. (Ah that my father had been so careful with his principal.) The interest generated, plus any gifts received over the course of the years, were the only funds put toward the construction of the buildings and grounds. Progress was slow. (Never touch the principal.)

In 1891 Edmund N. Brush, M.D., became the first physician-in-chief and superintendent. The asylum began a course of enlightened, benign care, guided by the principle that "no anger, no severity, no revenge, and no disregard would ever be shown the insane." Environmental determinism would have it that the place itself was enough to cure most. So although Dr. Brush knew there would be "unmanageable tempers, some violent and sullen patients" he hopes "much of the ill humor, almost all the disposition to meditate mischievous or fatal revenge or self-destruction would disappear" amid the "attractive corridors, parlors and bedrooms." The patients will enjoy a civilized ambience where "the table furniture, silver, and general service will resemble that of a well-conducted hotel." It was Dr. Brush's hope to "cure" most patients and then restore them to their "home and friends." For the untreatable, terminally insane patient the hospital would provide a long-term "refuge, a protection from himself and the world." After all, he reflected, "despair can itself sometimes be found to give place to cheerfulness."

I'm to arrive on the centennial. Perhaps there will be cake.

CHAPTER 17

Politesse

"I can never understand how anyone can NOT smoke," Mann wrote in *The Magic Mountain*. "When I wake in the morning, I feel glad at the thought of being able to smoke all day, and when I eat, I look forward to smoking afterwards; I might almost say I eat for the sake of being able to smoke."

I couldn't agree more. Nicotine, plus the 7,357 compounds identifiable in the smoke of a burning cigarette, is the least of the appeal. There's no hope of reducing the magic of inhaling and exhaling cigarette smoke to mere chemistry. The portion of the nicotine molecule that so effectively mimics the tasty neurotransmitter acetylcholine is a brief footnote to the nearly bottomless pleasures of smoking. Science will have to do better. I've found no satisfactory explanation for the way my mind and body agree to call a brief détente as I smoke. For the three or so minutes it takes to draw and exhale approximately 22 times until the paper and tobacco find the Camel Light's spongy, flameproof cellulose acetate filter, the idea of myself and the experience of being in my body align. I can always have another, because if there's relatively cheap magic for sale in the world, I find it time and again in the ritual of burning the fragile white paper-covered sticks.

So I smoke. Look at the clock. Smoke some more. How many hours? How many minutes before I leave 77½ Intervale Avenue to disappear behind the double, soundproof doors at 112 Church Street? For the last time? The sun hasn't even risen on Burlington, Vermont, latitude 44.49°N, longitude 73.23°W. September 10 sunrise: 6:24 A.M. I have so few hours to burn.

I wish instead of going to my 8:00 A.M. appointment at Dr. Kohl's office, where I'll meet my father and pick up whatever information he needs to get me where I'm going, I could go now, passing like a wraith through the brick walls in the predawn gloom. I'd sit silently in the darkness of the politely tasteful reception area, waiting for Dr. Kohl. I'm safe there. Eventually he'd unlock the outer door, check the answering machine, unlock his office, and disappear into his space. He wouldn't indicate he'd seen me but he'd know—we would know—he'd seen me there. Hell, instead of going to Baltimore I could occupy the same chair there all day, unobtrusively observing as he came and went, collecting and discharging patients. I could pretend, as I always do when I spot one of his patients either waiting for the next appointment or leaving the one before me, that those other people don't exist. Fakes. Liars. Nothing to him. Quiet as I would be, virtually invisible, he would care only for me.

Sadly, I do have an 8:00 A.M. appointment to keep. There will be no sitting in the waiting room all day. Long has that first appointment of the day been mine, Mondays and Thursdays. First. One more time. Best. In my mind lurks the suggestion that if I'm being hospitalized I must be exceptional—although maybe not in the way I'd like.

For a year and some that feels like the entirety of my fucking life I've been waiting to feel the charged moment when the door opens and he looks at me, taking me in, deliciously assessing, deciding about me as I step through the public door frame into privacy, drop my bag by the chair, and turn to face him. Once in the chair I'm excited as a blooming girl set before her birthday cake with bow-tied gifts piled around awaiting eager hands. Six months ago he noted as much to himself: "Almost every time she sits down here she looks like a contented child settling in to be doted upon." Now, for the first time, I don't want time to pass—I just want to sit here in the safety of my apartment.

Why can't time move now as it did for the past year, the hours between appointments stumbling, slow as redemption in a 1950s western you're watching because you might as well fuck that two and a half hours into oblivion with an overfilled bowl of salty, cheesy popcorn—as not. Like a lizard I take popped kernels hand to mouth, lifting them as they stick to the wet of my protruding tongue, carefully measured time dripping. One by one. Minutes. Slow as the progression of nine-point type marching in tight, mean lines down the longest, most boring book. Title Page. Dedication. Table of Contents. Introduction. Preface. Chapters. Notes. Glossary. Appendix. Index. Addendum. Margins half an inch all around. For so long I urged the days until Monday away and then cursed Tuesday and Wednesday, as if their only purpose was blocking passage until Thursday rolled in.

As it always does, however far my faith slips, the hour eventually comes. At least I can trust that and now, here it is, September 10. The ritual. First, Henry's Diner, where I'm useless, acting like a fool without a book at midnight and a delayed flight twelve hours out. Before I have time to put myself in order

over coffee and toast the ugly 8:00 A.M. is nearly upon me; time
to walk around the block to his office, where I'm supposed to
see myself off to an unknown that once done can't be undone.
I've been caught in a self-made snare so effective escape requires
self-annihilation. I won't say good-bye.

His car is there, hot and slick as always. I make my way past
the reception desk and the empty chairs. A fresh benefaction.
But not this time. I've just arrived and we're nearly done. There
are three of us. It's all business with my father there. Unforgiv-
ably steady, the clock's tick-free modesty can't be blamed this
time—or ever. But I do blame it. However politely, it has silently
betrayed me by signaling me out the door twice a week—sometimes more often. Who made the rule that fifty-five minutes is
enough? I'll blame the whipping boy, Freud, but for now it's the
clock that keeps his terms. I wonder if I could shatter it with
a toss, small and large gold-plated hands, heart-points flying.
Would it grace the air, detached, spraying seconds in droplets as
it fell to the floor? If that didn't work I could go inside, where it
keeps its purpose behind a churning mechanical hum, to bend
and break the pieces. Or I could simply smash it down on the
shiny table to stop it. But what of the masterful electricity, argu-
ably the true culprit? Clip, cut, pull the plug? However it's done,
I'd like to dismantle the whole with the violence it's due, at least
temporarily eliminating the mechanism of my departure.

But the send-off is in motion. Dr. Kohl's hand extends to
offer his grasp. A shake? What can he mean? Shake hands as if
we've completed a deal? Met politely at a conference and hope
to see each other again, knowing we won't shake? Thanks for
dinner and I'm sorry I'm fucking your wife shake? You're a little
shit and I'll crush you, but people are watching so I'll follow

convention shake? Surely it's the good-bye and we have a deal shake? I'm numb.

I've never shaken his hand; I've hardly ever touched him, except for those riveting moments when he wheeled his analyst's chair close to me to examine, clean, and bandage my burned arm. That was touch.

But this? Out of years of polite training—"*politesse,*" my Dad would prompt at the least impudent glimmer—I extend my hand. Skin to skin. His unblemished, callus-free office fingers graze the freshly laid Band-Aid covering last night's handiwork on my palm. He's close enough to see my cheek. I'd chosen the most obvious, most visible spot. Fuck you. It didn't matter anymore. The game was up. More fresh work there, more fresh work on my feet. How can Dr. Kohl let go, sending me off with nothing more than this stale ritual of a formal good-bye?

Willing time to release the warp speed it takes on in this room, I won't yield. I'm walking out that door? That door I've walked out of so many times with the greatest regret for a two- or three-day absence? Now this? Weeks? Months? Years? Forever? He releases my hand as I petition the moment to show some sign of promise. Anything, really, will do.

PART II

*Ya know, I ain't never been in an institution of
psychology before.*
> —Jack Nicholson as Randle Patrick McMurphy
> in *One Flew over the Cuckoo's Nest*

Do you like plum cake, Monster?
> —Lion from Lewis Carroll's *Through the Looking-Glass*

*But I was feeling febrile even then—for the air up here
is not only good against the illness, you know, it is also
good for it, it sometimes brings it to the surface—which
is of course a necessary step in the cure.*
> —Thomas Mann, *The Magic Mountain*

CHAPTER 18

Humiliation Olympics

As humiliating experiences go, third-place ranking goes to the time I confessed to my father over a Tanqueray and tonic while perched on a stool at the Oak Room in the Plaza Hotel that I was pregnant and getting an abortion and sure, I could use the extra cash. Then taking the bills and feeling like a sexual being and therefore like a big, slutty whore dumb enough to get knocked up and greedy to boot. The honorable second-place ranking in my humiliation Olympics goes to a discussion I had with my father about whether or not I was sexually molested as a child, including speculation about who it might have been—the boys at the end of the driveway in Woody Creek, who always seemed creepy? Or that babysitter's older boyfriend? Or lovely Hester, the foreman at the Ranch, whom I adored but got confused about? As if that weren't bad enough, I said, "Yes, I'm sexually functional," leaving the conversation knowing I'd said too much, more than necessary, because in what universe does anyone other than the person you're fucking, your doctor, or your best friend care if you do or do not achieve orgasm during sex? But surely in first place, the gold secure, is being escorted by my father onto and off an American Airlines flight from Burlington, Vermont, to

Baltimore, Maryland, to be checked into a hotel where I will be kept under guard for the night only to be delivered up to a psych ward the next day.

My father is worried and doing the right thing because he figures on a vague, paternal level it's all his fault and he should have seen this coming and how could he let this happen to his daughter and now he'd better do whatever the shrink says to fix it because he doesn't know what to do and maybe he never did. His endearing chatter is awkward. This is an emergency. And he can't possibly talk about it because the chance of saying the right thing is close to zero.

So he doesn't say shit and the air is as thick as the pillowed clouds sliding in appalling stillness past the oval frame of the scratched acrylic airplane window. The red-white-and-blue of the American Airlines logo on the blade of the wing cuts through them without disturbance and yet each one appears substantive enough to walk on, like the massive thunderclouds from *James and the Giant Peach* the Cloud-Men cavort upon, "huge hairy ghosts" chucking hailstones at the peach as it sails through the sky under power of hundreds of seagulls harnessed by Silkworm's rope. Dad read me the book before I read it myself. Dad, here in the next seat adroitly folding and turning his way through today's *New York Times*—"Strawberry Comes to Rescue as Dodgers Remain in First . . . Cuba Rationing Cigarette Sales . . . Police Seek Missing 8-Year-Old Bronx Girl . . . "

When I get there, will there be leisurely days spent padding around in tasteful pajamas or will muscle-bound, tattoo-sheathed orderlies watch patients wander the hall clad in paper slippers and flimsy mint-green hospital gowns opening at the back? Both options are false, lousy with film and fiction, derivatives of too much culture. Likely, patients will wear their own contemptible clothes just as I will. Still, the idea of spending all day—possibly a week, two tops—in pajamas is a pet I can't quite release. My PJs must kill.

We're at "Harborplace, Baltimore's Exciting, Dynamic Waterfront." That night before I go in I locate them, brazenly offering themselves to me, dangling from the tidy rack of like Persian-style pajamas in Men's. I can't fail to recognize them. Their lonely occupation of the grubby mall in the bowels of the Marriott doesn't help. Surrounded by the aura of hopeful emptiness defining all unprofitable retail locations, this Brooks Brothers' simulacrum of upper-class privilege gleaned from its 346 Madison Avenue flagship has been further corroded by its location across from the Piercing Pagoda, offering a two-for-one special: "Nose and Navel $55." This is my final hit of in situ consumer transformation before I go in.

They are my unforeseen denouement with their placket front, five fat tortoiseshell buttons, finely hemmed length of identical material as drawstring, slim fit, and gaping fly with no buttons—not like I have a dick to stick out of it in the middle of the night in the dark, but if you locate navy and hunter-green plaid pajamas in madras so fine you want to lick it, and it's the last shopping day before the big event, you lay down the card. "Sign here." These are the pajamas.

My father has exchanged pleasantries and credit card information with the desk clerk in the hopelessly empty lobby of the

Marriott. The key to room 335 in hand, we're soon in it, pulling open the heavy draperies. Baltimore's harbor spins beneath, animated by the movement of boats, water, and wind. I press the red power button on the sleepy remote. The generic hotel room attempts a degree of self-importance with the uncluttered right angles of the desk, table, door, window frame, heater, and full-length mirror doing most of the work. Accurately matching one another, two immaculate queen-size beds add to the effect, while the chrome luggage rack announces the impermanence of our presence. The affected gentility will be demolished as soon as clothing, toiletries, shoes, and unmade beds blur the edges, spoiling the symmetry. Leaving the flickering television light to fill the vacuum, I go to pee.

My dad sounds as though he'd rather drown himself than speak when he says, "You have to leave the door open." The volume and tone read timid, his voice overlaid with embarrass- ment I can identify without seeing his face or gestures. Before this moment, the two of us have hardly spoken about what I've done or what I'm doing, and then only in the presence of Dr. Kohl, preferring instead to focus on the process of getting where we're going fast.

He's been my distant keeper, certainly in mind; but the literal enactment of the role, as my jailor, flattens me. He's doing as he's been told. Instructions I heard and Dr. Kohl wanted me to hear, saying them as he looked at me: "Don't leave her alone. Not for a minute. Don't let her close a door between you. Don't let her out alone for a walk or a coffee or a cigarette. Watch her." My cheeks and forehead flushed then as they do now—the blood beneath the skin on my cheeks inflamed as the opened-up capil- laries warm.

I'm fine. You don't understand, Dad. It isn't like that. I'm not going to burn a hole in my skin right here in the bleached bathroom with you ten feet away. I'm not sweeping aside the dwarf-size guest shampoo to make a seat; turning on the hair dryer as background noise; tearing the lid up through the laughable white paper Sanitary Seal to make an ashtray of the toilet; choosing, lighting, inhaling, and homing in on my spot. What I do is too sacred for this cheap space.

Silent, I open the door to pee in the unnatural exposure the open air between my father and my exposed ass creates, vaguely hating my compliance along with the door's failure to complete its function of shielding this intimate act from an outsider. My piss hitting the water sounds just as it should—loud. The steady stream of free airplane Diet Coke coupled with the sour coffee at the airport before takeoff exits my body, hot yellow liquid flowing into the waiting toilet bowl, where it mixes with cold Baltimore water to make its way down the pipes and away in one pressurized whoosh.

My father sits on the bacterially rich hotel bedspread somewhere out of view, the perfumes of our humiliation mingling in the sorry air box of room 335.

CHAPTER 19

One Big Disappointment

The Arrow Cab driver who picks us up in front of the Marriott seems tired, as if it's the morning after a night shift. He looks the way I feel after barely sleeping in the queen bed, an outsize extra-firm hotel pillow straining my neck as I listened to my father's steady snore not two feet away. As I would gaze at the enviable, unblemished smoothness of a woman's thigh or the perfect mocha tautness of a muscled arm, I study our driver's elegant neck. I'd rather think of anything other than what's happening to me or how ugly the once alabaster skin covering my right arm now looks to everyone but me. So I ponder his possession of the maximum load of melanin (and its cousin eumelanin), speculating that for him to possess such skin, his family tree never branched far from the ancestors who retained the distinctive traits they shared, refusing outsiders who didn't fit the norm. Perhaps he descended from East African Nilotic people who, amid Africa's vast genetic diversity, retained the trait for the darkest skin, somehow keeping this highly mutable genetic feature intact thanks to geographic isolation, a cohesive language, culture, and the splendid resources of the fertile Nile River valley.

Whatever his history he's here now, in Baltimore, Maryland, where his skin shines despite the light it absorbs. He's radiant; a postmodern Wallace Thurman relegated to being a poor man's chauffeur in a reality ordered as neatly against him as a game of cheater's Monopoly. Lost in my reverie, trying not to think of where I'm going and the mess I've made, I wonder what the sun feels like on his skin, how the surface melts creamy white suntan lotion into a glossy slick, like when I manage a lovely dark tan and the Coppertone melts into it quick as lard on the surface of a hot cast-iron pan. I imagine shedding my pale mutt pelt and trying his on for measure. I could drive off in the taxi, look for a fare, smoke a cigarette between pickups, go home to a familiar bed.

"Sheppard Pratt, 6501 North Charles Street. It's in Towson," my father leans in to tell the driver. Giving directions and paying the fare are his job. I'm the child. I can ask questions but I've agreed to do as I'm told.

I'm not a bad fare, almost a catch, really: nine and a half miles, eighteen minutes without traffic. As we move down East Pratt Street I press the button to lower the window, feeling instant relief from the chilly silence of the cab. Hot air gushes over me and with one humid pant dilutes the car's interior.

The driver's eyes and mine meet in the rearview mirror when the window comes down. Despite the air-conditioning whirring on max, he's not going to tell me, "Roll the fucking window up, it's hot outside." It's obnoxious to put the window down but I don't care. It occurs to me this minor act of rebellion is weak; I could make a scene just to fulfill the psych patient cliché. Maybe the driver expects a little drama when driving a bandaged girl and her duffel to Sheppard Pratt. I'm one big disappointment.

We approach the hospital and the cab slows in strict adherence to the fifteen-mile-per-hour speed limit—no rush on my account. I absorb the scale, landscaping, and grandeur of the sweeping lawns and massive brick buildings. The imposing elements of semi-evolved Gothic Revival structures with their steep roofs, painfully sharp peaks, intricate gables, arched doors, and decorative windows form islands surrounded by green grass flowing like liquid into and out of the generous open spaces between them. The whole communicates civilized bucolic ease with the ready gloss of a healthy, well-tended endowment.

The architecture is supposed to be slightly medieval. It's also quiet, beautiful, formidable, and more than a little alarming. Even if the grounds and buildings were designed to look like residences—not a prison—the appearance of the place spooks me. The cab stops at the tasteful "Admitting" sign. The antiseptic, distinctly bureaucratic feel of the reception room contrasts rudely with the world just outside. After several papers have been signed it's time for my father to leave. How reckless I am. By handing myself over to the care of unseen doctors and nurses, knowing almost nothing about the rules, expectations, or dangers of the closed world I'm about to enter, I've made a giant bonfire of my life and decided to walk away, letting it burn. My father's departure makes this all real.

He looks miserable in his moth-bitten gray Shetland sweater hanging over butterscotch-brown wide-wale corduroys, the folded-sewn cuffs just hitting the tops of worn, cushioned brown leather kitchen shoes. He's what Roald Dahl calls an "eye-smiler." Forget the face—it's mostly obscured anyway since he's all forehead and beard. But those two dominating features highlight the intensity of his kind blue eyes. I look right into those eyes after we embrace for the final good-bye. The tears are messy as my nose begins to run, the salty liquid and snot marking the end of the costly job of maintaining a veneer of courage. I'm collapsing in on myself, my father's beard scratchy on my cheek as we each try to hold on.

CHAPTER 20

SDB

THE SHEPPARD AND ENOCH PRATT
HOSPITAL ADMISSION NOTE
SEPH SOCIAL WORK ADMISSION
PSYCHOSOCIAL ASSESSMENT
WITHIN 72 HOURS

Medical Record Number: #54847
Date of Admission: 9/11/91
Chief Complaint: "Burning myself"
Age: 25
Race: W
Marital Status: S
Religion: none
Referred by: Dr. Adam Kohl

I have to assume it was more than summoning Bush, Reagan, Carter, and Ford in the correct order and my ability to repeat three objects and remember them after one minute—cat, key, flag— that led to my assessment as "Intelligent, verbal." The nurse identified me as a "casually dressed well groomed WF." I was "polite and cooperative" during the interview. The intake form notes that I've had an increase in SDB-Burns (self-destructive behavior) and that I "do not see a problem" with the behavior "except in rxns. [reactions] of others" to its results. I was not labeled **Retarded, Below Average, Average,** or **Above Average.** The Gross Estimate of my Intellectual Functioning: **Superior.** How happy that would have made me, had I known it at the time.

On the next page, under "**Diagnosis: Axis I**" the chart reads "Depression, maj. 296.23 Bulimia R/O Dissoc D/O R/O MPD." Under "**Axis II**" is "def. 799.90" and under "**Axis III**" "numerous burns on arms, face, leg." The remaining **Axes, IV** and **V,** are blank. Under "**Initial Treatment Interventions (Diagnostic, Medical, Psychiatric)**" are four entries:

hosp for safety—pt. quite self destructive

watch for infection of open wounds

Pt's EDsx currently under control

Dissoc workup

I was given a primary diagnosis of major depressive disorder, single incident "Severe without Psychotic Features," along with bulimia and the ever-scary flavors of the decade, dissociative disorder and multiple personality disorder (MPD), that must be R/O—ruled out. The 799.90 under Axis II means defer the diagnosis. Watch and study to appraise the truth of the answers I offered alongside my behavior. Sort the "polite and cooperative" from the lies patients invariably tell. Put me in play.

The intake nurse conducts a standard interview meant to compress years of memory and an iffy scaffolding of fact into a page and a half of handwritten notes. Everything I say sounds trivial and wrong. I'm rigorously downplaying but I mean it when I say the burns are "really not a big deal."

Brevity is my goal, achieved by divulging as little as possible without explicitly lying or being uncooperative. Keeping the story of my life and appearance brief comes easily. I'd never seen the woman before and yet she expects me to answer the following questions: "Why are you here?" "Why do you burn yourself?" "Can you describe your childhood?" "Are you married or in a relationship?" "Did you complete high school?" "Did you go to college and graduate?" I'm aware she likely knows the answers to many of these questions. Her purpose is to see if I can explain my history with a logically connected string of words. I suspect her main goal is to determine if I am actively psychotic. My goal is reassuring her that she is doing her job. I figure if I put her at ease I can be on my way. So that's what I do.

Where am I going? The paperwork is fully inked. Now they have to actually do something with me. I can't stop thinking about which ward they will put me in. They must have halls for those prone to violence. That's where they station the beefiest nurses and an extra hall monitor or two. There must be a children's ward, a sad hall to hold fragile minds that have disappeared from this world to another. Surely there's a place for pure crazy. I hope I'm not going there. I'm depressed, bulimic, and self-destructive. I have no history of violence or psychosis unless you count what I do to myself.

What about a ward for people who have just grown too tired to perform? I dream of death but have never tried to die. Perhaps there's a politely crazy hall that separates the sad and hopeless from the insane? That's where I'd like to go; where inmates share a semblance of normality and where civilized behavior remains in effect—a place to exit the world without making it final; a sensory-deprivation tank set one degree above body temperature, 99.9. Silent as snow, dark as bat velvet.

Released from intake, I'm flanked by two nurses, one on each side. I follow in step with them down a fortress-worthy corridor into the nucleus of the building. My talismanic pink Converse high-tops convey my docile body down the hall. The nurses aren't talking or touching me but I'm pretty sure they would yell at me or grab me if I tried to step out of line. I walk while holding on to the objective idea of the action. In seconds I'll glimpse my fate and once I do, I've agreed to tolerate it for at least seventy-two hours—probably longer. My jailors get to do with me whatever they like and I have no reason, beyond Dr. Kohl's recommendation, to trust this place.

I might really be in for it. I should have left—extracted the maximum cash advance from my Amex and made a spectacular disappearance. India? Thailand? Brazil? In their matching white uniforms, the nurses resemble a pair of trained white mice, their hyper-attentive eyes searching and alert, as if a cat's around the next corner. Or do I have it all wrong and I am the cat?

We pass identical doors punctured by windows set at eye level so a nurse, orderly, doctor, food-service worker, or janitor can peer in to see if anyone is waiting on the other side. In here, there are no good surprises. This peeking routine must be part of the workers' safety training and I'm sure it's effective in preventing assaults and escapes. The brutality here is well disguised. The contrast of the fine crisscross of metal filaments over the windows against the backdrop of the hall's grandeur signals an awkward evolution of the space's use. Is there an impermeable door with unbreakable glass for me or are they taking me somewhere else? I can't quite grasp I'm about to be locked up, much less what that will feel like.

It strikes me that this is a good time to make a scene, no matter how minor. Before I'm locked in. But I'm not that kind of girl, as has been proved. There's a quiet magic in control. I need to play nice and there's nothing I can do about it. Not yet.

I've taken this further than I intended—if I did intend anything. Therapy. Burning. It's as if I started laughing in a silent room when I was supposed to be quiet. The attempt to stifle the noise and gain control only fueled the laughter, but there's no stopping because I enjoy letting it take over more than I've enjoyed anything for a long time. It had been glorious fun until I realized I couldn't stop if I tried.

I swore I wouldn't be easy for Dr. Kohl to diagnose—no 908.3 for me. I proved that point. We all want to feel special. But along the way I lost track of what I was doing. When I burned myself again I knew I was breaking the contract I'd signed. But it wasn't so much a decision as caving in to the inevitable. Still, how the fuck do I find myself in Towson, Maryland, being escorted down a long corridor by a couple of nurses in bleached party dresses?

I'm terrified but trying not to show it as I pass through a door to the right looking exactly like all the other doors except there's a metal sign printed beside it: B-1. Nurse two scurries to keep up, padding just behind, pantyhose swishing above thick-soled white lace-up sneakers. They're starting to show some wear. I feel a flicker of pity for her but it doesn't last. It's much easier right now, in the raw aftermath of leaving my father behind, to shut down all emotion. I do this so well I convince myself I'm not feeling a thing. Watching, as if I'm a third party, as the heavy metal door closes. It locks on the inside. You need a key to get out, not to get in.

I'm on the wrong side of the door. The forms signed, a thin folder makes its way through the building with my name typed precisely on the tab. Contained inside you would find everything these people know, alongside all they think they know. The system has eaten me and now it's digesting. The waiting Arrow taxi driver has driven his fare back down Pratt Drive. By now, my father sits in room 335, the TV on too loud.

CHAPTER 21

Enemy Cover

A third nurse waits inside what is to be my room. Prim in her starched uniform, a high, slick bun in strict control of her hair. She's breast-free and straight as a dowel, a shadow of her overweight coworker. Exuding steady patience reserved for intake, her gaunt face declares, "I don't mind being nice until my shift ends. I'm good at my job." The extra-sweet introduction exposes gaps that ought to be filled with some indication of sincerity. Why answer this automaton of the Sheppard Pratt induction team? I've now officially given up on polite. What immeasurable satisfaction to desert the wearisome social contract. No more offering waitress-daughter-patient-student-girlfriend-savior comfort. I've bailed on the familiar duties of gratitude. I can be as bad as I like. I'm barely even Dr. Kohl's patient anymore.

A smart little button of a bellhop or an orderly acting in such capacity has been at his job. I suppose I should have tipped him but now it's too late; I never even saw him. A hippo felled on the industrial nap of the carpet, the duffel gives itself to gutting. Zzz-ziiiippp. The taller nurse's ass presses against the fabric of her uniform as she leans in, revealing a bulge where the elastic of her underwear liberates the excess flesh of butt and upper thigh. Item by item they work as a team, sifting through the bag's entrails, touching, turning, shaking, examining, deciding. The cartons of Camel Lights are no longer mine, except they miss a pack tucked deep inside the kangaroo pocket of my faded Deerfield hoodie. Four lighters and three books of matches, confiscated.

The underfed mouse holds one book at a time upside down by the spine and shakes, the open pages facing the floor. I witness. Silent. Obedient. I've tucked a straight razor in *Buddenbrooks*, fresh and bright as a live sardine. The 604 pages flop, the fragile spine of the aged binding weak, crumbling, yearning to crack. I imagine the thin ink-patterned pages skittering to the floor, free, the words fluttering and humming as they make their way down. I see the razor falling on top of page 370, page 371 dropping down to lie on top of it. Enemy cover. Why didn't I choose a different book? Something newer. Tighter. A book with integrity. I'm sure *The Magic Mountain*, with its sturdy yellow paper spine and fine 716 closely packed pages, would never open itself so promiscuously. The big nurse gives one final vicious shake to Mann's first full-length novel, as if she can sense the weightless razor, impossibly sharp, hiding motionless inside. *Buddenbrooks* does not betray me.

There isn't much else to find. They've missed the second razor as well. It's tucked inside *Anna Karenina*. A matchbook deep inside the key pocket of my Levi's also escapes them. They take away rattling pill bottles—Prozac and Trazodone—piling them with the rest of the hazardous material emancipated from my possession. Not only lighters, cigarettes, and pills but pencils, pens, cuticle scissors, nail polish remover, a pink disposable Daisy, my scarred red leather belt, and a plastic bag containing shampoo and conditioner. I'm almost impressed with their thoroughness.

A brown blanket conceals the stiff mattress that's now the central feature of my habitat. A pawed hodgepodge of personal rubble dents the blanket's taut surface, claiming the space as mine. It's a magpie's paradise.

They're gone. Door ajar. The scene is plain as a college dorm room—two single beds, two desks, two chairs. Overhead light. Its austerity suits me. I'm in the hospital because I burn my skin and the behavior isn't socially acceptable. In the most objective sense, the line between landing here and remaining on the outside falls on the differences between public and private, shame and pride, voluntary and involuntary.

Men and women the world over scar themselves as a means of linking identities and common values—loyalty, war-worthiness, prowess, aesthetic pride, or honor. The scars of prisoners and bushmen make group identity visible and permanent. The tracks down a junkie's arm mark a broken tribe while serving as identification; when she's buying junk they're the best proof of not being a narc. My burns do the opposite—the secret of them separates me from anyone who doesn't know they exist, much less what caused them. They are private—Dr. Kohl was the only one who knew about them until, of course, I blew it up and landed myself here.

Some people assume wrongly that burning or cutting is tantamount to trying to kill oneself. Not so. Shrinks have a term and even an acronym for what I do: non-suicidal self-injury (NSSI). That's because even professionals confuse self-destructive behavior with a gesture toward death. Actually, what I do staves off suicide. Without it, I might not be able to say I've never tried to kill myself; without it, I'm not entirely certain I'd be able to make that claim. That's part of the reason I love my scars. They track my successful feats of self-preservation. The power I feel when I burn myself trumps fear, turning suffering on its head by making it a pleasure in its own right.

It's time for induction. I'm to tour the hall—a walk through the T-shaped unit with its wreck of tattered furniture cluttering the common room; TV room, where patients sit silently staring as light twinkles behind the screen of the talking box; men's and women's bathrooms; two shower rooms; two quiet rooms. The view through the open doors lining the hall to the left and right of the central common area reveals more bedrooms, duplicates of mine, plus one large dorm room with four bunks making eight beds. All rooms have enormous windows framing the ample span of cut grass and 100-year-old trees.

There are no curtains anywhere to block the light—or to hang yourself with.

A pay phone mounted on the wall directly across from the nurses' station awaits a purpose. The enclosed professional space hums, a cozy nest filled with voices, laughter, the jingle of the hospital phone—a warmth passes through the glass of the medication window and spills into the hall, where it brings life to everything within reach. The shelf and sliding door of the med window resemble the convenience-store cashier windows I've shoved dirty bills through, grateful for the late-night dispensation of Zingers, Bud, and Camel Lights.

Chubby mouse appears before me only to launch into a rehearsed explication of B-1's rules, her disproportionately small mouth painfully articulating words, their precision gummed by the most excruciating pauses. Rather than listening I imagine her words pouring out too fast to hear, flowing down her white uniform, a hot stream of silver liquid falling over the ledge of her giant breasts.

Since I don't want to listen, I ponder requesting a copy of the rules so I can read them. How quickly I could decide which ones to follow and which to skirt, avoid, ignore, disregard, or otherwise disobey. Deciding against interrupting, I listen in spite of myself while looking around, up at the spots on the faraway off-white ceiling, down at the gray laces winding through the chipped white paint on the metal eyes of my pink high-tops.

1. No entering another patient's room for any reason.
2. No physical contact between patients.
3. Medication distribution: 8:00 A.M., 12:00 P.M., and 5:00 P.M.
4. Showers by permission only.
5. Report patients dangerous to themselves, staff, or other patients.
6. No leaving the unit other than for a meal, therapy, or a scheduled activity.
7. Phone calls may be placed or received 5:00 P.M. to 9:00 P.M. with written permission from the patient's therapist for general or specific "phone privileges." Time limit for all phone calls: twenty minutes; ten if anyone is waiting.
8. Smoking permitted during designated smoking times three times daily between the hours of 9:00 A.M.–9:10 A.M.; 1:50 P.M.–2:00 P.M.; 7:30 P.M.–7:40 P.M.

CHAPTER 22

Well Documented

Being on Suicide Observation (SO) secures my status among the patients. Nobody gets too near a new SO. Even on a psych ward suicide is distasteful. I suspect there are few people here who haven't considered it or actually tried it—usually more than once. Why obviously flirt with darkness?

The inaccessible outdoor foliage of the hardwoods, rolling lawns, and rowdy gangs of squirrels are framed by sturdy shatterproof glass. I can only look at it. To release a little tension from my brain I write one of my shitty poems I call "fragments" in a notebook. I study the sounds while I wonder at the lack of motion. There's nothing for me to do, nowhere to go. I'm simply locked up. I don't touch the food on the dinner tray that's delivered to my room. Instead I lie on my bed facing the window until exhaustion takes over. I sleep.

It's Friday, day two, heading into what I will learn is the deadly quiet weekend. As I discover, there's no schedule for me. I must first see The Doctor. I haven't been assigned my therapist, group therapy, or therapeutic activities. The program has not been unveiled—my very own personally designed schedule for wellness.

Until then and until my SO lifts, I'm not allowed off B-1, nor am I permitted to close the door to my room. I am allowed to use the bathroom even though there have been incidents of girls drowning by sticking their heads in the toilet and even one who creatively filled a trash can with water for the same purpose. The nurses get a visual of me on schedule, usually in my room, every twenty minutes. At night the nurse shines her flashlight right on me to be sure I'm there—breathing. Check.

The weekend's stagnant doctor-free hall expires as Monday saunters in late. They're back, the army of professionals here to mix up the monotony and make me right. Dr. William Simons, head physician, is off on his rounds, more than on time. He's looking trim, his cheeks and chin and lip freshly shaved, pink on white, smelling of expensive soap, ready to chat. I'm not dressed and not noticeably alert, my bed little more than rumpled laundry beneath me. I'm not talking to this man.

As I quickly learn, decisive male voices signal rounds each weekday morning as the senior supervising doctors work their way through the ward, stopping to chat up the patients on the hall, perfunctorily knocking on the door to each room, never waiting for an answer before entering. The doctors speak in normal voices (not the hushed tones the nurses use), appearing larger as a result. Dr. Simons's five minutes with me feel perfunctory: "How are you feeling today, Ms. LeFavour? Sleeping? Good. Good. Settling in?"

The nurses are another matter. Female to the last, they behave cautiously, unsure of me and what I'm capable of. It's tempting to surprise them but then . . . they're likely difficult to surprise, requiring gore and drama beyond my present abilities. So I remain a blank, dangerous as any void for its unknown quantity. Perhaps I'm not sure what I'm capable of either. I have no immediate plan to take to the razors, cigarettes, or matches, but I do like having them there. As the doctors who ordered the SO know, inpatient bulimics have close to a 40 percent rate of attempting suicide. Adding self-harm and depression to the mix results in an even more sobering percentage. I probably deserve my SO status, if only out of respect for the statistics.

Becoming an indoor cat at a psychiatric hospital in 1991 requires meeting a certain criterion—the objectively irrational self-mutilation I enjoy qualifies me under the category of "a danger to oneself or others." Is that how I find myself here, on the other side of an extraordinarily thin line between sanity and its absence—one that I can't exactly remember crossing? I'm not at all convinced I belong here. And yet part of me is ready to be taken care of under the thoroughly infantilizing conditions of SO. My childlike dependency on Dr. Kohl has found its ultimate expression. I hope I can hold on to the fantasy that he's taking care of me; turning against him now that I can't see him or hear his voice would leave me hopelessly detached.

The bed next to mine is briefly occupied. I don't talk to her or look at her longer than necessary to assess the damage. I'm not mean to her but I'm also not making the mistake of taking care of her if we're going to occupy the same room for the next . . . who knows how long? It's easy to put her at a remove. I couldn't care less what she thinks of me. She's her own problem just as I'm mine. The last thing I want to be is her friend, confidante, or sympathizer. Before I'd know it I'd be sitting in for her mother. I'm too porous—whatever mental equilibrium I can achieve is subject to disruption.

She's a cutter. Blood arouses some people; it might arouse her, the gory immediacy fueling her ritual self-mutilation. As little as I've tried cutting, I suspect the delicate yet determined hand required for a really deep cut is beyond my abilities. I've never applied enough pressure on my instrument to make the cut really count. The force combined with the sharpness of the instrument produces unpredictable results. I prefer the control of flesh combusting in layers. Temperature squared and multiplied by seconds equals depth: $T^2 \times S = D$—or something like that.

My luck interferes: she's discharged before my anxiety over her company becomes too much. The room now securely mine, admits must be slim. The insurance revolution churns, policies shrinking, mental health care benefits stingier by the month. Empty beds augur the limited stays that will be the norm of the future. I'm in possession of the gold standard of insurance policies: with just the tiniest deductible, I have a $2 million inpatient cap. The hospital verifies the information on admission—all good. I'm the golden goose.

Liberally spent money ensures I remain alive and unharmed. I take to the pablum of solicitude like a doll, even if I'm unnerved by the experience of the ever-open door, the flashlight bobbing around in the dark, the staff eying every movement, my presence on the hall and state of being alive on record every twenty minutes. The scrutiny of SO comforts me before it morphs, turning me feckless, like a footnote to my own breath. I've never been so well documented. Now, nurses with clipboards nestled against a range of breasts from meaty to bud-like, pens in hand, record me. Check, present.

CHAPTER 23

Safe with My Sister

The reality of being kenneled takes only a day or two to shuffle right up close.

B-1's doctors and nurses are supposed to call the patients on the unit a "community." It's a tenet of "milieu therapy" intended to foster patients' interdependence. As far as I'm concerned, the idea that becoming dependent on others on the ward could be beneficial is the obvious front to a snap trap smeared with peanut butter and bacon grease. However much I might belong here—or not—I recognize that attachment is a danger, not a goal.

I miss smoking alone in the dark, the cherry glowing bigger and hotter with each drag, quiet blackness my only other company. But I'm here in a crowd, escaping onto the scratchy brown wool blanket, where I read, hours building into days of pages—Thomas Mann, Jim Harrison, Leo Tolstoy, and Ernest Hemingway. I indulge in the last only when most pitiful, most nostalgic for my childhood. He may have been a misogynist and a drunk but the Nick Adams stories, especially "Big Two-Hearted River," power-blasts away a ponderous dread, bringing me to where "it was cool in the shade, sitting on a log." Effortlessly I'm back in time, camping with my sister in a tight clearing, gathering dry sticks, making a fire, grilling a pork chop. We're somewhere, out beyond the house, having come just far enough to count the night as an adventure, Whitey my dog circling in the fragrant, fatty air. My sister keeps me safe.

The defining characteristic of B-1 is collective boredom. What I see are aimless, unhappy individuals wrapped up in their pathology. The TV's always on, patients sitting in groups watching daytime shows. I stay away.

Plucking an immaculate white towel from the rack while a massive gray canvas wheeled hamper collects the dirty ones from the previous day and night is my greatest luxury. A pineapple round on a paper plate topped with a scoop of chicken salad, a white bun so airy it can't possibly be food, a tub of Fleischmann's margarine, a cute mini-carton of milk, and a tapioca pudding earn the slightest glance. The removal of the offering is accomplished by my placing the tray and its untouched contents on the floor in the hall outside my door. Room service, please.

Waiting out my SO, I eat little and my clothes fit better each day. I couldn't be happier because I like nothing better than lying on my back seeing my hip bones jut up to serve as tent poles for the elastic on my underwear. I'm not there yet but the sight of my rib cage showing its shape ever so faintly above the divot of my belly button feels better than any kiss, just as thighs not touching at the top where that vicious fat likes to settle redeems my mood for hours. Many girls here are too thin but I've never been there so I wouldn't know what it feels like or even if it exists for me.

My chivalrous father hasn't deserted Baltimore. He finds me a copy of Mann's out-of-print novel *Joseph and His Brothers*. One of the nurses delivers it to me with a note. I imagine him wandering used bookstores, searching the shelves only to find copy upon copy of *Death in Venice*. Perhaps dreading the finality of leaving the state of Maryland or hopeful Admin might call, asking him to retrieve me, he lingers. The *New York Times* I request can't be delivered to the hall, the bound cylinder having a history of disappearing en route to the patient, falling in among bored doctors, nurses, social workers, administrators, and orderlies. As suggested, my father puts a mail subscription in my name instead. It's not exactly "home delivery" but it communicates a terrible finality.

Before boarding his flight back to California, my father arranges for a weekly delivery of fresh cut flowers. He purchases a tall, tasteful, glass vase. An inspired gardener, he chooses deliberately; a chef with an acute sense of flavor, scent, movement, and color, he doesn't mildly appreciate beautiful things, they matter to him. Flowers, like food, wine, and books, are among the handful of interests he deems worth pursuit.

Too bad glass in any form, given its propensity for becoming shards, has long been verboten on B-1. He replaces it with a brass goblet decorated with cavorting Greek goddesses, their Dionysian abandon etched into the dark metal. Looking at it, I wonder how consciously my father selected the design—I suspect the joyful scene was meant to be cheering. Serving its improvised purpose, the unbreakable goblet holds fresh water and a sequence of bouquets arriving as steady as the week itself at the same hour each Monday—airy French tulips in the lightest pink, brash gerbera daisies in supersaturated flame tangerine, flawless stock in undiluted white clusters. I'm sorry for their grim life; they're too good for the place. Their scent, texture, and color suggest the unavailable green growth on display beyond the windows. I imagine eating the blossoms, ingesting the fullness of their beauty, and then spitting back the spent petals, stamens, and pistils.

On Sunday night lightning turns the sky and trees on and off as if a child has been set loose to play with the divine switch. On my now familiar bed in the dark I envy the intermittently visible trees and lawn. The rain slicks the grass as dead leaves form a reflective gloss on the ground. Snail paradise. I tap into the memory of wet, cut grass stuck to bare skin from toe to ankle. The itch I feel atomizes the aspiration to escape, one that refuses rest. If I could only walk and walk until I was lost enough to remain that way.

My sister Nicole and I have always been walkers. We stuck together, by turns suffering and giggling, over the two miles we trekked to the school bus stop at the Ranch in Idaho, the temperature five or even ten degrees below 0°F. It was precisely as far as we had walked in Aspen, but back then the banked snow loomed above us along the road or we sank up to our knees when we took the trail along the irrigation ditch. Later in Nepal, without a Sherpa, we hiked the seemingly endless miles of ascents and descents from the village of Jiri to Namche Bazaar at 11,000 feet elevation and from there to Gorak Shep, just a day hike from the lowest of the Everest base camps.

Above all else, we were tough, which left scant space for letting our guard down long enough to realize we wanted anything else. As spoiled as we were by travel, books, and food, we were uncommonly self-reliant.

I was safe with my sister next to me. When she was there nothing terrible could happen. She's too courageous for that, her soul big and certain of itself. Encased in our greasy, puffy down parkas, layered long underwear, turtlenecks, felt-lined zip-up snowmobile boots, wool hats, mohair scarves, and OshKosh B'gosh overalls, we walked through the black morning under the auroral Idaho starlight. The passage through came on fresh and dangerous every time but we never faltered.

I can hardly speak to her now for shame at my breakdown. I've kept to myself so long and now I've failed the endurance test we always passed together. My will is spent. All this inside hearing, the noise behind the 11s, blurs my senses. I am deeply, inexcusably weary. I miss those days. I miss what my sister and I were to each other.

CHAPTER 24

Passing Plates

Days three, four, five, six. It's September 16. I gaze at the cut flowers in their metal goblet. I don't deserve the flowers but I adore them. I try to be rational while the subterranean river of 11s tugs at reason. The din of movement and voices on the hall wears on my ability to hold a critical perspective. At my worst moments I'm fixated on Dr. Kohl's betrayal. I'm not sure I have a choice about giving in—or not—to the destructive pull of the 11s. They form a powerful current: get the *Buddenbrooks* razor and put it to use.

The magic scares me; it's not a thing I chose. It chose me a long time ago and now it's grown bigger, wrapping itself up in the burning, entwining itself with Dr. Kohl, fueling my desire to stop time. I sit on the edge of my bed and muster the courage to break the rules. This doesn't come easily but I have twenty minutes until the next check mark goes beside my name, indicating I'm present. That's twenty minutes of privacy and I need a fix on myself only a burn can deliver. Digging out a cigarette from my secret stash, I manage to light it. I'm in a panic. A nurse or patient is sure to smell the smoke. But I've gone this far so I hold the cigarette to my calf, pressing down with all my will, as

I always do, until it becomes pleasure. But everything is wrong. There isn't time. I can't focus. I can't turn the pain into anything useful. Cheated out of my only real pleasure, I snuff the cigarette out between my fingers, wrapping the butt in tissue. Now the superficial burn hurts—at least I have the mild, residual pain soon to form a blister filled with clear fluid. That's something.

Like a guilty teenager hiding the stink of burned marijuana, I sweep my arm through the air. Opening *The Magic Mountain* to the dog-eared page, I go to Hans Castorp's familiar losses. His failure of courage comforts me, making me feel human. He's my most sympathetic ally here, where time drags on formless and purposeless. I'm a mess. I taste salt on my tongue. It's either a trace of a word I've just read or the residue of squandered heat, the crystallized remorse for everything I've done to land myself here.

Allowing myself to relax into indifference, I doze, nightmares coming at me from a source I'd rather not know. Dreams of near-death escapes, knifing, slashing, and forced sex acts gather as if the most sadistic strands of my imagination have shown up for sport.

I hold on to logic, breathing to steady my mind. I know I shouldn't stay long at the Mad Hatter's Tea Party, moving one place down amid the absurdity. I need to object to the pointless action and the nonsense, but the part of my brain I cool with a lit cigarette goes on uninterrupted. Before I yield to the pressure of doing myself real harm with a razor, I call Dr. Kohl from the pay phone in the hall, exchanging a $5 bill for the roll of quarters a busy white cap in the nest pushes through the med window.

Wiping the receiver before I put it to my ear, stuffing the quarters down the slit, I register each making a satisfying click as it drops and falls into place. My fingers run up and down the ridges of the phone's shiny metal cord. Listening to the rings, imagining them sounding on the other end, causes adrenaline to flood my limbs in great, terrible pulses. He's there, at home in his house overlooking a stretch of Lake Champlain. His wife hovers nearby, the star of the graceful life spread around him. This is the airbrushed scene I've imagined every time I've called him.

She picks up. I ask for him, my tone more polite than it's been since I left his office a week ago. The familiar patience of his voice settles me instantly. My mind skitters into happiness by tapping the feeling of a static version of myself playing outdoors with Nicole. This childhood idyll is so clearly set in memory that it comes to life in a moment, flooding me with faith in Dr. Kohl's promise of a better time. I'm seven, wading in Little Woody Creek, thinking I can catch a rainbow trout with my hands, touching the slippery bodies as they zip past. I'm wet and cold and the river rocks barely hold me but I don't know that. It's spring and, for the first time since the snowpack melted, I'm in shorts and a T-shirt and the sun warms me. This nostalgic fairy tale fills the bigger, badder losses. Joy. He's close now. I can sense his presence as if I'm solidly in the room with him, 55 minutes to go.

I tell, fingering the loneliness, the razors, and the cigarettes in my room. I make a show of disdain for the nurses who've missed them but, having no heart for it, I let it go, giving it all up to him willingly. The time goes too fast. Hard black plastic receiver in hand, I tighten my grip, willing the unidirectional seduction to last as long as I can keep it satisfied. Slipping. Metal on plastic, I put it away, releasing him back to his life.

Spent, I lie on my back in my room in contact with the familiar scratch of the blanket, waiting for the inevitable shakedown.

In less than ten minutes two nurses arrive to silently ransack my things—again.

"The hall received a call from the patient's psychiatrist in Vermont. He reported that she has just called to say that she had razors and cigarettes hidden among her belongings in her room. A thorough search was made of the patient's belongings and razors were indeed discovered. The patient was continued on SO throughout the week."

I watch them but it's as if I'm not there. *Buddenbrooks* isn't so loyal this time; taking a beating to the spine, it gives up the razor in a flash of silver. The second falls from Tolstoy. It rests on the floor for a moment right where it lands. It's a harmless object without intent but I can't remember ever being able to look at a razor without thinking about cutting myself with it. It's almost a relief to see it go.

My carrot for getting off SO dangles: therapy. It can proceed when I'm allowed off the hall. I need an unstated number of clean days to earn the status of Hall Escort. That's not all. The doctor–nurse–social worker powwow to determine the length of my stay, plan of treatment, diagnoses to rule out, and therapeutic activities will now take place on the 23rd, three days later than planned. I'll be asked to join them in conclusion so that they can tell me all about myself. Finally end the SO? Begin a pharmacological experiment? Give me a Rorschach and then some? All I want to know is how long I'll be here. I could do with a lit cigarette and privacy. Days—7 days to go.

CHAPTER 25

Looking-Glass Cake

I've been warehoused for nine days. The TAG Heuer watch I ordered using the hall pay phone arrives. Long since inspected through the plate-glass window of Tick Tock Jewelers, 185 Bank Street, Burlington. I don't have a lot of nice things but I wanted this one. Now it's mine. As Dr. Kohl liked to say, I "cathected objects not people," which is a fancy way of saying I form deep emotional attachments to objects in ways that are unusual and perhaps even harmlessly pathological—if there's such a thing. Depositing emotional investments in objects rather than people protects against the possibility of rejection while providing an idealized connection that, unless I lose the object, remains under my control.

That's why my favorite pink sweater isn't just a sweater— it's a talisman. I've prepared myself to form a particular relationship with the watch as a symbolic barricade against the tyranny of time here, on the inside. The watch also represents a tentative gesture toward rapprochement with the 11s, as if by so subtly acknowledging their power, the power of the numbers on the watch I will worship, I can get on their better side.

The contrasting fair blue face of the watch, bright as Turkish tile, is framed by the stainless-steel bezel; and the industrial link bracelet wraps snugly around my left wrist, locking into place with a satisfying click. The heft of it balances the bulky white gauze encompassing the whole of my right arm. The cat's-eye glow-in-the-dark painted hands move precisely as the second hand sweeps around the face smooth and sure as time itself. I've never bought such an expensive object nor worn anything I'm so certain I like. It augurs trickery. If I'm locked in B-1's regimented space to be mandated by a clock—waking, rounds, smoking, mealtimes, bedtimes—I'll be worthy of keeping the hours. As it turns out, the Amex and dirty pay phone are still good for something.

The monotony of routine builds as the days span out, my frustration mounting as the consciousness of imprisonment in the absence of "treatment" of any kind accumulates. They're testing me? Or am I just going to be warehoused? This is it? I'm doing what I can to conjure the good stuff: the self-contained lightness and purpose of cross-country skiing over a well-packed track when the temperature hovered around freezing, allowing just enough friction for glorious speed; the irrational joy of watching a snowstorm from the window as the shapes of familiar objects lost their edges, softening into mere bumps of downy white; listening to my father read a book I'd heard thirty times before just so I could stop movement while loping around inside the world the illustrations brought to life . . .

Cards and gift boxes begin to arrive. My twenty-sixth birthday is upon me: 9/20/91. I choke on the flood of goodwill. The sickening vulnerability I feel when I think how all these cards and gifts come from people who now know I'm not what I once seemed is more than I can absorb. New friends, old friends, coworkers, family—they're coming as if in answer to a whistle to suffocate me with their well-intentioned sympathy. I suppose my family has spread the word in an effort to yield a virtual deluge of support. My cheeks flame at the thought of how ungrateful I am, while the embarrassment churns in my stomach, slowly turning to cement.

Matt sends packages with mix tapes—Tuck and Patti, John Hiatt, Bonnie Raitt—mail, and reports of my cat. One of the packages contains my XL red Woolrich union suit and the note, "I thought you would also appreciate having your jammies because they're so comfy to snuggle in." This was the boyish charm I'd fallen for. I feel my grandmother's warmth and affection in spite of the Hallmark card featuring a mouse holding a birthday cake on a background of peach paper, "For a Special Granddaughter," and inside "With many loving wishes for a birthday that will bring / All that's bright and happy and the best of everything!" Indeed! The endless cheerful notes and small gifts from my father's wife, Faith, contain no pity, just concern, warmth, and generosity. My friends send lighthearted postcards about nothing. I appreciate their lack of pained earnestness.

The ongoing gifts of well-thumbed fruits, nuts, and vegetables and lengthy letters from my dad made me weep, a mix of longing and humiliation flooding me at the extent of his generous efforts to cheer me, fix me, support me in the ways he knows best. As a broken object I've let him down, my failure to remain intact putting emotional demands on him we're both uncomfortable with.

"Enclosed you'll find a late birthday present, gleanings from

the farmers' market this A.M.—hope it all gets there in reason-
able shape. I worry about the carrots and tomatoes. The plums,
from baker Edie by the way, may seem like little bullets but try
one, you'll like 'em. Same with the nectarines—'Should be eaten
out of hand, crisp like an apple!' says the grower. The almonds
are from the backyard and I dried the figs." Followed by, a week
later, "In the package are a few more Jonathan apples. We're really
right between the early and late apples and next week should give
me better fruit pickings. The dried fruit is organic—no sulfur."

I treasure my sister's wacky sheets of recycled paper from
Boise, usually the back of a political poster she'd been putting
up around town, often decorated with line drawings of small
animals that manage to combine cute with weird, every other
available space filled with her tiny writing. Brave, my sister oper-
ates differently from me. Her vulnerability, enthusiasm, and
optimism match her natural generosity. The raw truth of her
letters, her concern, and her expression of how important I am
to her make me really cry—a messy state I try to avoid. I put
the letters away.

I want to be in the world freed of the apparatus of thinking
about being in it. The letters of my name on all this mail are one
random trail, meaningless. I spell nothing. I don't bother much
with seeing myself through others' eyes; I'm too busy seeing
myself through my own eyes and everything about this scene
feels unreal. I'm confused by all the goodwill.

The birthday. Some party venue this is. The only cake they had
was white, so they delivered their oversize sheet of sugar. I imagine it passing through a metal detector or sliding beneath an

X-ray so the orderlies can check for razors. Or was it one of many in a dedicated basement birthday cake freezer stacked with white cakes identical to mine? I imagine the slabs thawed overnight in the dark kitchen so that at 11 A.M. the following day the cooks in their whites could send the cakes up. Wherever it came from it looks like all the other grocery store cakes I've ever seen, except the French groove tip used to pipe along the base has so many finger dents the frosting looks unintentional. Two pink sugar paste flowers hard as dry mud form a cluster—if you can call it that—in the upper right corner. Settling in to a dirge played as a birthday song, the colored wax melts, fiery stubs closing in on roses and icing. Covered in wax. A wish? Quick, blow the fire out. Parceled and sliced . . . Pink rose frosting flower for me, please. It's my birthday. The cake is all sweetness suspended in slippery shortening. I chew in faith, swallowing. A wish? Did I blow out candles? Or is it a dream, this birthday cake and the gathered ghouls chasing bites of cake around paper plates with useless plastic forks? Garbage heaped: clear plastic bell, cards, gifts, crumbs, pink roses, uneaten lettering, smudged frosting. Fill it up. Overflowing with kind thoughts and good wishes, food dye, and flour. Dump it. This party's over. Rather than cake I eat confusion for afternoon tea. As Alice says, "I'll never go THERE again! It's the stupidest tea-party I ever was at in all my life!" Party? Birthday party? Tea party? But of course: "'You don't know how to manage Looking-glass cakes . . . Hand it round first, and cut it afterwards.'" I didn't know.

CHAPTER 26

Characterologic

Today is the day. Once I hear the locked door of the unit slam shut I know the rest of the patients on the hall have gone to breakfast. It's so quiet I can hear the words coming from the TV someone left on across the hall two doors down.

The Diagnostic Summary and Master Treatment Plan are ready. I'm scared. Ten days on SO lockdown, my determination wilting, the delusions of persecution folding in on me as if I'm an empty box of lo mein. They have my razors, cigarettes, and matches. They've never seen the minor burn on my calf—it's been covered by pants or pajamas. If my mind is under close scrutiny my body, with the exception of the burns the nurses and doctors know about, remains unexamined.

I've not left the hall, slept uninterrupted, or been alone for more than twenty minutes. Masturbation, the only sort of abandon I can come up with that doesn't involve reading or lighting a cigarette, presents difficulties. Timing dictates all. The door is never fully closed, as per the rules. How would it be to belong to Dr. Kohl—to feel his hands on me? The thought is all I need of desire. Once I'm in motion, of course, the danger of getting caught adds a frisson. I rub one out, but its insufficiency only heightens the desire to burn a fresh hole in my skin.

I shouldn't be thinking about this as I stand here facing a circle of professional eyes pointing their X-ray vision at me. Do they know I've fallen in love with my shrink? It's entirely unoriginal, after all. Whatever's in their minds, they're ready to report it to me, judging from the stacks of paper they've amassed. Nurses' data must be the bulk of the material layered into the authority and observation skills of the doctors on rounds, who pop their heads into my room every weekday morning. The data must be thin; I haven't had a sustained conversation with anyone since I arrived. The collective aura put off by their doctor–nurse–social worker regalia gives them the authority they need. I'm listening for the answer to only one question: "When can I leave?" I stand timid, the bandaged arm a pink elephant announcing itself—except it's white. I'm wearing my high-tops, black pants, and favorite sweater for safety.

Present at the meeting: Dr. Robin Weiss, Primary Therapist; Dr. William Simons, Attending Psychiatrist; Georgine Schildknecht, RN; Janet Cohen, LCSW; and Terry Wilpers, OTR/L. Their report contains what I already know:

> The patient has been withdrawn and isolative on the
> hall, spending time pacing with a Walkman on and
> reading quietly on the hall, avoiding contact with
> other patients. She appears to choose which staff
> and occasional patients are worthy of her attention
> and will be cooperative and will be talkative and
> forthcoming with them while excluding all others . . .
> The patient is clearly very intelligent and verbal and
> is extremely motivated to engage in therapy . . . She
> appears to have signs and symptoms of depression

over the last couple of years. There is clearly evidence
of personality disorder and a question of dissociative
behavior as well.

They make me sound so likable . . . so much fun.
The first thing they do is hand me my schedule:

A. Individual Therapy, Dr. W., 3 times a week for forty
minutes [sessions are even shorter on the inside];
B. Attending Rounds, Dr. Simons, daily for ten to
fifteen minutes; C. Family Therapy as arranged; D.
Activity Groups, most lasting 50 minutes to an hour,
including Art Therapy, Communication Skills Group,
Cooperative Task Skills Group, Individual Task Skills
Group, Recreation Therapy, Dance Therapy and Pre-
Discharge Planning.

Despite the official-sounding titles the activities aren't anything more than a foil. I suspect they can be dispensed with.
Quietly disregarding the bulk of the schedule should do the trick.
Glancing at the list, I don't imagine I'll be so busy as all this. I'm
not interested in the daily schedule of any single activity—I'm
looking for evidence of the total duration of my stay. I scan the
paper again.

Rounds. Okay. There's no avoiding rounds.

Straight therapy I'm eager to begin. I have nobody to talk to.
I don't expect more than a welcome distraction. I see I've been
assigned a female therapist, Dr. Robin Weiss, as per Dr. Kohl's
request. It certainly should eliminate the annoying distraction
of erotic transference. He must not think much of my fidelity.

Art therapy. I'm tempted by the idea even if it's a pilloried psych ward cliché. Painting and drawing calm me.

I glance at the next three items, each under the broader category "Group." I'll talk to the doctors if they talk to me. I'll talk my way around the nurses' rules as much as possible. I'll let the social worker know how much I value her advice on halfway houses, grooming, holding down a job, and paying bills. But I'll do nothing in a group.

As for recreation therapy, I'm pacing the halls no less than an hour a day—any break in the monotony of brown carpet underfoot would be advisable. Too bad as I read down I notice that recreation therapy could be more accurately described as aqua therapy. Not even I think it's a good idea to subject the oozing, open wounds on my arm, foot, and face to the water of a heavily used public pool.

Looking up from the paper, I meet Dr. Simons's perceptive eye. I don't think he's quite sorted me out, but I suspect he doesn't like what he's seen so far. Maybe I'm too together to be in here. Or is that what I hope he thinks? Looking right at me, Dr. Simons explains I will continue to "taper off all drugs" so that over the next fifteen days I can be "observed off Prozac and Trazodone." I'll undergo psychological testing. I am "Now released to the status of Hall Escort." My full schedule of activities can begin. I'm allowed to leave the hall with the rest of the patients on B-1 to take pleasure in their company and in the sumptuous meals waiting in the madhouse cafeteria.

But I'm still waiting for my answer. The mention of fifteen days is just the psychological half-life of the Prozac (a total of roughly three weeks when added to the ten days I've been here drug-free). Under Responsibility Level I hear him say one of my goals is to "learn to be a little bit more dependent" on my peers. He notes, as if in warning, as if he has read my mind, that "an attempt will be made to integrate" me into group activities. My resolute avoidance of speaking with the nurses or other patients thus far and my virtual nonparticipation in or absence from the mandatory daily hall meetings have wormed their way into my file. The sum of what they know is based on the physical evidence of my behavior before I arrived; whatever Dr. Kohl has communicated about my diagnosis; and the thin dossier containing evidence of my behavior on B-1.

I still don't have my answer.

They're all looking at me. The clincher forms, a bead of moisture on a cold metal surface: Dr. Simons says they've determined I have "severe developmental and characterologic disruption and distortion" that could "benefit by long-term inpatient therapy." What does this mean? "Characterologic?" Is that even a word? I'm well bruised by the time the number breaks from Dr. Simons's mouth. The words startle me as a bird might, had it escaped his lips: "Estimated Length of Stay: 6 months to 1 year."

I contain myself before the gaze of the five professionals holding my present and future in their hands after casually entangling the two in a tight knot I don't know how to begin to undo. I want to hear myself quoting Herr Settembrini as he admonishes Hans Castorp for his proposed length of stay at the Berghof: "'Don't you know there is something frightful in the way you fling the months about?'" But I drop nothing more than my gaze; I'll merit no further cause.

CHAPTER 27

A Thing for Lit Cigarettes

I cringe at the nurses' contact with my skin when they change my bandages in the vestibule of their station. Having them see it up close feels like a violation. But it's not just them. The vast landscape of the wide-open wound ready to be smeared with snowy Silvadene ointment is visible to anyone who passes through the hall. I behave fairly normally; it's the severity and extent of the burns that seem to earn me legitimacy as a nutcase among nurses and patients.

There's a palpable sense of horror at what I've done that I pick up in the expression of distaste tinged with fear on the nurses' faces. I'm not crazy like Bird Man, who sits in the common room talking eloquently to no one in particular, of finches, common and obscure. I'm not claiming to have eight, ten, fifteen alternative personalities who walk, talk, dress, and behave in their distinct ways, as the cluster of MPD (multiple personality disorder) patients do. I'm not the one who tried to kill myself. Once, twice, too many times? And they think I'm spooky because I have a thing for lit cigarettes?

Dr. Simons's voice reverberates through my skull. Time can waste itself: "6 months to 1 year . . . " I have no use for all that time puddled at my feet. What matters at the moment is the contest I seem to be losing with myself. A growing part of me wants nothing to do with opening my eyes in the morning, reading my book, picking at my food—even the idea of seeing Dr. Kohl again and returning to my small life in Burlington, Vermont, is receding. Dr. Simons's sentence feels like a joke I don't quite get. The prospect of staying in this place for six months, never mind a year, is at once impossible and dangerously appealing. The appeal of being responsible for nothing, free to disintegrate, sleep in my pajamas all day, talk to nobody, never brush my hair, is growing familiar. I'm afraid if I let my resistance down I may never want to leave. As Hans Castorp settles in at the Berghof he tastes this danger, for "at that there swept over him anew, from head to foot, the feeling of reckless sweetness he had felt for the first time when he tried to imagine himself free of the burden of a good name, and tasted the boundless joys of shame." Ah yes, shame. The 11s are chipping away at my rational self and right now they're more real and compelling than anything in the confined environment around me. I have nobody to talk to and if I did have someone I wouldn't risk telling him or her this, the deepest of all secrets. To do so is dangerous, pure folly.

Exerting my most rational self to stay intact, I again create enough critical distance to calmly study my options as I stare at the cyclamen plant the florist delivered as this week's alternative to a bouquet. The punctuation marks of crimson blossoms float over the mottled heart-shaped leaves. They testify to my father's belief in beauty to cheer and strengthen me. I imagine all the flowers I've ever seen, cut, wild, and cultivated in a superabundance of color, shape, texture, and fragrance, filling my room floor to ceiling, blocking the view, obscuring the ugly carpet, and drowning out the stink of cigarettes. It's pure witchery. I keep the image I've conjured like a mantra I can return to when I need it.

I've stopped writing what I call "fragments"—unpolished poems spewing rank as bile—because they're scary thoughts from some other part of me. A disturbing antidote to the 11s called Edlin parades as a named entity come to rescue me. The poems are a devil's brew containing mistrust of Dr. Kohl, "memories" of sexual abuse, loathing for my mother, and fear of insanity. I rationally deny them all, but when I apply pencil to paper I'm possessed, as if the letters and the words they make are dictated by an alien self speaking in tongues. No, I won't entertain the ways I could fuck with myself in this place by inviting greater lunacy. There's nothing I want here other than the liberty to go before I forget I want to.

I'm escorted to my therapist Dr. Weiss three times a week. I'm not in love with her; I don't obsess about her, I don't fantasize that we're together in bed, I don't repeatedly dream I have her arms around me only to wake imprinted with a sensual flush. I hardly think about her. She doesn't know me and she may well not like me. I can't blame her for that. I'm not all that charming these days. So if there was anywhere to get, we don't go there. I already have as much as I want from her. She's a woman in a chair with a pen and a job, gone before she arrives. She's the keeper of forty minutes three times a week.

She talks. She listens. Tell me about your dream. Tell me about your mother. Your father. Your sister. Tell me where you grew up. Tell me what you want. Tell me why you want to leave when you've only just arrived. Tell all.

Not so fast. She may think she can bring me back, convince me to settle in. I guess she doesn't recognize how reckless
a locked door feels when it traps you on the inside. I suspect
she can't, not with her keys—hall, car, house, office. Not with
her dinner reservation. Grocery list. Laundry load. Dirty dishes.
Pretty things to buy. So I tell Dr. Weiss what she expects to hear.
I won't let her too close. She's expected to write, file, and stuff
me into her briefcase as adequately accounted for. I hope she
thinks I fit nicely.

The first ten days on SO felt like a month—everything was new.
Since my induction into the hospital, the routine of meals in
the cafeteria and of therapy, time has sped up, but the rapid
pace is now as upsetting as its slowness once was. Six months
could pass without interruption; even a year could be one steady
stream of undifferentiated hours. The undertow of disappearance has been with me for a long time. I've dreamed of running
away, pulling out without a word, leaving a brief note behind or
not even that. Once the desire to give up takes hold the fantasy
builds, climaxing in the cowardly luxury of choosing not to live.
Staying in here comes awfully close.

I had quit my job at Community Action. Withdrawn from
my grad classes at the University of Vermont. Farmed out my
obese cat. Forwarded my mail. Turned off the lights. Set the
heat at 55°F. Paid the rent a month in advance. Shaken my
shrink's hand good-bye. Giving up the infrastructure of my daily
life was a little death I can no doubt recover from, but having
loosened myself thus far, how much easier it would be to leave
it all behind forever.

This unhappiness, the discomfort I feel in my own skin but hide so effectively behind an intact self-sufficiency, is less plausible when the hall hushes and its stealthy hours mount me like I'm their cheapest syphilitic whore. Listening to Herr Settembrini's advice to leave, I try not to ingest the air. I need to channel the clear-headed Joachim speaking truth to Hans Castorp's persistent question: "So no one had left?"

"No one was purposing to leave—nobody did leave very much, up here, as a matter of fact."

I strain to remember I belong on the outside. I'm busy declining the magic that's getting sweeter and greedier the longer I stay. Rest. Quiet. Acquiesce. I push to go but the other side plays to win; my resolve slips away, however hard I try.

To escape myself I shower often, even if getting there requires contact with the nurses. Patients must sign themselves, the key, and their contraband toiletries in and out: shampoo, conditioner, soap, safety razor. A nurse checks on me at least once while I'm in there, just to be sure I haven't choked on soap, drunk shampoo, or bludgeoned myself with the showerhead. I've come to love the shower room better than any other space on the hall. Hot water spilling down, light off, it's as alone and invisible as I can get on B-1: unalloyed blackness and complete privacy, even if only for a few minutes before the nurse knocks and unlocks the door to peer at my shiny wet nakedness through the steamy triangle of light flooding in from the hall. They hate it when I turn off the light; it freaks them out and breaks the rules. This makes me a little happy.

CHAPTER 28

Quiet Rooms

The dead zone of another weekend—no rounds, no therapy, no movement. This is number four and counting. The neurons I depend on are locked in a centrifuge set on High as I try to sort out the reverse hierarchy of B-1. There's no nice normal here or even the pretense of it; just degrees of irregularity. Symptoms are the measure of a twisted class system placing the sickest patients—dramatically unwell and in possession of the longest list of diagnoses and hospitalizations—in power.

Unsurprisingly the lifers—those who have come and gone so often they don't have a home beyond halfway houses and hospitals—form a tight clique. The price of belonging to their privileged group is maintaining the status of "super-sick." As Mann observes, "It was easy to understand that each patient inclined to make the most he could of his individual case, even exaggerating its seriousness, so as to belong to the aristocracy, or come as close to it as possible." The aristocracy. Yes, the women I call the Dowagers keep dramatic acts and gruesome symptoms on order.

This clutch of Axis I anorexics whose Axis II label reads MPD stick together the way the prettiest, most popular girls in high school do. I've learned to be cautious, quiet, and as invisible as possible in their presence. It's how I am, but never more so than here. I can only hope the social remove I instinctively maintain acts as a buffer against the practically inevitable iatrogenic effect of the psychiatric ward—that is, symptoms caused by the cure itself.

The uncontested Dowager of B-1 is a spectacularly wasted anorexic, Sherry. When I'm angry and bitter, hardened against my fate, I see violent red hair falling over sickly, pallid skin draped in loose folds over bones like unironed curtains. When I feel stronger I see her fiery hair as pretty, her pallid skin as like that of an old-world fairy. I discern in her demeanor gentleness that makes me sorry for the irreparable damage of starvation. To be here for as long as she has been is to suffer crib death—silently suffocating in her cage despite her youth and potential vigor. Whatever I'm feeling, when I pass her in the hall I erect a wall of indifference that's my most trusty defense. Avoid me. Avoid me. I keep my eyes on the carpet and walk, tall as my six feet will allow. I'm the Jolly Green Giant, twice or three times her weight, six inches taller. I make it my business never to speak to her, touch her, or touch anything she's recently touched, whether it's a couch cushion or a door handle. Anxiety over her illness contaminating me—as if that were in any way possible—leaves me feeling cruel and unworthy. She's abundantly unwell.

Sherry has been on B-1 for more than a year and that's just this round. She has the lead in the infamous cluster of MPD that Sheppard Pratt is becoming notorious for under Dr. Richard Loewenstein. There's an epidemic of sexual abuse at the core of the "recovered memories" that prop up the diagnosis. These dangerous snippets of fantasy-cum-fact mess with memory—that deeply unreliable source when it comes to sorting through one's own past. Even without the help of sodium amytal, age regression, hypnosis, or guided imagery what might I come up with if encouraged to do so? Dr. Kohl has never encouraged me to "remember" things that might have been no more than sense impressions, a valence of eroticism that could have been mine or someone else's.

I don't blame Sherry, Sweetie, or any of the other Dowagers for what they've become. Sweetie is my favorite for her gentle demeanor—all there is to discern from her virtually blank, clearly crushed affect. What she and the others are up to without meaning to be goes far beyond malingering, a particularly nasty term for faking psychiatric illness to gain attention. You can't fake anorexia, nor can you fake most mental illness. But the subjective quality of self-reported symptoms and the malleability of the mind up against the awesome authority of a doctor put many patients to the test. This is particularly true if they're ambivalent about who they are and what it might mean for them to get better. I should know. Being mentally ill, becoming a diagnosis, can so easily supplant the hard work of building a viable identity.

I'm not at all sure how well or ill I am. Deciding to pull myself together can't be reduced to nor accomplished by making a simple choice. I'm sure the Dowagers are trapped in a similar maze where motives, desires, fears, and hopes are laid out in confusing trajectories. The MPD patients aren't engaging in a conscious strategy to be sicker than they are; it's just that it's too easy to lead a patient with a weak, porous identity to various conclusions about herself. Presenting the option that there are two of them—or more—must be terribly appealing. I feel completely at odds with various parts of myself most of the time. It would be a relief to slap a diagnosis on this confusing state.

* * *

As part of my education Sherry gives a lesson in what the quiet rooms are for. Padded floor to ceiling, one of the two rooms has a cushioned table not unlike a massage table, but this one comes with four straps attached to padded leather cuffs to secure wrists and ankles. The other quiet room is just one big, empty, soft space. Romper room. The walls and doors of both are soundproof—sort of.

I've learned that earning a trip to the quiet room takes little effort. A fight with a nurse or patient will do it. Hurting yourself in any way. Even a verbal threat is enough. I'm not sure what Sherry did this time. She's visible through the porthole-size observation window strapped down from her red hair to her bony ankles, like a frog in a witch disguise pinned for Bio I dissection. Before she goes in there's noise, nurses shouting, shrill tones, an alarm buzzer signaling for additional staff and a doctor. (MDs must authorize use of the quiet room—it takes an expert to know when a patient is a real inconvenience, if not a danger.) All the other patients are told to return to their rooms.

"Lockdown!"

As usual I'm already in my room. To escape the emergency I read harder, focusing on Hans Castorp's pleasure as he admires Clavdia Chauchat from afar:

> *When he thought of her (though thinking is far too tame a*
> *word to characterize the impulse that turned all his being*
> *in her direction), it was as though he were sitting again in*
> *his boat on the lake in Holstein, looking with dazzled eyes*

from the glassy daylight of the western shore to the mist
and moonbeams that wrapped the eastern heavens.

I'm reduced to reading the sentence three times before the feel of Mann's vision takes hold, forcing back the noisy farce playing out in the hall until it recedes into my chosen fictive universe.

As it turns out, Sherry cut herself—for the third time and that's counting only this admission. Despite the precautions, a determined patient can usually find the means to slice open tender skin. A janitor in a blue work suit arrives with a bucket to scour the blood from the bathroom tiles, the stench of ammonia permeating the hall as he pours Clorox over grout.

When the agitated hall returns to a quieter than normal hush I pass by the tiny window, my full bladder standing in for bloodless curiosity. Glimpsing her, I'm not sure what to think of Sherry in that room, all strapped down and presumably sedated. Muted and stilled. I know I'm relieved she's not out here with me. I don't have to worry that she might sit near me or talk to me in the common area. It's less than nice I feel this way considering her misery, but I'm short on compassion these days.

The girl is a mess, as are the other Dowagers, any one of whom provides sufficient inspiration not to hang around B-1 too long lest I wake up one morning to find myself part of their sad cabal. Unfit for life—that's what I'll be if I stay too long or come back too often. As Herr Settembrini explains to Hans Castorp:

Do you know, Engineer, what I mean by being lost to
life? I know it. I see it here every day. Six months at most
after they get here, these young people—and they are

mostly young who come—have lost every idea they had,
except flirtation and temperature. And if they remain
a year, they will have lost the power of grasping any
other; they will find any other "cruel"—or more precisely,
ignorant and inadequate.

It's the very seduction I fear.

Never before and not since has a single diagnosis spiked as MPD did in the early 1990s, providing a fertile field for ambitious doctors, not to mention long hospitalizations; there were articles, books, and even fame to be had. Sheppard Pratt was called an "MPD mill" by some. There were empty beds to fill. Thank you *Gaslight, Sybil, The Three Faces of Eve, The Bird's Nest*. You've done your work. I want nothing to do with the dominant sickness here on B-1. The diagnosis of MPD at Sheppard Pratt is contagious—as if the cholera bacillus flowed from the unit's water fountain. The sanest part of me, the part that called Dr. Kohl to tell on myself and give up the razors, is desperate to leave before I drink too deep.

CHAPTER 29

Carnival Lights

It's Carl who divulges the cruel Sweetie details. He's informed. He's a regular. He has his sources. He's the only patient I befriend, the only person I have more than a five-minute conversation with—other than the staff—for the entirety of my stay. However unbalanced his paranoid schizophrenia makes his mind, we understand one another enough to become coconspirators who can share a few secrets.

Sweetie. A white sheet, as long as a standard twin bed. I imagine her with it wrapped around her body, sneaking it into the bathroom under her loose clothes, a hidden shroud wound tight around her airy anorexic form. Once she's there she knows where to go. She's been flirting with that pipe for weeks—possibly months. It's been taunting her with its easy availability, offering itself up to her, seductive as a dreamy poster boy who doesn't think she's fat. All better now.

Stringing the sheet up around the cold smooth metal isn't difficult if you stand on the sink. There's time during lunch. There's time when the hall falls quiet and everyone else eats—the nurses busy in the nest with thermoses of chicken soup, turkey sandwiches on rye wrapped in foil, cute little bags of chips manufactured to fit neatly into Kraft paper bags. There's time.

First, I bet she pulls her seventy-four pounds up onto the rim of the white American Standard sink with its perpetually toothpaste-gummed spigot. She then tosses the two ends of the sheet over the pipe and passes the ends through the looped center. Next she ties the two ends together with double square knots, one on top of the other. To tighten them, she leans her weight on them without closing the loop.

The sheet, pulled from her unchanged bed, smells of her— traces of oily scalp sebum and generic drugstore body lotion. The knot secure, she puts her head through the loop and tests to make sure it slides. She edges the sheet along the pipe toward the center of the room, calculating where her feet will dangle from the new position—well off the floor and just far enough beyond the rim of the sink to prevent regaining it.

She's done this trick before and she knows her feral instincts are stronger than her will to die. She will struggle to regain the sink. She will frantically pull at the noose that's held tight by her own weight. But this time will be different. This time will be a win. She's ready.

Leaning precariously, she balances to tie the laces of her sneakers together in an impossibly tight mess of knots. Her feet are cuffed. Even if her mechanical instinct, stupid and stubborn, tries to save her, frantically struggling back to safety, her awkward, useless feet will slip as one and the pushy will to breathe will be fucked for good.

It's just her hands that are the worry now. Gripping the sheet, reaching for the laces. She's weak but the will to live is tenuous—even when it's not. The knots holding the sheet to the pipe are impossibly tight. Her own weight, insignificant as it is, will do most of the work as the noose tightens fast and hard. There won't be any way to take herself down even with her hands free to grab at the fabric, her neck, or the pipe. It will be over too quickly. She's almost sure this time she'll get it done right.

Wanting nothing more than to stop time, weary, half eager, she readies herself and yet I bet she pauses. The tiniest splinter of fear prevents movement. Maybe a full minute passes. Standing. Noose slack as a fashionable French scarf draped around her neck.

Emboldened by a sound in the hallway, maybe she suspects post-lunch-hour movement, a nurse with a hint of onion on her breath to foil her careful work. Yea, noise? Then I'll be brief. Instinct makes her close her eyes as she pushes up off the sink as if jumping to clear a cliff as she drops into a swimming hole, arms up. Her body falls through the close air of the bathroom until the tension of the noose completes itself, gripping her neck on all sides. She can't breathe, so her mind and body join in a rush of adrenaline-fueled panic. Her dumb body flails wildly, writhing to find a way to breathe, just as she knew it would. The room dulls to gray as her oxygen-depleted vision fades. In time her body stills, dangling with something like cruel grace, the peaceful spin not quite a dance.

When they find her it is, as they say, too late. Was it too late? Too long? Too smart? Too careful? The hall alarm sounds shrill as the nurses rush to take her down. To save her. Not too late? Ghoulish gawking patients are herded like confused extras back to their rooms.

Lockdown!

The Sheppard Pratt paramedics arrive, gangly legs of the stretcher bouncing like a grasshopper's down the hall. Sitting on my bed, through the crack in my door I see her go. Out into the world. She's found her true winding sheet now.

Reports of Sweetie's fate filter through the patients on the ward; the consensus of the gossip is that she did it. Nobody seems entirely sure of the truth. Everyone should have known better. As Board Secretary Mr. Joseph Grape noted after the first suicide of a patient at Sheppard Pratt way back in 1892, "It is well known that insane people . . . possess abnormal cunning . . . and they outwit the most wonderful care that experienced foresight can devise, short of cruel restraints." Judging from the nurses' demeanor, from their grim silence and humorless movements, judging from the emergency hall meeting called especially for the occasion, I think she's won. They don't want to talk about that. They won't talk about it. They want to discuss how we, the remaining patients, feel about what happened. There aren't a lot of hands up volunteering thoughts, feelings, or complaints. All the sensible talk I expect to hear hovers, eventually settling down mutely, practically touching the carpet. Above it, still aloft in the oxygen we share, the word "copycat" gleams as obvious and impossible to ignore as the disembodied grin of the Cheshire cat. That's the real reason we're all sitting here; that's the damage good Dr. Simons wants to contain.

B-1's routine churns almost indifferently to life within hours but I'm cowed. The nest ramps slowly back up to its customary vitality with the filtered sound of chatter, phones ringing, and calls for coffee. One of the nurses freshens the communal candy bowl—tiny Mr. Goodbars, Hershey with Almonds, Krackel, and plain Hershey bars no bigger than matchboxes. Shiny silver foil minnows school in the trash can as the sugar makes it almost okay.

But I can't shake the moment the sheeted body sashayed on its wobbly litter down the hall and out the locked B-1 exit door. Seeing it go, I knew this wasn't the place to toy with minding such a hapless misery as mine. A waiting ambulance; carnival lights red, white, and blue spilling garish beams onto cut grass; a sheet hanging in a bathroom three feet from a stinking toilet. There has to be a more stylish way to wind it all down.

Surely I'm not alone. The Sweetie event must force every patient to savor the balm of a tenderly nursed antipathy toward life. I question the leakage of time and how I find myself mired in it again and again. The event prods to life a communally held immoderation as the electricity of death surges through B-1. No longer an abstraction or an easy acronym, its newly made gloss of reality practically glows. You can die here.

CHAPTER 30

A Splendid Woman

Grief has slipped on her best kidskin gloves to tilt the hall a degree or two off balance. The place feels screwier than usual when I find something new mixed with the usual morning routine. Amid the early swishing gurgles of water running and toilets flushing and the commotion of shift change I spot Juliet walking in the hall, eyeing vulnerable accomplices, teasing me with her youthful beauty and flashes of a shiny dagger. She's alert, listening, repeating over and over, "Yea, noise. Then I'll be brief."

As I pass their station the voices of the night nurses mix with Ophelia's almost inaudible whisper, an echo of the previous day, telling me that it's time to seek the bending willow, begging me to gather "crow-flowers, nettles, daisies, and long purples." The nurses, puffy-faced from dozing all night in an office chair, gather their purses, empty Tupperware, and go-mugs while communicating the overnight status of the hall to the perky, freshly painted faces of the incoming crew of day nurses. They don't seem to notice a thing.

As I wash my face and brush my teeth, these presences entangle me in their errands. Exacting geniuses wanting their way. There's Plath beside me as I spit and rinse, asking me to gather rags and towels and bits of cloth; she wants me to dampen them and seal every door. It's still early; most patients aren't yet up; we move quietly. Don't wake the children. Turn the gas to six.

The noise of the med line follows the return from breakfast in the cafeteria. "Take with food." The dispensing nurse pushes a Dixie cup of water and a ketchup-at-the-drive-in paper container with the pills in it through the slot in the window. A pale woman stands at the nurses' station oblivious to the orderly line. Of course, Emma Bovary, "extraordinarily beautiful and majestic as a phantom," begging for the blue jar of arsenic, protesting when the nurses repeatedly ignore her plea. But the nurse can't hear or see her—she's all mine. Again and again she tells them she only wants "to kill the rats that kept her from sleeping."

Smoke time produces a thick haze that drifts down the corridor to either side of the main room as if we madmen and madwomen built a fire but neglected to open the flue. I smoke my third cigarette in a row and return to my room. The hall goes mute as soon as the trance of my book takes hold, the new location broken only by the sound of the janitor running a vacuum back and forth directly outside my door. I manage to loosen and almost discard my present reality until the noise of the lunch line breaks my concentration.

I mostly look at my lunch in the cafeteria, where I sit alone at a table. Returning to my room, I nearly trip over the graceful, lanky form on her knees. Anna K. kneels there at the threshold repeating, "What am I doing? What am I doing? What for?" The red bag rests on the carpet next to her as she waits. I yearn to kneel down with her, join her chorus, and feel the vibration of the rail just before the rush of air and metal are upon us. It's getting crowded, these women appearing wherever I turn. I can't close the door with Anna blocking it, but even if I could my room isn't free. Lily Bart has fallen asleep on the cutter's empty bed. When I wake her she seems to "shrink from the glare of thought as instinctively as eyes contract in a blaze of light." Reaching quickly for a small bottle of chloral next to her she murmurs that she "must take a brief bath of oblivion." She explains, "Perspective had disappeared—the next day pressed close upon her, and on its heels came the days that were to follow." Yes.

Anna and Lily reappear in my room now and again but for the most part I remain uninterrupted. The early afternoon sun radiates through the window to warm me. I doze. Restless as the day drags itself forward, I pace the hall only to encounter Bertha Mason banging persistently at the unit's locked door. Seeking the roof, she's frustrated and wild with fury. There are no curtains to set alight. I'm far more in sympathy with Eustacia Vye; calm and contained despite Bertha's rants, she mumbles to herself as she keeps pace with me the length of the hall in her ravishing gray silk gown. "I must drag on next year, as I have dragged on this year, and the year after that as before. How I have tried and tried to be a splendid woman . . . "

The ghosts and the hours they pass through line up only to fall neatly into the grid. It's so dull I study the semantics of the blue paper menu hanging on the whiteboard by the nurses' station: "Dinner: Monday—Macaroni & Cheese, Green Salad, Roll with Butter, Chocolate Ice Cream; Tuesday—Salisbury Steak, Green Beans, Cornbread, Butterscotch Pudding; Wednesday— Spaghetti & Meatballs, Green Salad, Roll with Butter, Vanilla Cake . . . " only to be interrupted by the calm deliberation of a woman who knows what she wants. Woolf, taking her cane, fixes her hat and turns to me, her eyes pleading for me to help her find stones to fill the empty pockets of her overcoat. The murky bottom of the Ouse wants her.

Shaking her off, I turn back to the bulletin board. The menu and its meager strip of tape compete for space and attention with notices of minor schedule changes: "The SEPH Pool will be Closed from 5–6 P.M. on Wednesdays for staff use during the month of September"; bleached brochures for hospital-sanctioned halfway houses in the Towson vicinity; times and locations for AA, OA, NA, and ALNON meetings; information about the Maryland Youth Crisis Hotline 1-800-422-0009. I almost amuse myself considering what sort of trouble I might make if I called the Hotline from the pay phone. But whom would I report first?

Hours slide past before nurses and social workers begin knocking on doors to prompt attendance at Hall Meeting. Forced to participate, I reply with monosyllabic answers to "How was your day, Cree?" "Could you tell us about how you're feeling? Whatever you'd like to include." In a corner of the common room, I spot Portia quietly begging for coals, not for warmth but to eat; she will swallow fire. A woman after my own heart.

When I return to my room, the commotion of the lines for dinner and for meds is louder than the morning version of the same as patients peel away from their center, the frustration and monotony of the day undoing whatever sense of order sleep left them with. Amid it all, I spot Sexton. She has removed her glittering gold rings as if she's getting ready for bed but she's sipping a big glass of vodka. She appears lost, confused. But I can't show her the exit to the garage where her red Mercury Cougar is already running. I step away from the dinner line, making a pretense of helping her look for what I know is not there, sniffing the air for a hint of carbon monoxide, but all I smell is the furniture.

After the post-dinner lull, the activity of smoke time grows audible for the third time, followed by the changing of the guard from day to night shift. Cheerful chatting among nurses, the reverse of the morning's, passing clipboards and status updates for each patient. At last the lull of water running in the sinks, toilets flushing, and the dimming of the hall lights signal the end. I push open the bathroom door to brush my teeth, but in the darkness of the room before the light goes on I sense a determined, manic presence passing from one end of the stalls to the other. With the light on I can see her open eyes but she's sleepwalking, her nightdress trailing behind her over the dirty tiles as she rubs her hands together: "Here's the smell of the blood still: all the perfumes of Arabia will not sweeten this little hand." I stand to wash with her, showing her the soap in the hope we can together scrub away our misdeeds.

If I could "go away" with any of these women, I would. But there's no romance or glory to be had in dying now—or worse, trying to die—here. To say or think I'm "going away," as I often have said to Dr. Kohl, is evasive. The phrase masks the terribly enticing fantasy of death by disappearance. When I really think about it, the attraction of death—its drama and romance—comes on like a bright surprise. When it's on me as it is now I feel the calm of routine interrupted by a chaotic willfulness as the proximity of freedom explodes like a tropical tree in the night to reveal an obscenity of carmine blossoms at first light.

But there are no geniuses to spare on B-1 and I need to remind myself there's nothing cool or romantic about death. Unfortunately, B-1 is haunted and I'm locked inside. My sister, who can't visit but writes letter upon letter, is furious because she thinks I've tried to kill myself—perhaps a mistranslation from my father of the danger of suicide mentioned by Dr. Kohl or of the burning itself read as a gesture toward death. I want to tell her I wouldn't do that to her—to her of all people in the whole world. She'd be the one I'd stay for.

I wish I could promise her to keep my life but I don't exactly feel in control. It's gotten away from me, sneaking around my conscious mind, having found a better way in. Like the burning it's not entirely up to me anymore.

Rather than brood over how sorry I am to scare my sister, rather than encountering more ghosts, perhaps in bed with me, rather than guessing at the painful sources of Sweetie's despair and what it must have felt like to hang, I conjure a trick of undressing that begins with my pants: taking them down knee to floor, they sit rigid, almost upright, as if I were still in them to hold their shape; hands crossed over my stomach, I grab the hem of my shirt to pull it over my head before dropping it in a shapeless heap; arms backward, fiddling with my bra hooks, I free my breasts, more naked looking than the rest of me, they resemble the pasty skin around the black matted imperfection of hair covering my pubic bone as I slip my underwear down, stepping out of them one leg at a time; insignificant, the undergarments are mere rags on the floor. I stand, nearly done: unzipping my legs they fall away, going somewhere, likely nowhere near the floor; I cast aside my torso with the undoing of pearl buttons stretching from hips to neck before releasing my face with the pull of a ribbon that unravels a bow; only then unbuckling my arms like old-fashioned ski boots. Where my nakedness once stood I find myself gone. I learned the trick long ago all by myself; practiced by necessity, there's no rehearsal for undressing of this kind.

CHAPTER 31

Afoot Again

I've been here too long even though I can't decide if it feels like a year or a day since I was escorted from Admitting down the hall to B-1. The fantasy of Dr. Kohl is blurring. I want him back. Visitors are a distraction and a guilty burden—my grandmother, my friend Karen and her husband, an uncle. Now I'm on "No Visitors" and "No Calls" status. These goodies I take to my room, savoring the isolation as I would baker's chocolate. I've just been given permission to stuff the competing parts of my psyche away, shutting them up for a bit. They'll be back. For now, I am relieved to have everyone on the outside firmly there, far from me.

The sticker price of this deliverance from the world outside? I take to my bed. S. Weir Mitchell, M.D., the great father of women's "hysteria," wrote in 1875 in *Rest in Nervous Disease: Its Use and Abuse*:

> *As to women, for some reason they take more kindly to rest than do men, and will stay there, once in bed, as long as you wish, and longer sometimes. Indeed, he who says to a woman "You are ill, remain in bed for a month"—takes on*

> *himself a grave duty, and may not have the luck to get her*
> *afoot again, which is a thing to be thought of when trying*
> *some of these perilous therapeutics on your future patients.*

Mitchell couldn't be more right. Six, seven, eight weeks in, part of me doesn't want to get "afoot" again. Dr. Simons has begun to have a certain dangerous appeal; what was once loathing has turned into a minor crush on his executive confidence and self-contained demeanor. When he told me to "Knock it off" during morning rounds a few weeks ago I thought: Is that how you talk to your patients? "Heartbreaking" he then added, as if to the air. The arm? Me? The two together? "Knock it off" is a redacted letter I can see through if I hold it up to the light. I read he sees me in full, his gaze mixing with mine to encompass the condition I'm in and then past it to my capacity to stop burning, hiding razors, holding myself apart.

Though I swore off all group activities at the start I've submitted to art therapy: painting tiles, glazing and firing them. I'm calmer and more cooperative. I've discovered a nurse I like. We're not pals but I almost trust her. She doesn't condescend.

Even my in-house shrink, Dr. Weiss, has improved. Her efforts to comprehend my wish to return to Burlington as soon as possible have divulged my erotic transference problem. I tell her I'm fixated on Dr. Kohl. I am what Freud, among others, calls "the woman scorned." If my "transference love" for Dr. Kohl is an act of resistance to treatment, if it is specific to the analytic situation and fueled by Dr. Kohl's rejection, I'm not ready to see it that way. I'm not even close to renouncing the principle of my pleasure when it comes to Dr. Kohl. But confessing the dirty secret liberates a tiny corner of the shame I feel, dislodging it without setting it afloat. I've never told anyone how I feel about him other than to say, "He's very good" when my father pays yet another bill. I've been probing my relationship to Dr. Kohl as I sit through my therapy with Dr. Weiss. We get just far enough. My reluctant attachment to the inertia of Sheppard Pratt starts to take hold; this tells me it's time.

I've long since ceased being a person seeing a shrink because I'm lonely, depressed, shy, insecure, confused, bulimic, compulsive, isolated, angry, self-indulgent, and scared. I've entered a new category: I am a person who has been committed (voluntarily) to a psychiatric hospital. In the future I can't politely call this phase a "nervous breakdown." Unfortunately, the antique phrase is suspect, long since supplanted by a phalanx of clinical terms—schizophrenia, paranoia, psychosis, bipolar disorder, obsessive-compulsive disorder, eating disorders, various grades of depression from major to minor to morbid, and personality disorders of all kinds. None of the diagnoses so elegantly communicate the dissolution of the mental faculties "nervous breakdown" encompasses, describing as it does the fractured, split, and dislocated entity that's theoretically supposed to be a relatively integrated "self."

The so-called Three-Day Letter, a formal request for discharge I have the option to make, is my only way out. If I submit it I have a chance of leaving. The three-day process begins with a hospital committee review of the patient's chart and then, if its members decide involuntary commitment is indicated, the hospital puts the request before a judge to contest release. If the judge signs off the patient is involuntarily committed. They could recommend commitment but I don't think they will, nor do I think a judge would agree. In my mind the problem isn't the committee's or the judge's decision; the problem is the nature of their recommendation because it determines the posthospital outcome. If the committee permits me to leave, I need a proper discharge—not a contested one. That was part of the deal I made with Dr. Kohl. He won't see me again if I leave "Against Doctor's Orders."

I can oppose my father, Dr. Weiss, and Dr. Simons. But I'm not sure I can risk never seeing Dr. Kohl again. If I do it there may be no 112 Church Street, no Henry's Diner, no receptionist, no brown leather chair, no Daffy Duck print to admire by the door. Am I ready to be so extravagant? I fear staying at Sheppard Pratt longer as I yield to its temptations. Numbed by who I might become if I drift longer on the inside, I hang on to my purpose despite how impotent the prospect of that one vital casualty makes me feel: Dr. Kohl.

But I'm done here, even if I haven't really "done" anything at all unless it's locating the strength to put to the test my strange bargain with Dr. Kohl. It has taken me two months but if I find the courage to leave—or at least try to leave—I will be choosing myself over him. It's actually fairly remarkable.

Time to submit The Letter. I experience a flash of plenty when I know I'll do it. If I dally there will be no leaving, because I will have fallen in full and that, surprisingly, now seems worse than gambling on being turned away from Dr. Kohl's door. I can feel myself getting far too used to the place. It's now or never.

I ask for the official form from a squeaky nurse. She pushes it to me through the sliding pill window over the smooth divot where the tiny cups and so many hands have worn down the wood. It's probably fifty years old, this oak counter—maybe more. After checking a few boxes, scribbling the date, and signing my

name, I hand the completed form to one of the many indistin-
guishable bodies in the nurses' nest, each one neatly packed
into its own crisp white uniform, whatever its shape. With that
motion a series of irreversible legal procedures will churn into
action. I've risked civil commitment and Dr. Kohl. If I'm honest
with myself I know I wouldn't have taken the wager if I didn't
think I could convince Dr. Kohl to have me back—"Against Doctor's Orders" or not.

The next day I tell Dr. Weiss I've submitted the Three-Day
Letter. I'm ready to go. I've said I wanted to go many times
before, but this time she really listens. And then, for a change,
she tells me something worth knowing. She's been informed of
a timely mistake. Mass Mutual, my worthy insurance company
with Veruca Salt-worthy $2 million coverage, is not, as it turns
out, so very outstanding after all. There has been a mistake,
twice repeated.

My insurance, in fact, ran out after forty-five days. I've been
at Sheppard Pratt for two weeks without coverage. In my file the
mistake is noted: "This will be disputed with evidence from the
verification obtained on admission." Although I don't see this as
a gift, it is. I overlook the white satin ribbons and shiny bright
red wrapping paper Mass Mutual has just forced on me for the
shabby indignity of money trouble. The insurance gap is a boon.
For once—maybe for the last time—too little money is better
than too much. The hospital will have a harder time keeping me
without insurance; I'm a financial risk without proper coverage.
Can I or will I pay the bill?

When The Letter I've submitted arrives on the desk of good
Dr. Simons, he and his colleagues seem to agree they can't in
good conscience keep me here without coverage given my most

excellent progress. I guess "6 months to 1 year" sounded credible when the number was $2 million. After all, with that much cash to blow I could ferment sedately for eight years and nine months.

My Three-Day Letter is returned to me unprocessed the next day. It has seen neither panel nor judge. The hospital, represented by attending physician Dr. Simons, does not contest discharge. Then it all happens really fast, as I'm immediately scheduled for release in two days: Friday, November 8, 1991. Dr. Weiss, in consultation with Ms. Wilpers, whose job it is to oversee the transition to life "outside," confirms and documents in my file that I have an appointment with Dr. Kohl on Monday 11/11/91—two months to the day since I went into the hospital on 9/11/91. How symmetrical of the universe. How good of the 11s. After a stay of two months Sheppard Pratt has been generous enough to release me with a straight discharge and a prognosis of "Fair to Good." I'm deemed "Moderately improved." I'll take it.

CHAPTER 32

The Ceiling of the Profile

Ms. Wilpers insists we review the standard handout: "TIPS FOR STAYING OUTSIDE THE HOSPITAL." While she talks I amuse myself with visions of perching on the steep gables, lurking beneath windows, climbing the stately trees . . .

A few highlights from Ms. Wilpers's twenty tips:

- Don't look back to the hospital or how it used to be.

- <u>Strongly</u> consider a structured living situation for at least 3–6 months after discharge.

- <u>Have set appointment with outpatient treaters before leaving the hospital.</u>

She asks me to write three lists before I leave. Fine. I like lists enough, paper and words acting as magical vehicles of clarity and insight. First up, "Things I'm dreading" (my words, not hers):

1. Explaining where I've been.
2. Make place [apartment] cozy—now a mess.

3. Isolation—being without staff and support they provide.
4. Newness/familiarity of apartment.
5. Structuring time.
6. Food/eating. New routine.
7. Dealing with/reassuring family.
8. Establishing new level of honesty/relationship with friends and family.
9. Boyfriend/old relationships. Establish new pattern.
10. Finding a job.
11. Saying good-bye to old job/coworkers.

Second, my Supports at home, "outside" the hospital.

1. Doctor.
2. Sister/father.
3.–6. A handful of friends, Matt, and my cat, Billbob.
7. Exercise.
8. Computer.
9. Books.

Finally, I'm to draw up a list of Warning Signs that signal a worsening mental state:

1. More isolation/not answering phone.
2. Not really sharing anything.
3. Problems with food/bulimia.
4. Desire to burn.

5. Biting nails off.

6. Sleeplessness.

7. Extreme agitation/restlessness.

8. Withdrawal from activities.

9. Not exercising.

10. ~~Over-dependence on . . .~~

I cross this last one out. I'm thinking of Dr. Kohl, of course, but I'm not going to admit that to her.

The official discharge papers read as follows:

Discharge Diagnosis—DSM-III-R
  Axis I: Bulimia
  Axis II:Borderline personality with Narcissistic
      Features (principal diagnosis)
  Axis III:Healing second-degree burns—right arm,
      foot, cheek
  Axis IV: #4, severe—enduring circumstance
      (parental neglect)
  Axis V: GAF: Current: 60   Past year: 75

Although bulimia is my Axis I, or what they call a "principal diagnosis," this is just a quirk of the DSM that 301.83 is Axis I while other, seemingly more important diagnoses are considered secondary. My Axis II is the ever slippery Borderline Personality Disorder (BPD). It's not a pretty diagnosis and the prognosis isn't very good. The criteria, according to the DSM-II-R standard, are as follows:

1. *A pattern of unstable and intense interpersonal relationships characterized by alternating between extremes of over idealization and devaluation.*

I idealize Dr. Kohl. And my father. I'll give them this one.

2. *Impulsiveness in at least two areas that are potentially self-damaging, for example, spending, sex, substance use, shoplifting, reckless driving, binge eating (do not include suicidal or self-mutilating behavior covered in No. 5).*

Yes, I did binge and purge. And I spend more money than I have—always.

3. *Affective instability: marked shifts from baseline mood to depression, irritability, or anxiety, usually lasting a few hours and only rarely more than a few days.*

Yes, but I bet lots of people could say the same of themselves.

4. *Inappropriate, intense anger or lack of control of anger, for example, frequent displays of temper, constant anger, recurrent physical fights.*

Finally, a definite no. I do not fight, scream, or display my temper. I might be better off if I did.

5. *Recurrent suicidal threats, gestures, or behavior, or self-mutilating behavior.*

Okay, yes. This one isn't too hard.

> 6. *Marked and persistent identity disturbance manifested by uncertainty about at least two of the following: self-image, sexual orientation, long-term goals or career choice, type of friends desired, preferred values.*

I'm not always sure who I am, I don't kiss girls, I might want to be a doctor but I think I'll end up as an academic. I have always wanted to be a writer but I'm unwilling to admit that audacious ambition so I pretend I haven't. I am a bit shaky on friends and values.

> 7. *Chronic feeling of emptiness or boredom.*

Yes to emptiness, no to boredom.

> 8. *Frantic efforts to avoid real or imagined abandonment (do not include suicidal or self-mutilating behavior covered in No. 5).*

I admire the way the manual's compilers anticipated including self-mutilating behavior under frantic efforts to avoid real or imagined abandonment. I would have listed it here. Since I can't do that, I'll admit I get frantic when Dr. Kohl leaves town or threatens to leave me.

I solidly qualify for BPD by this standard—it's difficult to deny seven out of eight when only five are needed to confirm a diagnosis. But it seems that Dr. Adam Shearer, who wrote the report after psychological testing, wasn't so certain. Despite the discharge diagnosis of BPD (301.83), his report states, "Although some dimensions of her projective assessment, interview presentation and history would suggest borderline personality disorder, it is noteworthy that there is no appreciable elevation of the scale on the MCMI-II that taps the DSM-III-R defined features of borderline personality disorder."

The report, produced after several hours of psychological testing only ten days before I signed my Three-Day Letter, notes my response to the Dissociative Experiences Scale (DES) "produces an overall average score (20) which is on the low end of a wide range of scores generally suggesting significant PTSD or dissociative symptomology." Hooray! If there's anything to celebrate it's safe to say I've narrowly escaped the dread MPD. Then there's the Rorschach—those crazy inky blots that surely look like genitalia to all but the most pristine nuns. Beyond frequent sightings of penises and Georgia O'Keeffe-esque vaginas the report states:

> Ms. LeFavour produces a rather lengthy protocol . . .
> It's worth noting that her thought processes seem
> distinctly disjointed during the administration of
> the Rorschach . . . Although the resulting protocol
> was difficult to score, it is noteworthy that she
> displays quite meager capacity to produce "good
> form" and uncontaminated responses, suggesting
> that her capacity for effective reality testing is easily
> compromised.

He concludes that this indicates "considerable cognitive slippage to an extent ordinarily associated with a thought disorder." He then ominously adds, "Indeed, the index related to schizophrenia is significantly elevated. . . . It is also worth noting that there is an appreciable elevation of an index related to the risk of future suicidal behavior, though this elevation is just short of the level that has been empirically demonstrated to be predictive." None of this seems to be particularly good news.

Dr. Shearer writes in the Discharge Summary, "The most significant aspect" of my Millon Clinical Multiaxial Inventory-II (MCMI-II) is in the "scale related to aggressive/sadistic personality features." It's not just high. It's "elevated to the ceiling of the profile." He notes that "such personality features only underscore her difficulties in reconciling the cruelty of others as well as her own cruel and aggressive impulses."

Additional data in the report come from notes ferreted in my file by the spying white-suited *Mus musculus*, who noted that my "narcissistic personality traits" may have contributed to "my considerable difficulty accommodating to treatment," as evidenced by my objection to "petty" hall rules and "my inclination toward seeking special treatment." I might argue that failing to accommodate to "milieu therapy" demonstrates an unduly healthy response to the conditions on the unit rather than a sign of pathology. They backhandedly compliment my "fairly well-controlled angry responses."

In summary, the Report of Psychological Consultation states that my MCMI-II profile "does not suggest any indication of prominent Axis I psychopathology at this time . . . although she may have met the criteria for a major depressive episode in the recent past." In addition, these features, as tested by the 175 true-or-false questions in the MCMI-II, allow Dr. Shearer to conclude that the "most prominent dimension coming out of the test seems to be that of severe personality disturbance, including avoidant, narcissistic and passive-aggressive features." It's that fucking "characterologic" word again, this time laid out in more detail. He adds, "PTSD and/or dissociative disturbance certainly deserve continuing consideration in terms of longitudinal assessment." La-di-da.

PART III

It might be desirable to die; but this privilege was evidently to be denied her. Deep in her soul—deeper than any appetite for renunciation—was the sense that life would be her business for a long time to come.

—Henry James,
The Portrait of a Lady

If you were coming in the fall,
I'd brush the summer by
With half a smile and half a spurn,
As housewives do a fly.

If I could see you in a year,
I'd wind the months in balls,
And put them each in separate drawers,
Until their time befalls.

—Emily Dickinson,
"If You Were Coming in the Fall"

Everyone I like stays the hell away from me.
—Archie Bunker in *All in the Family*

CHAPTER 33

Safe in My Bed

The November flight to Burlington belongs to one more leg of a pilgrimage crowded with impending casualties. I can't muster the enthusiasm to qualify this as a homecoming. It's the familiar prescription for any illness minus the bed: "Bed rest, no excitement." Guiding my key into the lock for the first time after two months in a psychiatric hospital doesn't distinguish itself from the mix of disappointment and excitement I've felt many times before when, sporting a tan after a beach vacation, I've turned the key at once wishing for and dreading the sight of what I left there. Objects I never thought of or missed remain precisely where I left them: the single glass I washed before resting it on the drain towel next to the sink; the labels from the cashmere sweaters, ripped cardboard cartons emptied of Camel Lights, dried tea bags with the shape and feel of dead cockroaches litter the trash. It's all here. The familiar heavy quiet I've missed roosts easily on my shoulder—it's just me.

I can walk out the door and move freely down the street to the co-op, where I'll find a local Bartlett pear, biting into it to find its perfumed flesh unlike anything I've tasted in two months; I can order a strong coffee and my favorite sandwich, an untoasted sesame bagel with butter, Muenster cheese, sprouts, and tomato, and eat it over the same day's *New York Times*; I can light a cigarette at my kitchen table no matter what time of day it happens to be—and no one will be watching.

Putting the kettle on for tea and a smoke, I try not to pick a new spot. Once a spot is chosen, denial is nearly impossible to come by. Distraction. I wad up whatever thoughts I can to blinker my brain, filling space with words and books and lists and colors in an effort to displace the temptation to get at my own flesh. I don't want to go back—imagine failing within a day?

The temptation to clear the mind with a strong dose of cruel feeling and its wake of ablution suspends itself from the ceiling of every room. I miss the Band-Aids, nonstick pads, creamy white ointment, and most of all those frail filaments that once woven together form sturdy gauze. Rolled into a spool, this almost-fabric let out in one long ribbon might wind the circumference of my arm—or leg, or foot? But I can't have it.

I'm past hunger, my nerves setting my stomach into free fall. Chain-smoking with my tea at hand, I turn these matters over in my mind. No music allowed: the silence keeps the mental chaos in check. No Leonard Cohen or McGarrigle Sisters telling me it's time. As I stare at the loaded ashtray, my mind forms a daisy chain out of spent filters—pick the burned tobacco out and thread the white spongy remains on dental floss long enough to slip gracefully around my neck.

Listening to the jets pass, I wait for the clock to take the sun away. The digits are having their usual fun with me, winking 5:11 P.M. when I've avoided looking at them all day. I seek my bed. The numbers will wait for sleep to pull me to them and through to the other side. I listen for their symmetry, dreading the feel of them descending from the ceiling like so many spiders making their play for me. I won't feel them when they land but they will be there. Resting. Gaining strength. On me. Slowly spinning a net.

I catch myself, pressing my cigarette into the crystal rectangle that was my paternal grandfather's favorite ashtray. So I'm told. It's tomorrow soon and I can go to him: 11/11/91 is just hours away.

I conjure a childhood spell of snowy Castle Peak in the distance and the movement of white-barked aspen trees clustered in their neat groves like gentle herd animals. It takes but won't hold. The freedom of living alone is a luxury I've sacrificed a great deal to guard and yet I'm never done thinking of intruders. My friend Poppy, my mother's girlfriend's daughter, was with me in ninth grade the day we hitchhiked home together after school, taking a ride in a pickup with a guy we quickly identified as creepy. He insisted on driving us to the door of the tract house in Elkhorn. We weren't that naive. I declined to show him where I lived, and he let us off at the intersection; he was more interested than we realized. Getting ready for bed that night—Poppy brushing her teeth across the hall—I stood at the uncurtained open window in the warm air. Never far from thinking about what might get me, I checked directly beneath me before looking up at the spangled cosmos. I didn't exactly choose to see if someone was hiding there—it was the only way to quiet persistent fear, even if some part of me knew how irrational practicing these precautions was. The conviction that I might be right was so outsize it took courage to look—but I couldn't possibly not look. I'd been through endless rituals: checking under beds, in closets, behind shower curtains and doors. Never had I found a thing, but I kept doing it. That night, rather than the usual nothing, I saw the curve of a crouching back hiding, head down, so close I could have touched the plaid shirt. I was in my underwear, no top. I'd like to think that, backing away from the window like an automaton, I made a chilling noise worthy of a great actress in a horror film. If nothing more, it was loud.

This man embodied my fear, the big one that trumps almost every other natural, material fear. A man. After me. It's in my nightmares and in my mind almost every time I'm alone in the dark. I don't have a chance.

The man outside the window had seen my breasts; watching through the window, he waited silently. He was there while I painted my nails. Or was he? He wondered at me as I giggled at Yossarian's perversity in signing "Washington Irving" and then "Irving Washington" just to fuck with the authorities in *Catch-22*. He'd come for me—at the very least to see me undress, at worst to rip whatever remains of my comfort away along with my pink undies.

In my dreams, fears, and darker fantasies I'm tied up and gagged with my own ripped garments so he can stick himself in me and move with the violence of an animal until my guts bruise and the taste of puke and salt fills my mouth. But my body and mind would soon be gone. Putting my body away as I do when I burn my skin or when I can't think the same thoughts anymore just takes undressing all the way as I did in the hospital more than once.

But that time, just an overgrown kid, I was the victim of nothing more than my own imagination, the object of a prospective threat. The result of the Peeping Tom—how innocent that sounds—did nothing more than confirm what I believed to be true: that men were dangerous because they wanted something and would take it if they could. Desperate to escape the fishbowl of the house, we made a break for a neighbor's house to call the police. By the time they shed their small-town flashlights on the house and took their perfunctory report, the Peeper, whoever he was and whatever his intentions, was gone. My sister, Poppy, and I slept that night in a seedy motel on Highway 21 on the outskirts of Ketchum.

When we returned to the house in the safety of daylight to grab toothbrushes, our homework, and a change of clothes we discovered the creepy pattern of footsteps around the house. The sight of the boot prints sunk deep in the wet ground fossilized in my memory. They were the boots of a big man. Without turf or landscaping to hide his trail, we could see he circled the house repeatedly, like a predator circling prey. But then, maybe he was just trying to get a better view.

After two nights in the motel—Poppy was whisked away after just one night—there was nothing to do but go back to the empty house now crowded with fear. My mother, whom we called to tell of the unexpectedly dangerous house, thought we were being silly and didn't want to continue paying for a motel room when we had a perfectly good house to live in. Wherever she was—at the café, in Picabo, on vacation with Pat helping her spend all that Pacific Palisades green she'd inherited from her father—it was easy for her to say, "Get over it." Maybe she saw it from her own perspective, a loaded pistol under her pillow; likely as not she'd have shot the fucker in the face.

* * *

I try to convince myself I'm safe in my bed in my apartment at 77½ Intervale Avenue despite how quiet it is and how unfamiliar the sheets feel after my two months away. I'm used to the imperfect sanctuary of a bed. Waking, I'm sickened by a presence on me like a mean hangover. It wasn't just the Dr. Kohl or hospital era that's been full of these nightmares. Bad dreams have intruded on the false security of sleep with regularity since I can remember. From the age of three until I was nine, the appearance of my sister's long white flannel nightgown floating like an illuminated ghost toward me though the dark meant I was safe—or safer. When I frequently woke myself—and my sister—with an unthrottled operatic scream Nicole escorted me to my parents' California king. There I'd lie between them, a hangover of fear wet on me, terrified to move lest I be booted back to my own, now scary bed.

I remember that the oppressive warmth and heavy smell of my parents' adult bodies disturbed me, but the idle house surrounding me was the greatest presence just as the silence is now. Staring up through the skylight centered over my parents' bed, I'd fall into a depth of stars laid like a fine gauze of patterned lace across infinity. With no light for miles around to obstruct their intricate collusion, I took in the beauty and the awful depth those pricks of light suggested while the house exhaled around me. Then as now, marveling and listening were the best I could do. There's no chance for sleep.

CHAPTER 34

The Queen of the Universe

Henry's. I've arrived. I crunch spiced sugar on warm bread, anxiety mixing with smoke and sour coffee. The waitresses in matching maroon take a few orders, mostly at the counter, talking among themselves. It's early and the day is long. They don't seem to register they haven't seen me in two months despite the sign on my forehead: FREAK. Or does the sign read PSYCHO? PSYCHO-FREAK? Or maybe it just says LOSER and I'm flattering myself. There's no chance of reading the newspaper; it's just for cover. I stare at bitten cuticles, scars, and the gold rings I'm again wearing. They're welcome links to places and people. I smoke another, knowing there's a cigarette machine in the corner, right over there. Freedom.

I feel people looking at me. I'm now one of those people who frequent public places everywhere—buses, bars, park benches—who make other people nervous. My force field of isolation keeps me safe. You'd never casually ask one of these people over the back of the booth for the ketchup or offer to buy a drink in a bar or sit next to one on a bus unless the one seat adjacent to them was the last one open. I'd long suspected many of these people weren't as scary as they appeared and now that I've entered their ranks I know it's true. My natural, fluid movement between inside and outside remains stiff. I can't locate my public face as easily as I once could. Or maybe I don't care enough to make the effort.

Do I feel ashamed? Yes, though I'll pretend not to be when I see my friend Jess and ex-boyfriend Matt. The worst will be well-meaning acquaintances busy talking around knowing where I went when we both know they know. I'm almost sympathetic. What can they say? How was it? Happy to be back? You look great. I can smile and pretend it was nothing, move the topic along, turn it around with "I'm fine, how are you?" Mercifully it has to be gotten through but once. Pretending I never went anywhere is the easy way out—for them and for me.

The shortest waitress tips the brown-and-gold urn to fill my too-small cup. She's making her rounds. I sit as long as I can at my table, forcing one more cigarette down. When I go I want Dr. Kohl to be there before me, waiting. The locked exterior door to the building reminds me that his room is a place of business where we engage in a professional transaction. I want to open the door to see him bending over the receptionist's desk looking at some paper, that luxurious, thoroughly reliable warmth ready and waiting for me. I long for his encompassing smile, the one he never fails to offer, the one that comes freely, flooding me with his sympathy, admiration, affection, and interest. The contents of my stomach jump and squirm, the movement coming right up to my throat. I'm choking on the anticipation of seeing him again.

I slide out of the booth, money on the table, ashtray full, coffee gone, granules of sugar and crumbs all that remain of my toast. I'm not sure whether I'm walking or floating over the blocks to 112 Church Street. Door unlocked, inside in his presence, his eyes on me, I feel the sickness fall away as he unfolds himself, predictable and lusher than I remember. That smile and the eyes hold me. Once we are secure behind his closed door it's us. Bodies, but mostly words. I could swallow them but they keep longer this way, out there in the air between us. This is what I waited for. This is what I mean.

I tell him about how I mostly wanted to leave the hospital and how afraid I was of catching the dreaded defeat that had drowned so many of the patients there. I tell him I felt guarded with Dr. Weiss, careful of what I said. I liked a few of the night staff—the ones who saw me in the dark hall, who knew I hardly slept during their shift. I tell him I'm afraid of getting sent back if I lose it. And then there's silence because I'm not telling him anything—I've been talking fast but not saying much. Silence.

"Are you waiting for me to start talking?" he says, because "I'm over here trying to figure out where you are." That's when I know I'm home.

The fantasy of reunion runs its strange, unexpected course—I was detached but hadn't realized it until he asked me where I was. The pleasure of him knowing me is deep and terrifying. Now I'm here again, about to become his in a way I can't begin to imagine.

There's business to do. Unavoidable. He's taking my treatment in hand, setting limits, and insisting on accountability. He writes "Reentry" at the bottom of the chart, as if I'm returning to earth's atmosphere from space.

Contract

1. No self-destructive behavior.
2. An understanding that I can't do anything to hurt myself: burn, cut, alcohol, laxatives, vomit. Want some help understanding that?
3. Overeaters Anonymous (OA) 2 x week.

He writes, "Nails grown in; arm's healed."

If I fail to meet any of these three conditions—if I harm myself in any way—he will not see me. I will then have a choice: leave treatment with him and find another psychiatrist, or go back to the hospital. Although I'm not surprised, I'm cornered by the appalling alternatives.

Going to therapy four times a week, doing nothing to self-destruct, and attending OA meetings are my jobs. I'm not working. I'm living in my cozy apartment with my cat, Bill-bob; painting; walking; writing; and thinking about applying to grad school.

All of life outside his office is filler. When I'm with him I'm right back where I was before, clinging to the smallest nuance, rehearsing every word I can remember as I parse and peel his meaning, looking for what I don't know, what might save me. The magic signs.

The first week I confess that the desire "to burn is out of control." For now, I'm putting on paper whatever anxiety or rage or unidentified feeling is driving me toward the impulse. We review the steps that lead to a burn. It's not complicated: 1. Thinking about burning myself, often for days before it happens. 2. Choosing the spot. The two steps are entirely artificial since choosing the exact spot is when I get wound up and attached to the idea of carrying it out. I'm supposed to call him if I get close. I hope I can do it in time.

Day three. I fear I'm filling with a nearly palpable blasphemy.

"I'm really angry."

"It shows," he assures me.

I've been "feeling a sense of death close at my bedside at night—twice in the last week. It's a sense of death as a finality. A choice."

Rather than exploring this fear with me he says simply, "It's a choice for everyone. I've said it before, I do not take you being alive for granted."

I consider my options. I could leave, climbing inside an airplane to the smell of oxygen and steamed food, and buckle in for a nineteen-hour flight. My standard phrase, pre-hospital and now, is "India calls." It means I'm fantasizing about slipping into the soft, colorful folds of a sequined sari to evaporate in the foothills of the Himalayas: fine rhetoric to cover the chill reality of going for good.

I don't want "the burden of having to make things better. It's scary," I say.

He suggests that "what's scary is feeling connected" to him.

Whatever I had of an identity has been flooded as thoroughly as before I was hospitalized. I'm entirely overwhelmed by my desire to meld with him, become him, have him in every way. This internalization reflects how porous I am. Psychiatrists call this quality self-transcendence. I empathize with characters in films and novels to the point of failing to maintain my own identity—it returns, of course, but not before the other is consciously shaken off. This identity confusion is part of the transference; the separation between self and nonself. In my relationship with Dr. Kohl this line has become dangerously fuzzy. The name for this excessive attachment and rage is "transference psychosis."

Beneath my vulnerable, open surface a powerful and highly primitive part of me keeps tabs on what's acceptable.

"I'm trying to resist. Something has been ruined. Wrecked. I don't know where this leaves me."

"Another child left alone who defiles herself or was defiled," is his answer.

This part of myself resents and fears my dependence on anyone I let in too far. In falling for what he offers, in telling secrets, I've violated much of what protected me throughout childhood.

"I'm worried you're trying to steal me away from the magic."

"You'll pay any price to keep that" because, as he observes, "the constant presence is what is good." In other words, my crazy system is better than being fully alone.

The Queen of the Universe is alive and well—that's me, or Dr. Kohl's name for my internal tyrant. She sees things, as Dr. Kohl notes, "So absolutely one way or the other." This Queen keeps me to the crazy rules: which cigarette to smoke, what's "okay" to eat, why I can only drink coffee from my special mug, the significance and power of jewelry and hair, which article of clothing confers magic. Keeping hold of the rules is part of what makes it crucial to remain apart—to protect what remains of the real elements of who I am. I glance at my hour and wait to hear and say more. Dishonorable truths fall to the floor, where I hope to leave them.

At the bottom of the chart on day three posthospital he writes, "Therapy is about the give and take of intimacy." Beneath that he writes in big, bold letters with triple underline: "Boundaries."

CHAPTER 35

So Many to Choose From

The lengthy posthospital era is best summed up as a colossal bitch of complication; the longing and aloneness are unmanageable. After two months he writes in a note to himself, "Looks distinctly more intact today." I must have looked pretty bad in the immediate aftermath.

I come as close to dying as I ever have. Trapped, I spin in what the psychoanalyst Otto Kernberg calls "the extreme and repetitive oscillation between contradictory self concepts." Not only do I not know who I am or what I want; I don't know what I'm feeling from moment to moment—I have no way of naming what I experience.

So I take to my bed, where I collapse into the pillow while the noisy days get on outside, the sun high. I sleep past the hours warm and soft under a pillow of feathers. No matter how risky it is, I let my dreams think for me. When I wake up the light will have changed, but since time has nothing to slip around while I sleep, I absently wonder what it's done with itself. Smudged, I miss nothing about the days I lose. Happy to see them go, I fall back into sleep and, with nothing to wake me, I skip morning and go directly to noon.

He's forcing me to sit in a church basement twice a week. "Hi, my name's Cree and I'm an addict." It's all a big joke to me. I complain bitterly but he doesn't care if it's helpful; he's holding me to the original contract I agreed to when I returned from the hospital. Going to OA was part of that deal. It takes months before he lets me off, granting release from the circle of tragic metal chairs where the bulimics, active and former like me, look on. We can parade our apparent normality before the corporeal freaks surrounding us, but everyone knows how repulsive we are. Lacking the loop of pleasure in becoming ever thinner that feeds the anorexic, our weakness is an indulgence in abandon. Only we hate our bodies—hate ourselves—so fiercely we'll do anything to erase the effects of too many calories. At least the overeaters seem to keep it honest.

Never a God person and almost equally impatient with the so-called higher power—yes, given the magic 11s the hypocrisy reeks—I can't bear the leveling maneuver the confessional, handholding format demands. I don't want to be like them. My problems with food, eating, and my body aren't going to be subject to the burned-coffee-scented air. I want no share in this lot of humanity; my own is more than enough.

I wander the bike path for miles as it stretches up the northeastern flank of Lake Champlain. I trust the lake's violent, changing surface to take on the job of displacing the imprint of framed mown grass and trimmed trees. Glacial, the lake's blue-gray water, flecked with aquamarine and white, cuts any conceit. I've long admired this lake's enviable self-sufficiency; even on the warmest days its surface communicates an inhospitable quality, daring rather than inviting entry.

The holidays arrive and my father and sister want to see me. Strained is a generous description of Thanksgiving with my dad, his wife, Faith, and my sister in Saint Helena, California. Dr. Kohl demands I go to OA even there. I go once, utterly humiliated to admit to my family where I'm going. We cook the big bird and eat. The wine bottles gather by the recycle bin, the cluster expanding as the afternoon meal wears on into evening. It would make quite a contest to determine who's most grateful when the dishes are given over to the quiet hum of the dishwasher, when the leavings of the greasy turkey have been scrubbed out of the butcher-block counter, when the final late-night turkey sandwich has been consumed and the mayonnaise put away. We don't fight or raise our voices—ever. That kind of bad behavior is reserved for the catharsis of juicy, healthy, bare-bones fights with my sister, mostly contests over how we treat one another. She accuses me of dismissing her or not taking her seriously; I accuse her of being overly emotional, which edges a little too close to calling her irrational. Neither one of us much appreciates being called crazy. It's all painful but not fighting with everyone else is so much worse.

I return to my 77½ Intervale Avenue apartment and, after a restless night, I'm greeted by Dr. Kohl at the following morning's session with the demand I leave the nest of my apartment to move in with roommates. Impossible. But he ties the whole animal to the stake—me, the hospital, him. We fight. He wins.

My aloneness, how expertly I avoid spending time with people, has occupied the content of many hours between us. I make excuses, delaying the move as long as I can.

I arrive at a session that winter "feeling better, resigned, not in a rage." I tell him, "I'm just going through the motions of my existence. Why not kill myself, end this completely? But even that's pointless."

He suggests I'm giving up on ever being loved. He frames it unoriginally through a metaphor of the child—the part of me that refuses limits, rebels, destroys myself. It's her, my domineering three-year-old self, the one that learned to survive alone by being tough and never needing anything unless I could give it to myself. She's having a temper tantrum because I've opened up all these extremely painful needs by experiencing real connection with Dr. Kohl. Therapy has shown me what it feels like not to be so alone. Now I can't let go of how good that feels. My intimacy with objects and numbers pales in comparison with the way he makes me feel. Of the little I've allowed myself, Dr. Kohl says, echoing Miller, "the gifted child left alone to parent self is brutal." It's sad and difficult and perhaps impossible to say good-bye to the power of self-sufficiency. All the need leaves me feeling exposed. The process of putting this tyrannical, cruel part of myself away, even taming her, is risky because, as Dr. Kohl writes in my file, "She might kill you" first.

I find the temptations of suicide pulsing as naturally through my mind as the temptation to eat. Denied, each can be forced back, diverted, or otherwise foiled, for as Mann writes, "Reason is only virtue, while death is release, immensity, abandon, desire." Sticky, the thought returns, resilient as a cockroach. There again, the uninvited guest.

I indulge in fantasies, but I know it would be cold to slip away without telling anyone. I imagine it that way. I think I could do it. Banish their faces—my sister, father, mother—so I don't have to think about them when they find me gone. But I've never settled on just one plan, as all mental health professionals say when they ask, again and again, if you have "a plan." Only one? But there are so many to choose from.

I dream of dying but I want to live. I'm either all good or all bad. Dr. Kohl is the same. I hate him because he doesn't care about me or I love him more than anyone else I've ever loved because he's perfect. "Death and love—no, I cannot make a poem of them, they don't go together," Hans Castorp reflects in his dream.

Dr. Kohl notes in my file that he's "using the demands" to have roommates, go to OA, and do no harm to myself "to 'delete' the transference." He's forcing me to confront his imperfections, provoking my rage without doing anything unreasonable.

"I see you as a deity and everyone else as detractors," I say.

"Very destructive," he replies. "I can accept your dependency now, but it's not an acceptable outcome."

He can't stop me from believing he's the only person in the world who will ever understand me, the only person who can ever love me and know me fully. Despite this or perhaps because of it, I'm as angry as I've ever been about anything. I blame myself for wanting too much, for asking for what I know I can't have.

CHAPTER 36

Want to Fuck?

If only my skin were as tan and smooth as the milk-chocolate-brown string bikini I wore when I walked the seven miles that posthospital January day from the Anglin Fishing Pier along Galt Ocean Drive in Fort Lauderdale, Florida, to the breakwater leading into Lake Mabel. The bikini just encased my breasts, covered my ass, and shielded my pubic area. The standard loathing for the appearance of my thighs aside, a glance at my image in my grandmother's full-length mirror told me I almost looked good.

Walking the distance barefoot across the predominantly bubbly sand beach tested my endurance as with each step my feet sank into the coarse, dirty-blond sand. Before turning back, resting on the giant boulders that hold the beach intact, I absorb the ocean surface, alive as if sprinkled with crude glitter. I still possess the capacity for happiness.

I'd decided to spend Christmas alone in Fort Lauderdale at my grandmother's condo. I'd spent Christmas there alone once before, during my senior year at Middlebury. It's not a bad deal—right on the beach, view of the ocean, almost warm-enough pool, and a daily average high of 85°F. Now as then, the appeal of sun beating down on bared winter skin and all that lovely melanin it kicks up in response convinces me to avoid passing the time caged in my apartment while Dr. Kohl takes a holiday week off.

The walk fills me up, gives me a reserve of strength I can draw on before I set off on the seven-mile return. But suddenly a man my father's age is talking to me. It takes me a minute, as it always does, to realize he's not just sharing the view. I half listen as he tries to tangle me in lies about the ways I'm beautiful. He asks me up to his condo, pointing to the high-rise beyond the shallow dunes, "Just for a drink."

Walking away from his insistent, increasingly angry invitation in mid-speech, I feel spooked. The surprise of finding a quiet space only to be hustled out of it shouldn't bother me. I can't count the number of times I've been snapped into a defensive posture when I least expected to be. I can't get used to men so casually targeting me physically as if I'm emitting the signal I desire them. I fear that the signal I most frequently had on display back then was lit up in neon. It read: "Vulnerable."

I'm not special—being a target has nothing to do with what I look like, my string bikini or whether I weight 155 or 185 pounds. The overbearing male desire commonly directed at adolescent girls and women scares me. Others may be annoyed by it, while confident, happily lusty women may welcome it as an opportunity to play out their own desire. I love that my strong, athletic body—especially my unattractive but powerful legs—can carry me these fourteen miles under the hot sun and countless other places when strength and endurance are required. Because I'm not sexually game, trapped in rather than empowered by being perceived as desirable, I blame my physical self for turning me into an object. This alienates me, distancing me from my own flesh and ultimately prompting me to forsake my body.

Dr. Kohl believes my loose, frequently unsupervised child-hood was sexualized, with weak lines between private and public, affection and sensuality.

"Children who have parents preoccupied with sexuality themselves become preoccupied with sexuality," he says.

The pervasive nudity of friends, family, and strangers in the saunas, pond, and pools in Aspen and at Robinson Bar was not terrible. It was the 1960s and early 1970s. The iconic Hunter S. Thompson's distinctive presence in my childhood tells more than I can of that hedonistic environment. As he put it, "With the truth so dull and depressing the only working alternative is wild bursts of insanity and filigree." Later, life at Robinson Bar was lusty and loose in a way distinctive to the 1970s, with crass jokes about oral sex, bestiality, and Beatles-style doing "it in the road," along with *Penthouse* and *Playboy* magazines practically on display. Sex was simply a pervasive feature of these easy-going environments in which drugs, alcohol, and desire mixed naturally with regular nudity. "People were not so afraid as they are now," as Hunter said. "You could run around naked without getting shot."

That I was exposed to this sensual environment without feeling protected from it—or from much of anything else—is the source of the problem Dr. Kohl identifies. There was plenty of sleeping around in the big, wide-open bunkhouse where the crew lived, as there was in the lodge where my sister and I switched rooms and beds as often as we liked. I even slept in our ranch foreman Hester's "loft" above the wood shop—innocently—or as innocently as an 11-year-old can sleep with a man of twenty-five.

He was my first big crush—tall and blond and skinny with his handlebar mustache, worn Levi's, cowboy hat, and boots. How could I not fall for him? We worked on the horses together.

For a break we'd ride in the beat-up, faded blue Ford truck to the Sunbeam general store and campground. He'd buy himself Budweiser, Marlboros, and a Hostess Suzie-Q chocolate cake with cream oozing out of the rectangular edges, memorably coating the clear wrapping from the inside. He'd buy me Orange Crush and yellow Zingers. I'd peel the all-sugar frosting top off to eat first, then lick the exposed filling from the holes on the bottom, where I imagined a hydraulic arm and a piston-driven piping tip puncturing and filling each cavity with precision-measured "cream."

There were few if any limits set on what might be appropriate in this relationship and others. That my parents often didn't know where I slept between the ages of nine and eighteen doesn't mean anything bad happened. I fell in love with Hester first, then my Nordic ski coach, Kevin, who doted on me as his star athlete. Then, of course, Dr. Kohl. These adult men focused on me, expended time and energy to sustain a level of attention I craved.

The warm affection I experienced with these three men stands in bleak contrast to those who made their sexual attraction explicit. When I was a teenager living with my sister and no parents, boys tried seduction: the popular "back rub" that led to the unclipping of the bra hooks and rapidly progressed to the removal of the shirt. I didn't trust these high school charmers much more than I trust the man I just walked rapidly down the beach to escape. Later, I encountered an even more unprotected environment in Europe when I traveled there for my high school senior project.

My two-month Euro-Rail pass tucked next to my passport in the outer pocket of my backpack, I landed at Heathrow at age seventeen in the spring of 1983. The "project" I was required to do had no real requirements. It was more or less two months off with a research paper due at the end.

I met my father and his girlfriend, "C" Rose, in London. After sharing a train ride to Paris with them, I headed south solo seeking warmth—Cap d'Antibes, Saint Raphaël, Toulon, Cassis. Eventually I made my way through Lyon, Chamonix, Lausanne, Munich, Paris, and back to London. At our parting in Paris I'd arranged to rejoin my father and his girlfriend in a week or two—after they'd had some time together and I traveled alone for a bit, as planned. Sadly, I was hopelessly fixated on meeting up with them before I finished my good-bye.

Asphyxiated by men from the moment I boarded the train for Nice right on through to London, I defended myself but got no thrill from doing so.

"Want to fuck?"

"*Bonjour, mademoiselle. Vous-êtes seule?*"

"Get in the car."

"Can I join you?"

"*Vous-êtes libre?*"

"Please sit down."

"*Si jolie . . .*"

"Come with me."

"*Vous-êtes mariée?*"

"Are you alone?"

I avoided restaurants at night, kept in sight of crowds on quiet streets, remained shut in my hotel room after dark. Shirt buttoned high, head down, I felt under siege. The sanitation problem in nineteenth-century New York prompted reformers and historians to ask, "When did free-roaming pigs begin to be considered a public nuisance?" I can't help comparing the pigs to aggressive men given their equally "unreasonable interference with a right common to the general public"—in this case my right to walk the streets, sit in cafés, or read at the beach unmolested. Under pursuit I was reduced to sexual currency, a kind of medium of exchange with my body as coin. I was not the banker. Absent a sense of my own sexual agency given my age and character, I tried to stay out of circulation. As I wrote in my journal, "I feel like a whore."

I traveled that month without purpose, my teenage self abstractly pressured to have a good time. I wasn't certain what that meant to me. Capable but too alone, I began looking for my father's reappearance before it was possible he could arrive. Traveling with him, I could be a girl again. At hotel after hotel I waited, moving from one grubby room to the next, each time leaving careful instructions with Madame to direct any calls to me while religiously leaving the number of a succession of hotels with a friend in London we'd designated as our contact. I filled my days reading by the phone in a series of one-star hotels, envisioning the glad reunion between chapters while refusing to recognize the brain-numbing speechlessness I practiced to perfection as weeks passed without conversation.

On the make for a *pâtisserie* or *boulangerie* in every French town, I hid in my hotel room with a bag and a book, crumbs cluttering my chest. Stuffed on contempt, I cruelly traveled on, devastating countless *palmiers, mille-feuilles, éclairs au chocolat, friands noisette, crêpes au sucre, gâteaux au chocolat, petits fours, tuiles, financiers, Paris-Brests, religieuses,* and *pains au raisin.* My gleeful body, stunned by its luck, sucked in superior French butter, taxing the seams of my pants and the lace-trimmed confines of the bras I rapidly outgrew. Even my underpants stretched, the elastic weary of containing more than its fair share of flesh. Impressively steady in my consumption, over the course of four weeks I packed on fifteen pounds to add to the imaginary twenty I already carried in excess.

In bed after strange bed I hid, read, and ate while listening for the phone. The longing I felt then for a reunion with my father reminds me now of the endless wait for the next appointment with Dr. Kohl. Then as now, my self-loathing carried on, impressively resilient. When I am free of the spell of a book it litters my writing with a litany of earnestly scribbled resolutions. In my journal and even out loud to myself in empty hotel rooms I called myself fat in the third person: "Cree is fat, fat, fat and getting fatter, fatter, fatter."

As I finally discovered through a phone call to London several weeks in, my father and "C" had found it rainy and chilly in France. They had traded up two weeks ago without leaving word: France's wine, pâté, and damp hotels for Mexico's tacos, tequila, and arid heat. I fell out of myself, slogging on, despondent but relieved the wait was over. I scribbled in my notebook, "I feel painfully alone—maybe a hard case of disappointment. Shit. I will <u>not</u>, however, cry."

In daylight I sat in cafés reading the *Herald Tribune*, soaking up tall beers with my *omelette jambon fromage*, adding in my schoolgirl French, "*Encore une bière pression, s'il vous plaît.*" I'd figured out how to stay warm and liquid, relieved by the way the alcohol shaved the edge off anxiety. Biding the time until I could return home—I had to finish at least one month of the two I'd planned or admit terrible defeat—I beat back the darkness by decaying in a familiar sugary daze, empty bag crumpled, pages turning, journal filling. Defenseless against the onslaught of fresh promises, my vows turned to lies as fast as I wrote them down.

Then as now, I fertilize the cycle of self-loathing, prohibition, and abjection with small doses of manic happiness that come on loan, swiftly returning to where they came from as fast as they arrived. It's just enough; these bursts of stubborn optimism, the determination to force it, keep me going.

Halfway through my trip I rented a boat on Lake Geneva, rowing out under the bright sky punched in by high peaks, their image doubled in the lake's surface. The water glittered and in that travel poster–worthy flash I'm aware that the world is extraordinary, but seeing my abstract self there from afar, I think to slide in, taking the dusk for a swim in the glacial melt before ebbing beneath the mirror, the wooden boat set adrift in the meager Alpine air.

CHAPTER 37

Sexual History

"Did you masturbate as a child?" Dr. Kohl asks me.

"Sort of . . . " is the beginning of the explanation.

As a girl I put myself to sleep with dark fantasies of boys taking me to the woods, tying me up, and doing what? Something. It was an unspeakable live-action film starring me, only I watched myself play the role of the desirable starlet. The images titillated me night after night. Maybe it was the humiliation that excited me, my part in it unwilling even if I couldn't stop playing it in my mind again and again as my body became light and strange. This routine bedtime fantasy was my normal. The image lulled me to sleep as I floated just outside my body, but its content was deadly secret. Who would I tell? Why would I tell? Impossible. It was all too, too far outside any language I knew. I don't know if it lasted a year or five years. Memory holds only repetition.

Now I wonder if the fantasies reveal a deep-seated masochism. Explaining the memory to Dr. Kohl, saying it out loud, made what was normal seem bizarre and disturbing, turning it from an inchoate memory into an aberration. Was I sexually abused? Was the fantasy planted in my preverbal subconscious or buried in memory just beneath the images?

We hash these possibilities over more than once but I have only the fantasy and Dr. Kohl does not encourage speculation. He listens and does what he can to make sense of the shameful confession, but he's not there to generate a sorry story to excuse past and present misdeeds. I wish it were that simple.

These girlhood fantasies shape my connections between sexual pleasure, shame, and humiliation. This helps explain why I've been "sexually attracted to remote, tragic, addicted, abusive men," as Dr. Kohl points out. (He doesn't mean physically abusive.) My first boyfriend, Rob, and Matt reinforced my isolation by caring so little. Each confirmed my ultimate undesirability. With damaged men I could hold on to the shame of being broken, unknowable, and ultimately unlovable. Conversely, the unavailability of the powerful men I fell for, including our ranch foreman Hester, my cross-country coach Kevin, and Dr. Kohl, offered the ultimate safety. With them there was no danger of consummating my desire. And yet by making them my objects I managed to subject myself to the humiliation of repeated sexual rejection.

The oedipal desire to sleep with the father is a therapeutic cliché. Like Hester and Kevin, Dr. Kohl doesn't desire me. After all, in my mind he's perfect. That means he remains neutral toward me. He's my psychiatrist, there for my benefit, not in service of his needs, whether they be for friendship, connection, or sexual gratification. Fantasizing about him shames and humiliates me—he's forbidden. No surprise, the excitement I feel neatly echoes my formative experience of arousal.

I lost my virginity sophomore year at Middlebury when I fucked the first and only guy who offered me his coat. I was cold and we were drunk and the gray, black, and forest-green British wool weave he draped over my shoulders charmed me as we walked in the dark, our path illuminated by the white snowbanks lining the sidewalk. Closing time at the late-night Middlebury bar. We began by walking home together up the hill.

My few forays into sexual contact had been no more than inexpert, usually drunken, self-conscious teenage fumbling doomed to failure. David was not a stranger but a friend I had a crush on that I never considered could be reciprocated. I didn't consider myself attractive. I lacked the flirty ease of more popular friends. He was out of my league: handsome, funny, smart, and kind, with plenty of girlfriends.

So when he kissed me in the dark of his off-campus house I kissed him back, warmed by his coat, surprised and pleased by the unexpected development. Into his room, onto a mattress placed ingloriously on the floor, we made our way, his charm in overcoming the awkwardness of what we were about to do a splendid gift, necessary despite the haze alcohol lent the scene. The shock was the unexpected violence of the act. He was a man, not one of the teenage boys I'd fooled around with a handful of times. Sex with him didn't involve fumbling; it was decisive. I hadn't imagined it could be like that. By the time he finished I was shaking. It was not a romantic response. He suggested we shower together to calm and warm me. Damp and steamy from the hot water, back under the blankets, we lay together until sleep won out. A few hours later, after fumbling for my clothes in the dark, I slipped away without a word, sorry to leave David behind but too afraid of being spurned in the light of the morning not to.

My sexual history didn't prosper. My avoidance of being seen in public with my first real boyfriend, Rob, junior year at

Middlebury should have been warning enough. I fell hard for him—an alcoholic misfit I chose because he was uncool and unguarded. He was sweet to me but a hopeless drunk, so I was safe from the possibility of real closeness. I'd chosen him so it would be in my power to determine how long to keep him and what to do with him when I'd had enough. I believed that, until I wanted him more than he wanted me. Little did I know just how sordid the whole thing could be, until the last time we fucked during my postgraduation stint at the family newspaper in the autumn of 1988. Again, it involved the great dignity of a mattress on the floor, this time at his apartment in New Haven, Connecticut. It was one time too many.

The pregnancy that resulted was an alien occupation. The cells growing in my uterus were uninvited. For as long as I'd wanted a piece of Rob, once I had it—really, really had it—it felt as though the worst of him had taken up residence under my skin.

I scrubbed myself clean and pretended the abortion never happened. Dr. Kohl thought part of my sadness was mourning the loss of a version of my neglected, baby self. This not-baby represented a chance to undo my own messy childhood. When I thought of it this way I couldn't help feeling sorry and wondering if getting rid of it was a mistake. I was twenty-three on 11/11/88. I flew to Vermont with my loyal friend Karen for the procedure because that state allowed earlier termination than New York.

When I was home alone on my futon in Schenectady a quick binge and purge left me emptied out and calmer. For some reason, as I lay there, it occurred to me to masturbate. Yes, I was twenty-three, but I'd never had an orgasm and I did not masturbate—not counting the girl fantasies that involved no touching. But I'd been pregnant—and suddenly I was not.

The primal reality of the violation gave permission or necessity as my hand wandered between my legs, pushing the elastic on my underwear down around my thighs, relaxing enough to feel what happened when I spread my legs and rubbed that dainty protuberance until the warmth wasn't just on that one spot but all over down there and my muscles tightened in a spectacular effort to hold back the pleasure until I couldn't and it went beyond me, happening most intensely in my brain, where the release of tension ventilated layers and layers of fury and confusion.

It was the bottomless sense of abandon that finally got me there—the fuck-it attitude that split my prim, scared, prissy, too-good shell open long enough to let me experience sexual desire. My body had again betrayed me but I'd discovered a way to tamper with it for my own purposes, definitely one worth pursuing. When I tell Dr. Kohl about my first orgasm and that it occurred that night, postabortion, he calls it an "indulgent punishment."

It's true. I'm grateful for the release of an orgasm, and the closer I get to wanting to burn myself the more I find myself lying on my back somewhere just private enough, fingers moving me toward that momentary transcendence. It's a half valve that draws me back into a missing center. What Dr. Kohl calls an indulgence applies equally to the act of burning myself. The shame about my body's responses to bad thoughts that began when I was a very young child with visions of sexual humiliation has been supplanted by fantasies of Dr. Kohl masturbating me or of me simply masturbating in front of him. He tells me what to do and I imagine him in charge. It tops me off every time.

* * *

"Maybe you're burning to close off sexual feelings," Dr. Kohl suggested at the height of the pre-hospital crisis in the summer of 1991.

My evasive reply was, "I'm not very sexual and unless I'm with someone . . . well, let's just say I don't masturbate a lot." Sometimes I masturbate what might be called a lot—say every day for a week—then I won't go near it for weeks on end, as if somehow I've forgotten that I can, if briefly, go elsewhere that way.

"Burning is a way of defiling herself, was defiled before in images of boys, sexual fantasies," he writes in my chart. It's true. I can't resist the furtive, the dirty, the forbidden, the salacious. He has no interest in my body other than when I destroy it by smoking, bingeing, vomiting, drinking, or burning my skin. Maybe he's my perfect man—my ultimate object of fantasy, not because of who he is or how he sees me, but precisely because I know he doesn't want me sexually. This is a man who can be trusted to talk to me, not fuck me.

CHAPTER 38

Borderline

Dr. Kohl's high-wire act is to manage the demands of the paternal and sexual feelings I have for him while fostering independence. Before I went into the hospital we were revealing and dislodging the sludge of thoughts, memories, and emotions. He thought his work then was getting me to connect to him. A lot of the pre-hospital talk circled around my anger at not having more of him, even if no quantity could ever be enough. It was as if back then the rebus of my erotic transference hadn't yet been fully assembled in my mind or his. Rather, it skimmed through the air in fractions, lodging next to every word, look, and gesture.

I know it's sick and wrong, but sometimes I find myself half wishing for some ghastly event in childhood, something that would make all this bad behavior comprehensible, even excuse it. Of course it's a mercy my half efforts are never to any avail. My history as this sort of victim or survivor is lost in fantasies of boys and penises, wrapped up tightly in all that shame. If there was a transgression, a taboo act, or use of my body I couldn't consent to it's gone now, perhaps having left behind an invisible imprint on my preverbal mind or a physiological trace that's part of me.

It's not that truth doesn't matter; it does. But I already know enough about my loose childhood. The work I have to do doesn't involve focusing on some ur-moment of violation that would magically explain who I am. That an "event" or "pattern" could explain everything is a fantasy. Believing in such an "event" reduces the loss of safety I felt as a child to a sideshow. This lack of protection constitutes the central damage I withstood. I've spent so long convinced that if I were just better, more worthy in a thousand different ways, I could back then have earned the full attention and undiluted love I yearn for from Dr. Kohl now. Had I earned that regard from my parents, had I been secure and tended, I wouldn't need to wonder if a dreadful violation occurred.

Genetics has likely stuck me with a biological vulnerability to emotional instability and depression. My mother can't be counted as happy and her father was wildly erratic, moody, violent, and difficult. That I struggled as a child to form a solid, resilient sense of self in an environment in which my emotional responses were devalued, questioned, oversimplified, mocked, or, most likely, ignored didn't help. The persecution I felt, the idea that I was in a set-up universe that could come crashing down at any moment, was a way of structuring chaos. I am important in this twisted universe of special objects and 11s.

Now I'm stuck like a dervish in a whirl of transference and countertransference with the single object I've elected to rescue me. I'm good at sucking Dr. Kohl in by compelling him to take care of me. I'm not above seduction through pleasing him. I'm as playful, smart, funny, hardworking, and attractive as I can be, even if none of it gets me the ultimate prize—him.

Dr. Kohl has never been oblivious to what might be called "boundary seductions," moments when the limits of the psychotherapeutic relationship blur. He made a decision early on to expand our relationship beyond the confines of 112 Church Street. Phone calls at all hours, a prescription for Silvadene burn ointment, rules about how to live, examining my wounds and bandaging my arm, sending his receptionist with me to the dentist—these were all on the edge, but he offered them to me as a way of trying to parent me, gain my trust, and connect. And yet my "libidinal demands"—such a sexy phrase—must be exhausting. Whatever he thought he was doing pre-hospital to nurture me is now, in the posthospital environment, up for grabs. Now he knows precisely who and what he's dealing with. He knows what I'm capable of; now his job is to sort out the symptoms and their origins.

Framing me as "borderline" seems useful to him. A diagnosis may begin with a DSM checklist but it doesn't end there. In fact, the psychoanalytic model uses no such list except when practitioners are forced to engage with insurance companies or are conducting clinical studies. For a psychiatrist trained as an analyst, as Dr. Kohl is, diagnosis begins with three basic categories: neurotic, borderline, and psychotic. Each term, terrible as it sounds, comes with symptoms that correlate with developmental deficits at various ages. These complexities of breast-feeding, egos, superegos, good and bad objects, sex and death drives, oral and anal phases, bonding, fantasy, reality, individuation, splitting, projection, repression, mirroring, reflection, and deflection are beyond me.

Dr. Kohl knows that intense transference, testing, and acting out often occur in cases with patients on what I'm going to call the "spectrum of borderline personality disorders." He does see me on this spectrum. On 12/2/91, he tries to separate the behaviors that go with the diagnosis from what he sees as my experience of it as a condition: "PTSD and BORDERLINE feelings: intense affect, apperceptual difficulties, social adaptiveness, extreme over-idealization and dramatization, affect instability, identity disturbance, frantic attempts to avoid abandonment."

PTSD is relevant as a secondary diagnosis. Some who experience heightened emotions as children—fear, sadness, longing—without any way to control or escape these emotions perceive feeling itself as dangerous. This dual diagnostic lens paired with symptoms of depression organizes my treatment. The clincher is that the symptoms hide behind my famously intact social facade. Oh, and I idealize the hell out of him.

I'm not sure how much it matters that by the end of treatment Dr. Kohl slaps a "BPD without sexual abuse" label on my file. (He adds the caveat because bulimia combined with BPD is considered by some in the field as prima facie evidence of sexual abuse.) Dr. Kohl dances continually around the question of my diagnosis when we talk about it, never fully pronouncing me as a person with BPD, as if "having" such a thing were like having diabetes or scoliosis. To treat this particular psychiatric diagnosis this way would bind me to it, making the work we do less meaningful and the central goal of changing my behavior pointless. Even if I meet the DSM-III criteria for BPD, even if I neatly fit the description an analyst of the object-relations persuasion might call "Depressive-Masochistic Character Structure Operating at a Borderline Level," these labels aren't a cover or an excuse. (Oh, that they were!)

So what good is the diagnosis to me? Most usefully I can reflect on the cluster of behaviors, symptoms, and emotions and try to head them off by pulling them apart to expose the underbelly of the problems various behaviors resolve for me—burning, vomiting, isolating myself. The worst I can do is label myself "abnormal," "sick," or "mentally ill." I've long since concluded that humans are fundamentally weird creatures. I burn myself with cigarettes and that, along with a raft of other traits, qualifies me as borderline—not the other way around. It's not *because* I'm borderline that I burn; the burning makes me borderline. This is a sneaky, essential distinction I'll be working through for quite some time to come.

Not surprisingly, under this large, shoddy circus tent of a diagnosis come behaviors that may have succeeded in eroding the analytic space. Part of this might be read from the affective intensity, the emotional tenor, of the exchanges between me and Dr. Kohl during sessions. I toyed with his emotions and tested his allegiance in the most sadistic way as I burned myself and looked forward to showing him the damage I'd done. We fought and argued and grew too close, occasionally pushing the proper limits of the relationship because he wasn't going anywhere and neither was I.

The certainty that Dr. Kohl wasn't going to just catch and release me, given all the vomiting, burning, and suicidal threats, might have undermined the central work of creating an intimate space based on a shared intellectual engagement. The lofty air of pure talk was, after all, part of what I initially fell in love with and is in large part the plane psychotherapeutic treatment is intended to exist on. But to treat me with a more traditional emotional coolness when I was at an age that wasn't quite full adulthood, when I arrived with a fragile belief in human connections and a well-evolved set of internal conflicts, might have driven me away. I'm sure Dr. Kohl fostered the emotional bonds I formed as well as he knew the risks that came with them.

CHAPTER 39

Guilt→Sex→Excitement

Dr. Kohl's posthospital limits and demands defined by our contract carry a rigid formality that is meant to reenact the parenting I never had. The agreements I've made with him are meant to hold me accountable to someone other than myself for the first time. And yet they have had the effect of also making me more dependent on him. I fight with him over the rules, angry and alienated from him one minute, sucked back in by his gravitational pull the next. I feel that he's laying these scourges in my way for the sake of provoking a fight. I hate him for it.

"I'm really tired of this therapy shit," I tell him in an expletive-ridden outburst at the end of December. "I can't believe I have to check about cutting my hair. It's mine. Fuck this. I'm leaving. Such a fucking game. OA is such a game. I play your fucking game. I go there just like you're telling me to. HOW DO I KNOW I'M NOT BECOMING SOMETHING I DON'T WANT TO BECOME?"

"You fear control by a masterful source," he answers. It's the 11s again and the connection between him and some external power turning me into something I'm not. For all I know this is the same power that's made me a chameleon all my life—as if there's a broader sense of falsehood in the universe that continually manipulates me to serve its purposes—the purpose of the people I encounter, the purpose of keeping me isolated and in doubt. When he prods me to socialize I resist and complain.

"I'm totally isolated and have no friends, no one to hang out with."

"It's hard to have friends when you have to control everything," he says. True enough. Although it's worse than that—what I need from friends is gratification, maybe even homage. My capacity for real friendship is stunted. As insecure and inferior as I often feel, the independence I rely on arises out of a sense of omnipotence. This is the charming "fuck everyone and everything" part of me.

Maybe that's why I fight so hard to be alone with Dr. Kohl as the sole object of my attention. If the demands he makes are intended to loosen my narrow focus on him by moving me into a wider, more social world I'm determined it's not going to work. After all, I have him and that's really all that matters, even if posthospital he's less the confessor than the strict parent.

Back then he was coaxing a needy toddler to trust him; now he's trying to manage a rebellious teenager by setting rules and limits. We fight over whether or not I'll agree to go back on an antidepressant. I question why I would I go back to it when it seemed to have no positive effect on me and carried now, no less than before, the great inchoate danger of compromising my "real" self—that ever-present danger of "becoming something I don't want to become." We do math together because I'd always believed I couldn't be good at it. I also had the Graduate Record Examinations (GREs) to master if I was going to apply to graduate school. All of these small attentions are his way of holding me accountable, taking care of me, and helping me normalize my relationships.

Despite the structure and thrice-weekly appointments (I went from four to three in January 1992) I don't trust what's happening to me. The nightmares, mixing sleep with waking, are crazy-making and come in concert with the blinking 11s; I'm not done questioning my sanity. I can't seem to make sense of the inside and outside—how false the world feels and how scared I feel.

"Maybe the only true authentic you is crazy and you only pretend to be sane," he says, half teasing.

"Yes . . . " I answer tentatively. It's as if he's instigating, forcing me to confront my fear because he trusts I am sane.

"If anybody knows you're crazy . . . " he says with a smile.

"You do." I finish for him. "Only you'd say I'm not . . . "

At the bottom of the page for the day he writes, "The sanity uncertainty and confusion come from internalizing two disturbed parents. Mother is ill, beyond the alcohol. She feels better with Dr. Kohl or sick friend because it is clear to her who is sick or well." Not able to trust myself to judge, I use Dr. Kohl to hold me intact when nothing else in the world remains steady.

"I got very close to burning myself," I tell him in mid-January. "IT'S SUCH A GAME."

"I made you a deal in here or you're out," he reminds me.

"Fine—you won't go along or be nice to me, so we can have this little game. I perceive myself as not having a relationship with someone." In other words, I'm trying to convince him that it feels as if my connection to him has been reduced to a game of chicken, a practical engagement in which he props me up and makes the rules while I flounder. I'm doing what I can to resist the progress he's trying to make by throwing myself at him as explicitly as possible. Our energies have been siphoned off into a defense against the goals of therapy through intense transference. I'm resisting change by clinging to him.

"You can't have me, so you will have no one," he suggests. I'm not answering this pointed, loaded statement so I head for the arsenal.

"I can't make that leap from burning is a big deal to it's acceptable."

"As if the ends justify the means."

"Yes," is all I say. I'm not entirely sure what he means. I honestly don't think the burning is a big deal—still. I guess he means that feeling better by cauterizing my desire for him can't be justified.

"No one was there as a child to talk over stimulating yourself or the guilt and shame you felt." As usual he's leaping to root causes, but I'm right with him.

"I actually thought of that. Felt totally forbidden," I confess.

He then writes, "GUILT→SEX→EXCITEMENT."

As Freud noted, the analyst must "keep firm hold of the transference-love, but treat it as something unreal, as a situation which has to be gone through in the treatment and traced back to its unconscious origins." Dr. Kohl is attempting to get at the root of the dynamic between us and around burning by tracing the transference to its origins. He must bring "all that is most deeply hidden in the patient's erotic life into her consciousness and therefore under her control." Whether or not Freud overemphasized sexual drives isn't in contention—it's fair to say he did, not to mention how he framed female sexual desire. But in this context his point stands; Freud got a lot of things right.

In April Dr. Kohl writes out a few goals for treatment to himself:

1. Help her, free her to expand relationships, loving, nurturing, "out there."
2. Deal with transference to prevent unbearable dependency.
3. Expand her "appetites" by supporting broader experiences.
4. Help her learn to fight for and express her needs.

I'm putting up a fairly heroic resistance to his efforts. I cut my finger "by accident." I've talked my way out of going to OA. I'm sick of people.

I call him to tell him "I'm toying with cigarettes. Close . . . " Then at the next session I say, "Saturday and yesterday I held cigarette close to finger, never directly . . . looks different now." In other words, I sort of, very mildly, burned my finger.

"It tests, pushes, by escalating something . . . After I got off the phone it did seem crazy to do it. I didn't even want to. When it seems not good it seems stupid, not horrible. I've never been concerned it was wrong. Only hurts me."

"Been abused." This seems like a non sequitur.

"No big deal I'm burning myself."

"What?" Then he realizes I don't mean it in the present continuous tense with the latest minor burn I've just confessed to, one of many I haven't told him about. I simply mean it as a thing I do in general.

"I dreamed Nicole was burning her arm. I was freaked, horrified."

"You've been through it all," he says, not that helpfully but with sympathy.

"Yes . . . burning seems meaningful in relation to trying to survive. Not a big price to pay in order to survive." I'm determined to defend the practice—as I say, it doesn't hurt anyone but me.

In his notes for the session he observes, "Eased up on the OA limit and she's pushed this [burning] boundary." Then he lists my "4 choices," none of which he ultimately forces me to make:

1. Drop out of therapy.
2. New therapist.
3. Back to OA (I let her out of this), math,
   roommates, no burning.
4. Hospital.

There's nowhere to go, nothing to do with how I'm feeling, other than to keep coming back. So I unload my misery at his feet. He's not afraid of it and he never tells me to put it away even when I give up.

"Being alive is a put-on and a fake."

CHAPTER 40

Musical Chairs

Eventually Dr. Kohl's patience wears out as I delay finding room-mates and a house to share with them. He sets deadlines to bring in the classifieds and prods me to approach the people I'm acquainted with through my former job. Finally, under his threat of not seeing me anymore, I throw myself in with a former coworker and her friends, who are planning on getting a house together. One is my friend Jess. I love and trust her but spend no time with her. Our friendship is truncated by her girlfriend, Olga, who, unlike Jess, brings with her jealousy, neediness, and other obligations of friendship I'm generally allergic to. The other three, one man and two women, are distant acquaintances. It's done. I'm moving.

I leave my apartment on 4/1/1992, quickly undermining the purportedly positive effect of my roommates by staying in my room, door closed, music up loud, writing. More useless words, practicing the only form of deliberate concentration I know. I write more poetry and then write what I can about Dr. Kohl, but I lack perspective; it's litter. As I'm so practiced at doing, I hold on to a presentable veneer for display when passing through the kitchen or catching one of my roommates on the stairs. The only

good part of being there is seeing more of Jess by frequently sharing a smoke with her on the front steps. It's easy to get smaller
and more invisible by the day in the big Victorian I share with
so many bodies. I have plenty of practice hiding.

I wish and don't wish to hear someone else in the house.
Book in hand, cigarette burning, I write and pass days secreted.
Voices in the kitchen, feet on the stairs, I have no idea how to
break the familiar pattern of feeling dispossessed.

Not long after moving, when I'm alone in the house, I lie in
a hot bath drawn in the shared bathroom, door locked. Turning
the lights out, I'm a body suspended in warm liquid, the slosh of
water and its scent in the dark more a temperature than a thing
to take in with the nose. I float bodiless. I imagine my familiar
outline, nothing to show above the waterline but two buoyant
breasts and a patch of black pubic hair. And my head, of course.
I try to relax, but all I can think is how natural it would be to put
my mouth beneath the surface and forget to breathe for a while.
Soon I could forget even the dark and the warmth I sought in
this element. Too bad I know it will take more than a fantasy to
finish me off. The body is unwilling. I suspect it takes a churning
ocean far from shore to drown at will—and then it's not will that
does it but hypothermia or a riptide or so much salt water in your
mouth you can't breathe after a while because every time you
cough to force it out of your lungs you gulp down more of the
liquid that will eventually suffocate you. As Anne Sexton writes,
"Real drowning is for someone else. It's too big to put in your
mouth on purpose." So I give the fantasy away and climb out of
the tub, squandering the hot water. The drain makes a sucking
sound for me, its one and only tired metaphor.

Turning the light on, I stare in the mirror at the reflection of my naked body, the legs I loathe; the arms, wide jaw,

broad shoulders; and the breasts, really my best feature. Firm. Proportional nipple. Not too big but definitely big enough. I can't look long—my face is blotchy and hideous; my cheeks and eyes, off-kilter, are horrible. Tongue stained a foul brown from too much nicotine and caffeine. Fine blue veins passing across my forehead feed me, making my pulse go whether I like it or not. I look to the noisy drain and cheap, molded white plastic tub, entertaining the idea of making a terrible mess of it with one of the razors I hoard. Forever quiet, no march of hours, no voice, mind departed. Did I say fuck you? Struggling to listen for myself, I wrap my wet body in a towel and tell the thought to go away and play.

Without burning and vomiting—my recourse when I need to let go of myself—I don't quite know what to do. The less of me there is, the lighter, the more I feel the power of denying desire. Then there are the 11s and their favorite toy, the cigarette, goading me to take to burning as the psychic eraser I long for. I'm left to loathe my body, the material self I can see clearly enough to hate. There's no dimness dark enough to hide.

The options before me: 1. I can go back to the hospital and rot or find a pipe and a bedsheet. 2. I can trust Dr. Kohl not just when I'm with him but beyond 112 Church Street, play by his rules, and come up with a reliable version of myself even if it's one certain to be fake. 3. I can "leave," which is to say die now.

The strongest grapnel holds; Dr. Kohl keeps me in place.

Once the move is over I focus on finding a job, if only to get a tiny piece of normal back. I've been cashing disability checks of $196.71 every month since 11/11/91. I don't recall asking for them and I don't deserve them, so by the time the daffodils, tulips, and lilacs have bloomed and withered, by the time Lake Champlain is busy with what looks too much like toy sailboats, I'm back waitressing at Sneakers, the popular breakfast joint that fills to overflowing with college kids every weekend.

Why go back there, given how much I hate the job? Because I know how to do it, it's easy money, and it's comfortable. I don't have to learn anything new or prove myself. Starting over isn't in me. They like me there. I always showed up, worked hard, and made the customers happy. Why not hire me back?

The mirrored backdrop of Bacardi, Myers's Rum, Gilbey's Gin, Tanqueray, and the rest obscures the reflection of my face, all smudged black eyeliner, dirty hair, and chapped lips. Such as it is, it's all a performance for the people waiting in the long rowdy line. I don't exist for them yet, the loud music drowning me out. In minutes I'll unlock the front door and click on the cursive neon "SNEAKERS" sign.

On this Saturday morning, like every other weekend day at 8 A.M., they rush as if I've started a round of musical chairs. Once they've claimed a spot they want me—all of them at once and not soon, not in a minute, but now. I deliver myself with a smile as if this is the best part of my day, as if there's nowhere I'd rather be than bringing them everything they desire while chatting them up as if we're old pals. I give it all to them as though I mean it, even when I feel pieces of me coming off and drifting to the floor with the jagged tops of the dups I rip away to stick on the nail for the cooks. Danny. Chris. Carbon copy. "Order up!"

By the end of the day parts of the customers are stuck to me, clinging with maple syrup and raspberry jam until I can shower. They always forget to pay for that, the part they leave on me as I question the quality of their hunger: *Scrambled, fried*

or poached?" is just the chorus. *"Coffee?" "Tea?" "Half-and-half
or whole milk?" "Skim?" "Honey?" "Orange juice?" "Mimosa?"
"Bloody?" "Salt?" "Omelet?" "Cheddar or Swiss?" "Wheat, white,
rye, pumpernickel, or English muffin?" "Granola?" "Yogurt or milk?"
"Fruit, no potatoes?" "Side sausage?" "Patty or link?" "Side bacon?"
"Full or short-stack?" "Blueberry, banana, or plain?" "Waffle?" "Real
maple?"* Between sets of beverages, condiments, meat, eggs, and
bread I take to the bathroom, lock the door, and turn out the light.
The dark and I rest together. A full minute of muted disguise
replenishes me before I emerge into the light to take their money
away from them, greasy bills, sticky coins. I'm greedy for it all
no matter how unclean.

After my shift at home, peeling my clothes off, I leave my
T-shirt and jeans rumpled on the bathroom linoleum, my pockets bulging with wads of $20s. These, the distilled bounty of
messy 5-, 10-, 25-, and even 1-cent coins, mixed with $1s, $5s,
and $10s, I scooped off empty tables with the wadded paper
napkins, cold mugs, and hollandaise-smeared plates. I feel a
vaguely pleasant physical fatigue after my nine-hour shift, a sense
of completion. *Heinz ketchup bottles consolidated and wiped; soggy
thawed cartons of orange concentrate diluted with tepid Winooski
tap water; Bloody Mary mix replenished with a potent cocktail of
V8, black pepper, Worcestershire, and raw horseradish; floor swept;
hot-from-the-dishwasher silver bundled in white paper napkins; bar
sinks drained; till balanced; tables and chairs sprayed and wiped;
pocketed apron in the laundry bin.* If only I were so orderly. I stink
of bacon and home fries.

Waitressing corrupts the authenticity I've been working
so hard to locate. After acting the part, staying in character for
nine hours, I need to degrease my skin and hair as much as I

need to mop up the shamefully artificial banter, charm, smiles, and affability I serve up all day.

"It sucks for you to be a waitress. You get paid more for faking," Dr. Kohl observes. My tips would take a serious dive if I behaved the way I feel. I'm working four days a week. My charm serves me well, even if it means sometimes I don't know what is me.

"It feels separate from me. Not my life." How handy; it's almost as if I've gotten a proxy to do the job for me. I've certainly had enough practice. I've done this job, the first requirement of which is effortless agreeability, since I was 11. I quickly learned to seduce my customers, inveigling them into giving me more of what I wanted—money. It's no different now.

The raw, red scars, with angry keloid ridges on the inside of my elbow, add a new dimension to an old job. The occasional customer will look at my arm and blurt, "Wow, what'd you do?" or "What happened there, burn?" A few even persist when I try to put them off with "Long story," quickly moving on to, "More coffee?"

"No, really. What'd you do? Grease splatter?"

I'm astonished by this audacity as much as by the fear and curiosity the scars elicit. Unlike the unmistakable vertical scars on the wrists of suicide survivors, my scars are an enigma—open to interpretation, guesses, and casual speculation. I learn to shut down the conversations I don't want to have. The irregular, not pretty marks are mine as much as they're irrefutable evidence of who I am now. I'm oddly proud of them, each one a stamp of time when I thought I might disintegrate and yet managed to find a moment of calm, a modicum of pleasure, a sense of coming back together by experiencing pain and making a new hole-scar-to-be. They're as much "me" as my nose, eyes, fingers, and breasts. Skin may be permeable—as I've proved with the incursions I've made on it—but it heals.

Whether I'm waitressing or just walking around there are invariably many different kinds of looking going on, mostly in hot weather when my full arm is open to view, scar tissue etched in pigment-free contrast to the tan skin surrounding the pattern of circles, lines, and irregular shapes.

"At least now I know why people are staring at me," I tell Dr. Kohl.

I also emphatically tell him I will never allow a skin graft to cover the scars. Never a stigma, they are, as Nathaniel Hawthorne wrote, "something to be sorrowed over, and looked upon with awe, yet with reverence too." I love them.

CHAPTER 41

I Can't Pretend

Throughout the spring and summer more burns and eventual suicide hang prophetic, as if the choices that matter were made long ago. It's cold and wet into early June; my favorite patch of white and crimson peonies flattened by rain. I've bitten my nails and taken off my jewelry—again.

"Men think long hair is a great thing. By chopping it off I can eliminate harassment from men. I look hideous with my hair short."

"It's your hair, why don't you keep it?" is all he can say.

"Like fragments," I say, describing how all the encumbrances of beauty were insignificant bits—nothing to me. I'm also referring to the poetry I endlessly write as fragments. I don't think much of the poems either.

"Skin on arms," he suggests, making an association between the word and the skin I destroy.

"Proves how tough I am," I say.

"You are tough, but magic isn't needed to prove it true."

"Opposite of fragment is WHOLE," I observe, "but scary and artificial." I am on some level purifying myself *for* the 11s.

If cutting this part of myself away makes me less of an object at work and on the street I don't mind—even if or maybe especially since doing so goes against much of what I've absorbed about feminine identity. I'm resisting inhabiting a self dependent on and defined by physical attributes. Maybe disfiguring my arm is a dramatic version of the same impulse.

Dr. Kohl has been trying to convince me to take a different antidepressant—this time it's Zoloft. I went off the Prozac in the hospital and never went back on. For weeks I've been carrying around the once crisp prescription ripped fresh from his official Vermont state pad. It's now wrinkled and tattered around the edges.

"If you choose to take it it's a way of taking responsibility for managing your own feelings," he says. I fill the prescription.

"I have the pills," I announce at the next session, "I just choose not to take them."

"Then you should question whether or not you want to be here." This is scary. I take the pills.

Again and again I dream of being in bed with Dr. Kohl. When I have the dream I wake happy and peaceful, as if a spell has been cast on me. We're in a big bed—just crisp white sheets and our entangled bodies. The sensation of the dream imprints itself on me, the image an erotic trigger I'll return to again and again. There's the scent of sex—it is after all a bed and we're in it together. But I never have explicitly sexual dreams. Their most prominent feature is the lush serenity of being everything to him in the immediate present. I am protected—safe in a way

I've never experienced. I hold on to the fullness of the dreams when I wake but the warmth slips away, drifting into the mean daylight. All I can do is dream it again—and I do.

I'm riveted the first time I see him with his wife. I run into them at a performance of *Madame Butterfly* at Burlington's art deco performing arts space on Main Street, the Flynn. I've never encountered Dr. Kohl outside his office and I've never seen even a picture of her—although I've heard her voice plenty of times. The strange contact spins me into anxiety over how I look, what I'm wearing, if I can appear cool and at ease. My self-consciousness about being at the performance alone like the loser I am doesn't help. But it's his wife that really sets me off—she's beautiful.

"You and your wife look like a young couple. Entwined, connected, and attentive to each other," I tell him at the next session. I then add, "She's abrupt at times [on the phone]. I understand her tone of resentment." Why not throw in a criticism?

"Are you annoyed with her?" he asks. I'm so tired of that question. What does it really mean? Why is "annoyed" his mental and verbal crutch? What's wrong with displeased, irked, troubled, agitated, or exasperated? Even peeved would be nice for a change. I skip the question, which I suppose is rhetorical in any case, just part of the grammar of therapy.

Referring to his family, I say, "All these people get to have you most of the time . . . they're intimate with your life." Then I leap right in: "We don't talk about sex here," it seems uncomfortable, "it's so loaded." I assure him in the same breath that "I'm not preoccupied with these thoughts" about him and sex. He makes me feel less of a fool for bringing it up, yet again.

"Closeness has lots of feelings, now it has sexual feelings."

I guess we can talk about it.

A month later I dream of being in bed with him and another man at the same time. It was, I tell him, "All warm, nice, connected." The dream captures an otherworldly safety and contentment.

"Two people, now that's an improvement," he gamely replies, again sparing me the shame, rewarding my honesty with humor and understanding.

"Never a woman," I say, perhaps because I want to establish in this realm, as in every other, that I'm nothing like my mother.

"You're getting warmth confused with sexuality. It's an easy thing to confuse in an undemonstrative family that acted out sexually." He then adds, "And Hester didn't help."

He notes my "uncomfortable laughter" in response.

"Abandonment versus a gloppy sea of sexuality-affection is not much of a choice" he says. I don't offer a verbal reply. He suggests "we clear up sex to let the warmth come through."

I have no idea how to sift out the erotic from all that I experience as "Dr. Kohl." If only I were a prospector, I could pour water over my mind, tilting my head this way and that to separate the erotic bits. I'm sure I wouldn't give them up if I could locate them—I'd tuck them away forever.

In his assessment of the session he writes, "Abandonment theme in all above: tried not to let them pile up. Astounded by it. She doesn't realize what's happening here until so much piles up. Burning = the pain and the defense." He finishes with, "Finally beginning to develop boundaries between sexuality and warmth-affection."

A few sessions later I blurt out, "I want to come home with you." I say it before I can think about it. It's the most directly sexual demand I can muster; I've said I want "daughter status" and told him about my undeniably erotic dreams but I've never said I'm in love with him much less that I want to have sex with him. I can't quite admit the desire to myself in spite of his starring role in my erotic imagination. He knows how serious I am about wanting to be his, go home with him, never leave his side. Maybe I'm hoping for a miracle or maybe I'm testing him.

"To act on that would compromise you, make me anxious, and I couldn't honor our contract," he says without the least snicker. He then adds, "I've told you I can't take you home." He writes in my chart, "Not used to not getting the little she asks for. Can she survive her own rage?"

I churn forward, filling time between work and therapy; I mostly read, write, smoke, and eat candy—spice drops are my latest obsession. The hours stick to me. I am lonely but I don't want to be with anyone except Dr. Kohl. As Samuel Johnson wrote, "When I rise my breakfast is solitary" but "the black dog waits to share it." Tired as the metaphor has become it seems apt when again and again I find him there; "from breakfast to dinner he continues barking" and I, too, must ask myself, "What shall exclude the black dog from a habitation like this?"

Dr. Kohl sets me up to volunteer with an underprivileged children's organization called King Street Youth. He wants me to see and feel what kids are like—to see what a baby a nine-year-old is, how young and needy a thirteen-year-old is. Besides, good as our office dance is, all the talk and analysis aren't enough if after each session I go back to my room to think and write about him. The children's vulnerability and need get into my blood, just as Dr. Kohl calculated they would. Rather than self-destructing under the unfairness of their situation as I did when I worked at Community Action, I keep my perspective. Maybe I'm holding myself together because I know there's no choice. I don't want to check out—either by hiding in a hospital or by swimming out to sea. And yet the calm I experience feels deadly; chaos is invigorating.

Jay, the leader of the program, has a body I come to mark as my type—slightly round, not too tall, with soft features—and easy, understated manners concealing devastating confidence. I spend the summer daydreaming about him, flirting in my own feeble way while ostensibly nurturing children in need of attention and playtime along the sandy strip of Lake Champlain that passes for a beach just north of Burlington. When someone whispers Jay's dating a coworker on the sly (against company policy) I collapse into my humiliation, berating the misplaced ambition that could imagine he thought about me that way. I'm just another worker to him. How could I have the vanity-fed audacity to think I amounted to more?

On August 19, 1992, just short of a year after I was hospitalized, I succumb to the pressure of doubt—my brain ignites and there's no way out, no time or will to pick up the phone. Choose, light, inhale. I've known for days where this one is going—my foot, to the side of my ankle, where I can throw a Band-Aid on it. Taking a drag to fire up the ember and then holding it to my skin allows my brain to bleed out in a state of perfect concentration. Bliss. Time at rest, the world comes to a stop in that familiar pinprick of pain-pleasure. I want to stay, maybe light and use a third cigarette to really do it right, make a twin for it, all the while resting in the interior of my mind, where an inky calm holds. Keeping the hand in place, breathing, listening. All the months of abstinence had me missing the trance of pain.

I stop at one solid burn. It doesn't really matter. I've risked everything this time. This isn't a tiny blister. I've executed a solid 3rd degree.

In the guilty calm of the aftermath I want badly not to tell on myself. I'll be in Dr. Kohl's office the next morning. If I confess he'll send me back to the hospital as he promised. The burn is a direct violation of the contract I signed when I returned from the hospital almost ten months ago. I can't disappear there again. I'm not sure I'd make it out this time.

Emotional chaos is my private little hell. I'm in it now. According to the Buddha, we are all burning from 11 kinds of physical pain and mental agony: lust, hatred, illusion, sickness, decay, death, worry, lamentation, pain (physical and mental), melancholy, and grief. This sounds about right.

Despite my devout atheism—or maybe because of it—I think about what humanity has imagined over the centuries as just retribution for human sins small and large. More often than not there's burning involved—even the gentle Buddha framed it that way. The ancient Zoroastrians believed hell was transitional but the final stage of escape from its miseries required three days of purification in a river of molten metal. Nice. The New and Old Testaments are full of burning bodies, like those described in Jeremiah 4:4: "Cleanse your minds and hearts, not just your bodies, or else my anger will burn you to a crisp because of all your sins." Whether it's Revelation's "lake of fire" or the Hindu notion of "great terrible hell" (*Maharaurava*), with its thirty-five thousand leagues where "the whole ground glows like a burst of lightning and radiates heat in a way that is intensely painful to the sight, touch, and other senses," all the heat and pain in the literature reflect the extraordinarily broad figurative and symbolic power of fire.

But that's not all. According to the Koran's extensive treatment of hell, those outside the blessed fold of Islam will be burned in hellfire eternally, "Their torment shall not be lightened nor shall they be helped" (2:86) and "the Fire will burn their faces and they will grin therein, their lips displaced" (23:104). The gory details of heat, flame, and burning in this last passage and countless others can't be divorced from all the nonliterary witches, heretics, criminals, and vulnerable racial minorities who have faced infernos of sticks and straw.

Fire has always been the most expedient and thorough means of purification through a process Ray Bradbury, in *Fahrenheit 451*, identifies as watching "things eaten, blackened and *changed*." Have I tapped into an iconic desire to punish myself in this particular way or are cigarettes just handy and the burns they make dramatic? "Eaten, blackened and changed . . . " The words echo. Haven't I done enough? Is there an end or will this attraction to a ritual purification I can't quite fathom be with me forever?

That night I draw my foot up, ripping off the Band-Aid. The burn has formed a neat, perfectly circular crater now crusted white, its center deep in the flesh beyond layers of skin that failed to protect me. At any temperature higher than 111 degrees F (44 degrees C) protein begins to break down, quickly losing its three-dimensional shape. Since the cherry on a cigarette burns at between 878 degrees and 1,472 degrees F (470 degrees and 800 degrees C), direct contact with human skin rapidly results in cell and tissue damage. Higher temperatures simply mean the shapes change faster, eventually losing any semblance of protein as the dominant molecules of oxygen, carbon, nitrogen, hydrogen, phosphorus, and calcium fuel the flame. Perhaps that's another reason burning is frequently deployed as a means of torture and punishment. Heat is efficient and the mess is minimal. If you burn a body all that's left after a good hot fire are particles of bone, easily ignored in the ash pit until a stray dog discovers them.

The hole I've made in my foot elicits no emotion. My body serves at the pleasure of my mind, "disembodied, unconscious of flesh or feeling," as T. E. Lawrence writes in *Seven Pillars of Wisdom*, a book I love. I perceive all bodies as he does, "with some hostility, with a contemptuous sense that they reached their highest purpose, not as vehicles of the spirit, but when, dissolved, their elements served to manure a field."

I could pretend the burn never happened . . .

At my session the next morning I play verbal dodgeball with Dr. Kohl. I cannot tell.

But the obvious truth on my foot bothers me all day. Burdened by the compulsion to have nothing hidden between us, I can't keep this from Dr. Kohl, no matter what it costs me. Without the truth, without the whole deplorable story, I risk cheapening the emotions that make his attachment to me worthwhile. If he doesn't know everything I can't be certain of the authenticity of his reactions and words. If I lie or pretend, my relationship with Dr. Kohl will be as compromised and artificial as my relationships with everyone else.

It wouldn't have happened if I could hold on to him longer than the bag of Jelly Bellies I chew and suck over Ishiguro's

The Remains of the Day. Lemon. Tangerine. Lime. Green Apple. Raspberry. Grape. Lemon Lime. Island Punch. Orange. Pink Grapefruit. If I could prevent his shadow from shifting to the fringes of my consciousness the minute I walk out his door maybe I wouldn't have burned this hole in my foot. As it is I pass out of his presence just as I always do, with too much to manage alone; the good feelings escaping like a scent in winter while the bad ones, the ugly stuff, fall and crack open on the pavement, untenable without him to manage them.

Two days later. It's time to say it.

"I burned my foot last week, before the last session." I'm so nervous my hands sweat while my core flexes tight as a jungle snake ready for a kill. How could I discard him, risk the loss of him this way? All for one burn, thirty minutes max of postburn transcendence?

"And you didn't tell me? You paint pictures with words that aren't honest." I'm not sure what he means. Once again we go through the usual "I'm angry" "You're angry" routine. Lately, I can't decide if "angry" or "annoyed" is my least favorite word . . . it's close.

"I don't know myself outside of here. What you *really* are. I feel very confused. I just want to be taken care of. I'm angry with you, with everybody, yet I don't let anyone—"

"You want out of here," he says, interrupting me.

"I do and I don't." What an extraordinary thought.

"Your actions say you do."

I'm so beyond the limit of okay that I go ahead and say it. Like Nicole in *Tender Is the Night,* "I didn't care what he said" because "when I am very busy being mad I don't usually care what they say, not if I were a million girls."

"Right. Mine—yes, they are the actions of a person who wants to live alone, who trusts the 11s magic, who wants to hide in the desert. She definitely wants out of here."

"What did you think I would do when you told me?" he asks.

"Say 'Go to the hospital or you can't come here.' Now I feel like I can't come here anymore." Falling between the lines, I see what might have been. The tears come on hard. Banished. Ousted. All because I'm too weak to simply smoke my cigarette.

"My head says you should go to the hospital," Dr. Kohl says. "I feel like I'm on trial."

I know him. This is my communion; reprieve from impossible loss. I'm giddy but in no way emboldened. I have no doubt another lapse will seal my dread portion.

"Truth is," he writes to himself at the bottom of the page, "I feel responsible for what is happening to her. I can't pretend."

CHAPTER 42

Mamsy-Pamsy Parenting

Later that week I call for an extra session and spend time in the waiting room, just sitting where I feel safe and calm. Sometimes when I do that he calls me in between sessions with other patients to talk for five minutes. This makes me feel exceptional.

I tell him about my crush on Jay and the revelation of his secret girlfriend.

"I don't feel badly about Jay. It's like I dismiss it, get really hard, it creeps up later."

"All the bad feelings get put into the burn."

"Or onto the paper," I add.

"Do you bring any here?" he asks.

"I do. I will."

"Is there some concern on your part that I'm drifting away from you?" he asks.

"I was feeling life was impossible. Burning is *hopelessness*," is my nonanswer to his question.

"And why not tell?"

"Fear of having to leave you. I was very afraid."

"Why didn't you call me?"

"It was out of the question. I just didn't call. It happened really fast."

"An act of denying it?"

"I felt alone, assaulted on all sides. My body doesn't even feel attached to me in many ways."

"Somebody else hurt it," he says.

"So I left it."

"You sound sexually or physically abused to me."

"I'll never know that."

Dr. Kohl calls me "an outsider with insider insights" at Sneakers, at King Street Youth, with my roommates, with my family, even with my sister. "She dances so well verbally as to befuddle the people around her and maintain her aloneness," he writes in my chart. And yet, he observes, "She wins all the arguments by not having them; gets all she wants by not asking for it (or them)." Most people don't notice any of this and I'm disdainful of their failure to see through me.

"The way people respond to me is inconsistent with how I feel about myself," I tell him. "People are nice to me. If only they knew, they'd hate me. They're fools. I'm defiled. Born evil and different. There's evil in me that's tied with the 11s, secret. Makes the outside seem very far away and ghostlike. Left side is to burn right side, I'm a lefty after all. Right is foreign, not mine."

But the burns have made the right more mine; the burns are all wrapped up in the complicated effort to placate the 11s. Maybe I really do want to burn away something bad inside me. Historically, one way to get rid of the evil in a "witch" was to burn her alive. Just ask the Puritans—or Hansel and Gretel. By

destroying the vessel, the demonic spirit within is also elimi-
nated. Burning books has a similar effect; it rids the world of
the evil *in* the object while destroying the offending object itself.

"I need you working on what's going on here instead of splitting," he says a month later, in early September. A big chunk of
that work entails making an end of brief bouts of hating him
overlaid with a love that borders on idolatry. I fail to see him as
a normal, fallible human. I've turned him into a cartoon.

In a note to himself he writes, "I'm feeling frustrated with
her active way of staying separate, except here." Why bring him
off his cloud? His power to fix me, if he only would, depends on
this fantasy. Failing to accommodate nuance in him or just about
anyone else—including myself—brings out my most unforgiv-
ing impulses. It's me at my worst.

"Sad, angry, in my miserable little hole," is how I describe my
state without him. I'm reading, eating tons of candy, feeling weird
on Zoloft, and smoking, as he says, "like an alcoholic tending bar."

"I've been miserable all week," I tell him. "I would have
slept forever. Held a cigarette near my arm. Heat felt very good.
It's like I want to go to the hospital, leave my life."

In October when my mother visits, my most obvious symptoms
are briefly in check—burning, vomiting. Stubborn depression
combined with the frustration of my unrequited attachment to
him makes for lax progress. Not being "in crisis" every single
day over suicidal fantasies, vomiting, and burning leaves space
to talk about other things, to work on building a sense of justice
I can apply beyond the extraordinary space of his office.

I've arranged for two sessions with my mother. My defenses are keen. As Dr. Kohl points out, "Mother's arrival brings up boundary between feelings, thought, speech, and action. Afraid of herself." It's not a social visit. On Dr. Kohl's advice the first I see of her is in the waiting room at 112 Church Street.

"I'm glad Cree has found someone to help her. To talk to," she begins, turning to me. "I know it's difficult for you to see me."

"Why do you think it's difficult?" I ask.

"I make you angry, have made you angry," she says. Shifting to the burning, she says, "I know when it happened after one phone call. I had a huge argument with Nicole for trashing my apartment."

I'm astonished: she thinks burning myself was precipitated by an interaction with her.

"That had little to do with burning. I was angry but felt good, I told you that you weren't being fair to Nicole." My mother is nervous. A shrink's office is not her territory. "I try to keep myself from you in a lot of ways. You tainted me, I couldn't be myself," I tell her, my way of explaining why being around her is difficult.

"Are you angry I left your father for a lesbian lover?" Of course I was angry—I was outraged and confused at the time, but it's ancient history now. That's not what this is about.

"I mean our closeness before, in Aspen," I say, changing the subject back.

"We were close with riding and on pack trips," she admits.

"I feel a lack of meaningful experience, I gave myself away, you wanted something from me for some other reason," I explain.

"That's too abstract for me." She's not digging in that pile.

"Buddy," I say. She used to call me her "Little Buddy." It has become shorthand between Dr. Kohl and me for the imbalanced relationship between us. I was not a daughter to her—I was her adult caretaker and partner in crime. Dr. Kohl has suggested that my discomfort with this role has led me to devalue this adult, responsible part of me.

"I don't understand how you live your life. There's something empty. A lack of respect for the way you choose to live is scary to me. I wouldn't trust what came out of it," I say, referring to her alcoholism.

"At the time I didn't realize it was wrong, it was my way. I drank a lot and relied on you. Often when I was drinking you helped me: catch planes, I'd drink in the airport." Turning to Dr. Kohl, she says, almost as if she's proud, "She took care of me, got me to the plane on time. I drank a huge amount more in Aspen than I do now. I drank while pregnant with both daughters."

"Not fair," says Dr. Kohl.

She blows by that. "I'm still drinking, I feel in control of my drinking. I drink a lot less, I don't offend anyone. I used to drink until drunk; I don't anymore. I enjoy alcohol."

Looking her in the eye, I say, "I enjoy burning my arm."

The next day is no prettier. When her abandonment of my sister and me in high school comes up, Dr. Kohl writes in my chart, "Mother stated it was 'usual' and 'natural' to leave two young children to raise themselves."

When her drinking comes up again, she says, "At age 55 you don't think I'm entitled to do what I want?"

Of course she is. But I tell her very plainly what she'll get in return from me. "I can smile, be pleasant, some of it is genuine." But, I say, "That's all there is."

"I can't change," she says. I know it's true. "I want you to be my daughter." I pity her but I'm not taking her up on a soft reconciliation so familiar for its absence of thought, work, or sacrifice on her part. I recognize her bald unwillingness to change and what it has cost me—and her.

"You haven't earned it. Not listening to me, seeing me through your own shit. You have no idea who I am." I finish by telling her, "I was good at giving you whatever you needed in the past and I'm trying to change."

Dr. Kohl writes in his notes, "Both acknowledge feeling sick." Gutted is more like it.

After my mother leaves, Dr. Kohl suggests that she is mentally ill, not just an alcoholic. I have no doubt she's been depressed and deeply anxious all her life; more than that I don't know. I need to wash her off; the poison of her "I can't change" despair feels lethal.

"It's as if your mother's evil is inside you," he says.

"That disgusts me. Makes me want to kill myself to be like her." That she's chosen to be drunk rather than take care of me my whole life has repeatedly blotted out my worth—the sense I could possibly deserve the space, resources, and oxygen I take up.

I'm falling down the rabbit hole of his dreamy world, salty tears my medium—"'I wish I hadn't cried so much!' said Alice, as she swam about, trying to find her way out. 'I shall be punished for it now, I suppose, by being drowned in my own tears!'" It was a rational fear, as it turned out.

"You wandered in here with Matthew and got hooked on a new you. You're afraid to lose me but not motivated to change," Dr. Kohl says not long after my mother's visit, accusing me of not working hard enough. It's unusual.

"It's hard to be motivated when I'm sad." There's no pity or I've already spent my share.

"This can't be a vacation," Dr. Kohl says. "It's a real opportunity to change your life." He never says things like this to me.

If I'm a legitimate object of treatment with the aim of psychic metamorphosis it isn't for want of trying that I'm confused. Quite the opposite. But I'm too far gone. Letting up leaves me half drowned in that terrible salty pool with the Mouse, Duck, Dodo, Lory, and Eaglet. I've thrown open the possibilities of who I am and where I've been. Fevered, changeable, and unpredictable as I am, dangerous as it is, transforming enchants me; I won't leave it alone.

"Do I play with my life or engage it?" I ask him. What sort of person am I? Do I get to decide and if so, how? I wish I could just do it . . .

I'm less stable than ever before as my dependence on this quasi-father figure long ago mauled my defenses—all that tough bravado that once served me so well. The conscious mantra I've long applied to virtually everything that hasn't come easily: Work harder. Be tough. Pull it together. Don't be lazy. None of it stands a chance against what feels like a stream of incipient madness and a hopelessness that makes me think of dying the way I obsess over which carton of milk to choose. I've tried many times to dismiss anxiety or con myself out of depression.

At fourteen I wrote, "What do I fear? Is it that something is acutely wrong—yes—and suddenly it overtakes my mind and the ugliness and distortion that I see terrify me." At seventeen I knew I was just hanging on when I asked myself, "What am I doing sitting here alone? What's wrong? Is this a phase or am I destined to be alone like this? If I am I don't think I can bear it." I then added, "I can't stand the thought of this being my life."

Ten years later and I'm afraid death might get me. I don't know how to defend myself from despair if I can't just tough it out, put all the shit I don't want to think about away. Bury myself. It's dangerous to nudge aside the loathsome Archie Bunker parent: "Meathead!" "Why don't you just shut up?" "Just gimme a beer."

Dr. Kohl suggests I could use more of what Archie would call "mamsy-pamsy parenting." In other words, what I keep going back to is a harder, meaner disciplinarian—a role I've pretty effectively filled as I raised myself. Now, if I'm ever going to change I need its opposite, forgiveness, along with basic human contact. It all looks so easy on paper.

I have to try something different if I want to change the uneven lens through which I've experienced myself for the past decade and a half. My natural instinct to force myself into it with the 11s at my side is just more of the same. How, then, is it to be done? What else do I have but hard work and a steely will? What remains for me is more ambitious than all that—terrifying and entirely untried.

CHAPTER 43

Pocket Trick

In brief flashes beyond Dr. Kohl's office I'm beginning to locate a semblance of the tolerable stranger he sees in me. This benevolent self comes and goes as if I have poor radio reception, cutting out unexpectedly only to flare into fresh song. Nothing feels better than the stasis of feeling content in the present. Just breathe. I'm learning to stay in this place when I read in the bath, soaking quietly in full awareness of my extraordinary existence, of opportunities, possibilities, and surprises. In these moments the comforts of hot water, silky bubbles, neat letters, strings of words and bound books are enough. If only I can hold on to a little gratitude.

Even if I don't carry away much, as autumn wears on the sessions begin to steady me. In between I dream of living alone again someday, finding a better job, going to grad school, reading books I've never heard of. I'm working hard to remain present, embodied in and out of his office. I do my best to coolly analyze my mind when nothing feels right, beautiful, or worth the effort. Dr. Kohl recognizes this hopelessness sprouting from me before I do. He then talks me back to clarity and desire.

Depression can feel like pure hatred or terrible emptiness. It returns as predictably as a book briefly closed flips magically open to the page last read. I recognize the signs in my unwillingness to meet anyone's eye, touch what a stranger's touched, answer the phone, or make plans. I'm counting everything, looking for the numbers, choosing one object from seemingly identical objects—a pencil, a box of cereal, a Zoloft tablet, apples in the produce aisle . . . the list goes on. But doing it more often and putting more at stake in making the "right" choice signals the decline. I'm in deep when the decision isn't in my control, when seeking oblivion in any form starts to feel inevitable. Food. Pain-pleasure. Sleep. Dreaming of dying . . . the bidding never ceases.

Dr. Kohl says, "I'm committed to giving the courage in our relationship." I wonder if this means I can keep siphoning his off forever. I have none to spare. His words give me hope. Courage. Yes, I'll borrow his.

Sitting by the phone in my room in the oversize Victorian house I share with my dreaded roommates, I stare at my cigarette burning down, keeping time for me fair and even as no other measure. I could punch the buttons. I could listen to see if he can make something of me. Again. Before I can't anymore. So often I need more than I can make here with tea, a smoking cigarette, a cat, and a room full of clothes, shoes, and books.

When I do pick up the phone to call him, the sound of his voice washes away the fury, smoothing out the tousled thoughts. My longing spills over as I say, "You don't belong to me. I belong to no one." There is no denying this but he can and does understand and listen. That's enough. His kindness and composure blunt the painful need, weakening the conviction of my worthlessness while diluting the valence of 11s. It works until I can sleep, until the clock flicks 11 to remind me who's really in charge. They're often the best I can do to feel connected. It's a laughable system of measuring oneself—how frequently the numbers find me, signaling they're with me—good or bad. I imagine the feeling I have might be close to what it is to be truly devout. I'm Calvinist; right action is the only way to salvation even if it may not save me. I'm not crazy, I'm absurd.

The outline of Dr. Kohl remains limited by his professional stance. What I know best is the sound of his voice, favorite phrases, pet peeves, infallible memory, humor, intelligence, and the fragile gifts of humility I've learned to take on board but can never repay. I know the sight and smell of his fast, expensive car, the comfort and warmth of his tasteful office, the neutral waiting room, the blue Smith-Corona typewriter, and the lovely noise his receptionist makes as she taps away at it. I know he lives south of Burlington in the town of Charlotte with his independently wealthy wife and two grown sons who, judging from brief glowing mentions, he loves and is proud of beyond measure.

I know he hopes I'll go to grad school, get married some-day, and have children. I know he worries I'll end up alone, an alcoholic, an addict, or dead long before the good things he wants for me can catch up. I know the flaws he sees in me and always reminds me to be conscious of: how sensitive I am to rejection; how angry I get deep in; how I endlessly question authenticity; how much I hate sadness and all the things I'll do to avoid it. He worries about what I will tell my children when they see the scars on my arm. He recognizes my strange attachment to destroying myself that might never go away, but by saying it, knowing it together, we weaken its valence ever so slightly.

When I say, "My life feels really useless to me," he takes the statement more seriously than I do. However confused I might be, there isn't all fake and all authentic, mean or kind, worthless or valuable. I am not divided in two but too often I get confused about what is what—I live in two realities but they're of my making. Developing and walking around with a false/bad and real/good self makes the parts of me and their corresponding worlds opposites by definition. As the famous psychoanalyst D. W. Winnicott notes, "No human being is free from the strain of relating inner and outer reality." Failing to do so results in psychosis. I can only pray I don't have that—but it certainly feels like it when objects are animated in ways I have no control over or when the silent magic rules my actions or when I mistake waking for dreaming or when my birthdate isn't 9/20/65 but 9 + 2 and 6 + 5, otherwise known as 11/11. Or that "Cree," when numbers are assigned to letters, is 3, 18, 5, 5 or 3 (hold the 1) + 8 = 11 and 5 + 5 plus the held 1 = 11, 11.

"It's either you or the crazy spirits. Both of them are a strand of you and I accept that," Dr. Kohl tells me one day.

This feels important, as if suddenly there's room for the magic *and* me. I don't have to execute, banish, or even try to stop dividing myself. It's—I am—all of a piece.

Although I continue to pack my already sizable arsenal with evidence of his indifference and the incompatibility of money, love, happiness, and all the fucking rules of therapy, I try keeping and tasting kindness. By sparing and applying to myself some of the limited empathy and compassion I once expended keeping people at a distance, I'm less resentful of human contact.

Pleasing, praising, reassuring, offering insights, and listening without actually exchanging anything leave me hollow. No wonder I want to be alone.

Dr. Kohl says, "You've spent your whole life trying to be a good person because you've been so certain, for so long, that you're not." Fighting to prove myself worthy is a thankless, exhausting task I've yet to learn to believe in, much less complete. Given my background and innate character, the idea that I come by my symptoms and behaviors honestly doesn't let me off the hook for who I am or what I've done. But it does thin my contempt with a spritz of compassion.

Delusions complicate the business of claiming an identity—and all delusions are really just the uncertainty of sticking to the agreed-upon version of reality. But as Breuer explained in the case of Anna O.:

> Nevertheless, though her two states were thus sharply separated, not only did the secondary state intrude into the first one, but—and this was at all events frequently true, and even when she was in a very bad condition—a clear-sighted and calm observer sat, as she put it, in a corner of her brain and looked on at all the mad business.

Like Anna, as Breuer describes her, I have a consciousness, stronger at certain moments than others, that keeps an eye on me.

"Tuck me in your back pocket," Dr. Kohl advises, to hold on to the good feelings.

When I try to bluff myself using this pocket trick I have limited success reconnecting to the feeling I have in his presence, where burning never seems like a good idea. But I keep practicing. There's nowhere good to go. I tried that: white walls filled with anonymous witnesses made the hours pass too easily. Henry James knew the feeling, describing Isabel Archer sitting "in her corner, so motionless, so passive, simply with the sense of being carried, so detached from hope and regret, that if her spirit was haunted with sudden pictures, it might have been the spirit disembarrassed of the flesh." The quiet release of disappearing to a hospital tempts me still.

"We're back to the painful loneliness," he says when I question the possibility that I *can* change.

When I wonder where my thoughts begin and end, the bit doing the observing tries to locate a center. It's liquid. Who I am is far from fixed but I'm learning to remember to look for it. To experience sadness is to approach the rabbit hole and when I edge too close the fear kicks in and I think less rationally. That's when I convince myself that a remote part of me has the real control, whether it's my crazy obsession with 11s or the sobering fact that I never quite know how I'll feel when I wake up in the morning or if by noon I'll wish I were dead. Maybe by getting used to this unevenness, by tracing it to its source, I can edge closer to normal—whatever that might feel like.

CHAPTER 44

Lights On, Rats Out

"She's confused about the caregiving and sexuality of Rx [treatment]," he writes in a note to himself.

Of course I am! That's the idea, isn't it? Even if the love for him isn't meant to find expression between us, it's a sketchy outline for a relationship that will eventually, if we can do this right, be full of all the texture of touch, shared experience, mutual understanding, and commitment I want so badly to feel now with and for him. He does his job by striking a precarious balance between my feelings for him and how he positions himself in relation to me.

In August he wrote in my file:

Countertransference time: Is my concern about violating therapeutic neutrality of us being sexual (that being destructive in the long run) a burden of "us," (I'm eager to be relieved by her working on forming her sexuality in other relationship), or just a "figment" of my fears projected onto her. Develop this with her. 1. Therapy is an aloneness. 2. ☿ 3. Possibilities—the "object."

He was putting his training into practice, checking the possibility that to avoid the hint of sexual contamination in treatment coming from him he might be subconsciously distancing me more than was fair, appropriate, or beneficial to me. By sedulously avoiding bringing his own sexual feelings into the mix (even if he wants to be rid of me, I guess he's human), he was concerned he might be overcompensating by pushing me away too forcefully. He was eager, as he readily admits, to be relieved of my erotic transference. It's complicated. I don't doubt he's been doing his best to get it right—if there is such a thing. He's rigorously policing his emotional response to me, alert to his own potential for transgressing the therapeutic boundaries. The idea that he might be overcompensating to avoid such a transgression seems to be nagging him.

Even when I've tried to seduce him by dressing up, flirting, being witty, or explicitly stating my desire, I doubt I posed a real danger to Dr. Kohl. Even were these veiled offers coming from someone more enticing, he's likely never been in danger from these simple ploys. What Freud calls "crudely sensual desires" are "more likely to repel and will call for the doctor's tolerance." This is borne out in his note to himself regarding countertransference; it reveals more weariness with the situation than a valiant struggle to resist my fabulous allure. Not surprisingly, part of him is "eager to be relieved" of the burden of my desire and its continual pressure on him to "violate therapeutic neutrality" by bringing any latent or overt sexual feeling into the mix. No, the real danger is in what Freud called "a woman's subtler and aim-inhibited wishes which bring with them the danger of making a man forget his technique and his medical task for the sake of a fine experience."

Dr. Kohl has conceded to return my regard to a degree—I believe he has made me special, set me above his other patients, as I so wished he would. Has this created what Freud calls "a fine experience" for Dr. Kohl? Has Dr. Kohl chosen Freud's "middle course": accepting and returning the patient's fond feelings but withholding any physical expression of them? Freud writes, "My objection to this expedient is that psychoanalytical treatment is founded on truthfulness. In this fact lies a great part of its educative effect and its ethical value." To return the patient's feelings while knowing that it is a calculated half measure fails the honesty test. "Besides," as Freud notes, "the experiment of letting oneself go a little way in tender feelings for the patient is not without danger. Our control over ourselves is not so complete that we may not suddenly one day go further than we had intended."

I take Freud's meaning of "go further than we had intended" as warning against emotional and physical excesses. Perhaps, as Dr. Kohl's note suggests, he is overcompensating now for an earlier failure to keep the countertransference in check; maybe he once made errors, sending me signals that he was attracted to me or available sexually. Maybe the craziness that's practically strangled me with desire for him isn't all my doing but actually *our* doing. After all, you can't have transference without countertransference. Given all the ways he has tried to make me feel connected, secure, and attached over the years, it's practically inevitable that at some point he miscommunicated or maybe even simply communicated a sexual response I picked up.

If his countertransference hasn't been as regulated as it might have been, then what I've experienced as the therapeutic relationship's seemingly one-sided intimacy hasn't been entirely my doing. And yet, despite the resistance to be read into my transference—falling in love being my way of diverting attention from the real work at hand—Dr. Kohl did succeed in allowing my longing for him to persist. This, as Freud notes, is the only way, short of stopping treatment, to impel the treatment forward, to get past the resistance.

"Maybe I make too good a mother because not only do you feel taken care of here, you feel sexual feelings here," he suggests.

"Oh . . . oh?" is all I can say.

The psychoanalyst H. W. Loewald writes that the therapeutic process helps "to lift unconscious processes onto a new level of integration" so over time they can be consciously attended to—"to turn our ghosts into ancestors." It's one of the most basic Freudian principles. The material I've been digging up and rooting around in at 112 Church Street over the years may have been preverbal or simply part of a narrative that, though unremembered and unconscious, has integrated itself into who I am and why I react to the world the way I do.

One ungainly piece I've been gluing together is my natural impulse toward masochism. It's a pervasive part of me, right at the core, imprinted there from my baby days of comforting myself with vague sexual humiliation, from walking mile upon mile in subzero temperatures with my sister, from competitive cross-country skiing kilometer upon kilometer, from lengthy bouts of self-imposed isolation, and, most spectacularly, from holding cigarettes to my skin until every nerve dies and the pain and the pleasure have had their way with me.

A core dynamic attracts me to self-punishment, humiliation, and destruction as a means to power and safety. Maybe
that, too, explains why I've helped create such an impossible
situation with Dr. Kohl. I've enjoyed the denial, which, as Freud
knew, only fueled the transference love.

More disturbing than the idea that I seek humiliation through
rejection is the possibility that I harbor a masochistic desire to submit to Dr. Kohl sexually, what Kernberg calls the "price to pay" for
his "love and protection." This might be what Dr. Kohl is referring
to when he notes to himself my "willingness to sell myself down
the river for a smidgen of affection." And yet, the causes and
effects of what passes between us, in my mind and in Dr. Kohl's,
are overdetermined—there can be no single, no right answer.

I've never doubted the integrity of Dr. Kohl's effort to instill
hope and compassion in me and to direct my desire for him out-
ward. He has expressed its importance repeatedly, most recently
by telling me, "I am really worried you will end up so cemented
to me as to become cynical about intimacy." In his effort to pry
me loose he's been up against my will to self-destruct, the gamble
I undertook to at once keep him close and keep parts of myself
separate from him. He has been to me what Kernberg calls "an
unconsciously hated or envied helping figure." Burning has
served "the purpose of 'triumphing' over the envied object," or
at least it felt as if it served that purpose when I pressed cigarettes to my skin.

As Dr. Kohl sticks with me, remaining consistent in his
care, determined not to abandon me, he may have experienced
what Kernberg describes as "phases of almost masochistic sub-
mission" to my demands, along with "disproportionate doubts"
in his own abilities. I think he doubted himself at times, as is

evidenced in part by his comment that he felt "responsible" for the final posthospital burn.

Whatever he felt for me amid the messy mix of paternal, professional, and sexual impulses, he has passed every test I put to him. However much he has done for me—and it's more than I can measure—his greatest gift has been the essential experience of mattering to him. This is the magic I've felt in his presence and the experience of it transcends any of the negative effects the relationship has had on me. By burning and vomiting I may have trivialized the real essence of my struggle to find meaning in my life, but he didn't let that get in the way of the real work of imparting faith, hope, and a sense I could control my future. That's what mattered. If my erotic transference and burning have gotten in the way—if their expression is a decoy for raw pain and the far more shameful need to simply be loved and cared for—he has passed through the obstacles of our entanglement.

I think back to a pre-hospital session with him when he said my effort to get myself together, my promise not to leave or die, was "just the old you trying to give me presents." At the time he said, "It doesn't work that way." What I didn't understand then comes to me now: I need to give myself that present. I need to promise myself to live.

He's an example of human behavior, compassion, and steadiness I can aspire to even if I still, perversely, long to possess him in his entirety. If more or less putting me in the hospital was based on his fantasy of a "life-threatening infection" rather than the reality of one, if our bargain was a strange one with its "if I go to the hospital then the prize I get is him" logic, I don't care. Maybe he did what he did, struck that bargain, because, as Kernberg writes, we were "interlocked in a stable, insoluble, transference-countertransference bind" that could end only in a place where "the transference acting out" (burning) could be controlled (the hospital). I have no regrets, even though part of my identity now includes a stint in a psychiatric hospital. I'm now forever inside the crude line drawn around the "mentally ill." The line demarcates those inside from those outside who remain within the norm. The history carries considerable baggage. Being locked up taught me it's entirely up to me to get on with life—or not. It's a choice I make again and again but one I'd undervalued, never quite recognizing it as a true choice that belongs entirely to me.

Dr. Kohl assures me again, "I don't take it for granted that you're alive."

Not rationalizing or not acting on self-destructive desires, resisting them no matter what the reason has slowly built my self-determination. It's time to locate the most forgiving, kind, gentle threads I possess and press them to my skin. It's time to act as humble as I feel. I've been learning to manage anxiety, rage, sadness, and even lust by writing, reading, drawing, walking, and talking to people outside 112 Church Street. I want badly to burn myself and I think about it every day, many times a day. The inescapable agency of being spreads slow and splotchy as lichen on granite, but it's there. I've tapped what he sees in me. It's a version of myself that sneaks up on me when I'm effortlessly kind or generous, grab hold of an exciting idea, finish a book I can't believe I've never read, or write a sentence I admire. I'm trying to trust my senses and breathe slowly. I see flashes of peaceful attentiveness delivering the understated rewards I'm trying to hold on to. I want to cool my brain. Rather than burning away the pressure, I dream of dabbing Tiger Balm there, the mentholated icy ointment soothing away the combustion.

As exhausted as I am by month upon month of rules; the endless internal turbulence; the routine of sleep, therapy, and waitressing, I want to make enough noise to chase away the false expectations, memories, lies, secrets, and illusions—now, here, when I can briefly see them for what they are. Whatever has been scurrying around in the dark too long, blighting every pleasure with doubt, poisoning assurances of present and future happiness—it needs to go. Lights on, rats out. It's finally time to assess what I'm left with in the absence of secrets known and unknowable while taking care to guard the switch to keep the cruelty, cowardice, weakness, fear, sadness, and arrogance that put me in this unholy mess from slinking back in the minute it goes dark again. Because it will. Every one of my habits of mind will return, but while briefly cowed by the light I have a chance, maybe, of figuring out where I belong, what I want, and how to forgive myself.

Too bad rat urine is so loaded with information. The markings rodents leave wherever they've been are a form of communication. Maybe that's why the struggle to come clean and learn to hold happiness never ends; all the residue of sadness and self-loathing remains behind. Where there's an infestation, a black light reveals markings on nearly every surface; to get rid of it you practically have to burn the house down. Even when the rats scurry away from bright light to protect their big, sensitive pupils from the glare, even when you can't see them, they're there in the walls, behind the baseboard, on the skin, just waiting to revisit all they wrote, to remember, read, and reread the past.

There's no escape. But "the rat has an excuse" for its failure to escape the past. As Hans Zinsser writes in *Rats, Lice and History*, "As far as we know, it does not appear to have developed a soul, or that intangible quality of justice, mercy, and reason that psychic evolution has bestowed upon man."

CHAPTER 45

Set It Alight

I walk into my October 29, 1992, session with a haircut (it was just a solid trim!) and he accuses me of self-destructing. I'm supposed to discuss these things before doing them. I justify.

"I guess I wanted immediate gratification. I wanted to change my hair—like for a date." The date gets lost in the fury over my defiance and his desire to hold me accountable. Testing him, annoying him, pushing his limits—I never tire of it.

"Are you not here today?" he asks at our next session. I'm distracted and evasive during that early 11/02/1992 appointment, unexpectedly pondering the man who's about to take my solitary mind and celibate body for an airing. "The date."

"I don't really know why I've agreed to go," I tell Dr. Kohl. I'm nervous. "Obligation. I'm a loner. I will live by myself as soon as I get out of therapy. I envision living alone for the rest of my life." I say this half to piss him off, half in truth.

So why am I going on a date? Is it possible for me to entwine my existence with someone else's, trading out the solitude that's the essence of who I am? What if I mix myself up and lose the pieces? I'm just learning to live and now I'm distracted by the possibility of pulling apart that hard-earned safety. Why would

I choose to give that up when I'm just becoming familiar with myself in a form I can (almost) recognize as me?

The date—Dwight—and I first met at Middlebury College. We were there at the same time, but it's chance, proximity, the happenstance of friends in common that transform a brief encounter nearly five years after graduation into a life I never believed in.

By the time he appears I'm still busy stashing piles of tainted cash for delivering myself up, along with hash and eggs Benedict, to the hungover morning crowd. House-sitting nearby, he comes in to do what defines him—read, write, eat, and drink. I pour his coffee; give him a menu; take his order; deliver eggs, breakfast meat, and toast. We exchange awkward small talk meant to make our lives look better than they are—thoughts of grad school, GREs, leaving Vermont. Of course I'm a waitress and he's already a writer, a journalist for the *Vermont Times*, the local alternative weekly. I've applied to grad school. Anyone can do that. It means nothing unless you get accepted. He has a career; I have sore feet.

We fill the silence with questions about our college friends RWR and Karen. I never entertain the possibility that this guy might be gauging me in any other way than the way you might gauge any waitress you're barely acquainted with—wishing your table wasn't in her section so you can proceed to do what you came to do in peaceful anonymity.

I never give him another thought until the next day when my coworker Rachael calls me from the restaurant to gush, "A boy who sounded cute called and left his number. Dwight, I think . . . " I'm surprised.

After three days of uncomfortable anticipation—the phone and I have a patchy history—I call. He'd left his work number so it's not he but a receptionist who picks up on the third ring. Biting a stray nail until the salty iron taste answers my tongue, I say his name. "He's on vacation for the next ten days," she says. "Can I take a message?"

A message? No. Definitely not a message. I'll be scattering no evidence of being played. No wait, do leave him a message, can you just write, "You're an asshole." Who but the most mean-spirited person leaves a number and a name for a girl to call and then goes off on vacation, knowing he won't be there for ten days? Maybe I'm just another figure to him, one of many he's fished for—I'm nothing.

Face burning, I replace the receiver, cursing the gullible part of me for falling for an obvious ploy. Fuck him and fuck you, too, phone. I fall for the thing every time. Days and days gone. More than a week passes before I lay out my humiliation, explaining to Dr. Kohl how he called and set me up.

A tad less paranoid than I am, Dr. Kohl practically demands I call again. It was, Dr. Kohl convinces me, likely a mistake. No malicious intent. An oversight. Why would I not call when he returned from vacation? I must call one more time. I suppose, given my success in remaining mostly solitary despite roommates, he's eager for me to venture into any new relationship. Maybe he thinks I'm ready. Maybe he thinks I deserve to have a boyfriend who offers more than Matt, more than fantasies of him. It's been almost a year since I walked back into his office after my months in exile at Sheppard Pratt. I wonder how different I am now and what, if anything, has really changed.

That afternoon I obediently pick up the receiver to punch in the numbers I've scrawled on the back of a notebook. The familiar sickening trepidation makes itself at home in my gut. I prepare for the assault. The humiliation of rejection will be on me again. I'm asking for it.

Once past reception with "Just a moment, I'll connect you," I soon have a kind, easy voice in my ear, nervous but warm enough to erase the dread. He needs to be brave. He has to ask. For a date? We set a time to meet at the bar where everyone goes to withstand this sort of thing: the Daily Planet, a hardworking room hot with people, noise, and friendly waitresses.

What to wear? I'm past thinking I'm the kind of girl who meets the right guy. This date is part of my training—living with roommates, trying to make friends, saying yes to padding out my minuscule social club—to be less alone. But it always matters what I wear. Not for him but to get me through. There are the shoes. The sweater. The pants. Each one is essential for the company it brings me, the way it will hold me up amid strangers because I know it's there with me. On my side.

My trusty pink Converse high-tops protected me from Sheppard Pratt's corridors, bathrooms, and cafeteria. The rubber, the canvas, and I bonded against them. The pink wool KIKIT cardigan sweater twins the shoes. It does more than match. The risky, unusual fringe of pom-poms on the sweater's hem cancels any remaining masculinity the boyish shoes might claim, transforming the outfit into what I'd like to think is a mix of girlish, sophisticated, funky, and posh. The set goes on, slim white cotton tank top beneath the sweater, sockless feet, familiar, comforting jeans—jeans that don't betray me by not fitting or by making me feel more cowish than I already feel. Even if I am on the much thinner side of "I can't live with myself," not too fat relative to fat, no matter how much I weigh I'm always FAT. The word has a presence that skips alongside my body, waiting for the right angle or the right thought to pop out and show itself.

Right now, I'm not letting it. I feel okay. Ready. I leave my room on the second floor, closing it tight, thinking how soon I can come back to lie on the bed in soft pajamas and finish *Tess of the d'Urbervilles*. It won't be long. Dates don't last. Duty. Obligation. I can't hide from this one now. It's done.

There, by the window, he sits at a table for two. He looks as kind and harmless as I wish I felt at my best. Nervous, I take the empty chair and order a beer. I ask if he minds if I smoke, thinking surely that will be the end of it—he'll be repulsed by the disgusting habit, ask me if I mind not smoking, ask me why I smoke. Rather than all that, his face opens as if he sees Lauren Bacall with a Gauloise, those eyes of hers waiting for Bogey to set it alight. This he does not do. Not being a smoker, he keeps talking as I huddle and light it myself. Burying my relief in the nicotine, I find my pace as I hold the burning object with one hand, my pint with the other. It's going to be all right. I can do this. I'm not looking for the way out. Not yet.

CHAPTER 46

Ugly but Interesting

We talk and listen without trying, not noticing the hour, TAG Heuer silent and well behaved. The deflective maneuver of asking too many questions comes to a draw—he's a pro at that game, a match for me. We tell and ask—neither of us doing all of one and none of the other. Outlasting the polite brevity allotted for "a drink" in date parlance, we order pints until late. He walks me the short distance to the door of my loathsome shared house, where I pull the covers up with a giddy glee, astonished at remaining so long aloft on Dr. Kohl–free warmth and pleasure. This one's mine. For once my book, abetted by the pleasant whirr of alcohol, won't have me. It doesn't really matter; not even Hardy can better the pleasure of replaying the memory of him.

Not many second dates involve a two-hour drive in a nine-year-old Volvo station wagon to a used bookstore but that's what we do. "Wanna go to Rutland?" is a roommate's transcription of a message Dwight leaves that morning. The note waits on the kitchen counter when I come down that morning looking for coffee. A piece of paper understated as a grocery list.

We're off. Talking as if we know each other. I embarrass myself by hiccuping half the way to Rutland. Perhaps he's bored, thinks I'm a freak, wishes he'd never asked me along. It doesn't feel that way but then my judgment can't be relied on. The wreck ahead comes from liking him too much, too soon. If I were capable of reason I'd stop now. Too bad emotional control remains no more than an enviable intellectual construct.

Tuttle Antiquarian Books, 160 years old, forty thousand books. We wander the paper warren, the diversion of the find consuming stray awkward moments. Our eyes on the spines, we pull, flip, and replace books the way people do when they know what they're after. He buys H. L. Mencken, Lionel Trilling, Paul Fussell, and John Updike; I buy Anthony Trollope, Henry James, and Jim Harrison. We load our booty into the car before buying sandwiches from a deli down the street. We walk past chain-link fences; once charming houses, their front porches piled with boxes and plastic toys; dog shit ground so far into the sidewalk it's nothing more than an ugly thought even in my mind. The bleak atmosphere of the gray working-class neighborhood grinds against the fragile pleasures of our picnic. We're new to each other. I'm conscious of my body and words, of the impression I think I'm making.

I say, "Yes" to dinner that night at his apartment. "Yes" to 7 P.M. I bring expensive dried dates and a bottle of half-decent red wine. Because that's what you do.

Between the soft eyes of his eight-week-old black-and-white Lab mutt Hank and the flawless salmon with asparagus he cooks and plates I don't stand a chance. As I take my portion I never even entertain the option of telling him I'm a vegetarian. Eat the fish.

We retreat to his room for dinner to avoid his roommate, swallowing forkfuls of rich fish the color of winter cantaloupe. While we are lying sideways facing each other on his big bed, my expectations slip out the back. Astonished by how much I like him, how safe I feel in his unassuming presence, I'm all his by the time he moves the empty plates aside to make room for four elbows and two slim books: Galway Kinnell's *When One Has Lived a Long Time Alone* and Sharon Olds's *The Father*. If I'd been less astonished at his offer to read me poetry I might have suspected a setup. But I'm not cynical, because he's anything but. The words unload their simple force on me, covering the accumulated sludge of remorse, regret, longing, self-pity—all of it. Obscured. I'm lighter and calmer; I'm almost here on the bed, dropping down from the ceiling, where I've been watching the scene. He gently asks about the scars on my arm. As I tell him, he reaches out to touch them. Nobody has ever done that before.

When he asks if he can kiss me, a question I wouldn't have believed could be asked earnestly in such circumstances, he says it with a seductive precision tuned to an internal monitor I didn't know I had. I answer "Yes" even if I'm not sure I say the word out loud. I don't need to. Leaning in does the work for me.

I guess you could say I fucked the first guy who offered me his coat and I married the first guy who asked if he could kiss me. I'm a sucker for good manners and even for standard boy ploys that probably work every time. The kiss. Eating dinner on the bed. Poetry. A puppy.

I know I want the first kiss and the next and the next even if I lack that enviable, smoldering Lauren Bacall confidence—to steal the first kiss and then reply, when I asked why I'd done it, "To see if I liked it." He's the arts editor at the local weekly and a stringer for the *Village Voice*—generally pretty hip and respectable work as Burlington, Vermont, goes. I'm a waitress at a popular hash joint with an uneven schedule of early mornings and free afternoons. He gives me a key to his apartment so I can hang out or walk the puppy when he's at work in the afternoon. Unlike me, he's dated a lot and had plenty of serious girlfriends. But none of them, it seems, were perfect. Perhaps, soon enough, I won't be perfect either? The puppy stays, I go.

I suspect I've found in Dwight what I've been looking for. What I look like—good or bad—has always reinforced the break between what I consider "me" and my damnable body. When it comes to men my physical self works as litmus paper to identify the frauds and users shallow enough to care about my appearance. I'd fall in love with someone who thought I was ugly but interesting. At least then I'd know he meant it. Although Dwight has given no indication he thinks I'm ugly, I don't get the sense that he cares all that much about what I look like. He seems to like me because I'm one of the few people he's met who has read more books than he has.

Never outside Dr. Kohl's office have I felt as safe, real, and adored. Never, even in the presence of Dr. Kohl, have I been this greedy for someone who seems to want just as much from me as I want from him. The fear in my gut eases.

I want to be with someone if this is how it feels and maybe, just maybe, the evidence of what I've come to think of myself over the past two years snores softly right there next to me in bed. Allowing myself this, choosing and being chosen, collides violently with my savage interior. It's hard to believe I'm touching such grace.

I don't really understand it thoroughly but I'm vulnerable to internalizing Dwight—in danger of becoming him by gobbling up an idealized version of the potent figure I've fallen for. As Dr. Kohl notes, in my world love is finite and if I'm going to have enough for Dwight I need to take it away from him. I'm using Dwight to supplant Dr. Kohl. I use both to erase my worthlessness.

"Is it him you like? Or the idea he likes you?" Dr. Kohl asks, very gently.

I'm certain it's both but I'm also not sure it's possible for me to separate the two entirely. The linear fixation on Dr. Kohl has wavered, leaving me foolish but not entirely sated. When I'm not there I scoot away from him hoping to leave my shame behind, nestling closer to Dwight, where I know I'm wanted. I've swapped one obsession for another.

We spend Thanksgiving together at a big farm east of Burlington with a group of his close friends. It's a classic Vermont farmhouse surrounded by muddy pastures still green as wet moss. Organic everything crowds together in clunky pottery dishes on the long barn wood buffet table. Apple pie makes our offering, overshadowed by praline pumpkin tart I can't forget.

Before Dwight my days were ever emptying out, demanding more and more of me—reading, writing, walking, waiting, working, thinking. Now the days take care of themselves.

"I don't go somewhere else in my head when I'm with him," I tell Dr. Kohl. Flushed, I can't taste my own mouth anymore. Lips raw from kissing stubble, I'm uncertain of wanting so much, but there's no angle out. It's strange. I can't find the bottom of him.

Even my massive insecurity, my fathomless doubts, can't get in the way of a thing so sure of itself. Why keep to our own beds when all that matters is contained by our mixed presence? We're a couple. We have sex and then watch a show on the tiny black-and-white TV by his bed. I locate my coffee mug, a glossy masculine mahogany, like nothing I would ever buy. It's all mine every morning while I sit watching him sleep. He lingers long, pulling the last warmth from the night before coming to.

Pruning our lives to suit the conditions of coupling, we begin by not spending another night apart until three weeks later, when he leaves for his sister's wedding in Naples, Florida. He wants me to come along but we both know it's too soon—even by our sloppy standards. I miss him the way I miss Dr. Kohl between sessions, as though I can't breathe until he's back with me.

I tell Dr. Kohl we spent an hour just kissing.

"I've never done that before." It's "Great. Strange. Scary. Wonderful," I say. I'm unfamiliar with Dwight's spirited, sensual lust for food, drink, books, music, movies—and even for me.

"All the demons have disappeared. Eating preoccupation is gone. Burning makes absolutely no sense right now." I'm not giving the Zoloft any credit. I can be around myself when I'm with him without a constant fight between sides.

I think back to the hospital, now a strange memory I keep tucked away, muffled and well hidden. It hides in my mind like an exotic vacation that's so different, so transformative, it can't find a place to fit in the ordinary memories that make up the past. Instead, it stays to the side, its own enclosed arctic zone, hard to get to, a little dangerous, best left alone. I shove it away—or try to. Is there a tinge of shame? Maybe. Being there was the ultimate proof of a dark history I'm not sure I want to carry around anymore. Self-destruction of such an explicit kind with permanent results falls into a disturbing category. It doesn't matter exactly what I was, am now, or will be in the future. At some point I was crazy enough to do what I've done to myself.

How enchanting would it be if falling in love fixed me, saved me, and solved my problems. More than ever it's on me to decide what I want—not what I think I should choose out of duty, guilt, need, or obligation; not what I should do because Dr. Kohl wants me to; and certainly not what I end up with by not actively choosing because no choice is a choice. This is a lesson I've finally learned. No. I've confessed and analyzed and suffered and endured to get to a point where I can be with myself at least most of the time without flirting with tasty oblivion.

But I love to fall in and I'm pretty good at it. To lose myself because I'm distracted or led in another direction—salmon, anyone?—would be the worst possible outcome. I think of this when I'm having what must be too much fun getting drunk with him at our favorite Mexican restaurant, going through baskets of chips and salsa, laughing too loud as we tell each stories for the first time.

The drinking is new or renewed since college. As a freshman I drank Popov vodka with my roommate Heather, and spring of junior year passed most quickly with me and my friend Karen drinking pint after pint as we dissected our postadolescent disappointment. Taking on the abandon of drunkenness again with Dwight after several years of hardly drinking risks blurring my cautious, carefully guarded self-consciousness.

The salt-rimmed margaritas on the rocks collide ever so predictably with Dr. Kohl's sober credo—he calls it "ominous."

"You have a problem with alcohol," he says.

"I don't have a problem with alcohol," I shoot back.

When I continue drinking he says, "You're going to be getting yourself a new psychiatrist. 1. It's malpractice. 2. It's harmful to you."

I tell him I'll stop but I don't. Drinking carries a hedonistic appeal Dwight identifies with my exotic childhood and what he frames as my badass, chain-smoking persona. There's an unhinged quality about me he finds exciting and dangerous. I'm taking it for a spin.

The treachery of commingling appears risky but inevitable. On 11/11/92 I'm five minutes late for my appointment with Dr. Kohl. It's precisely one year since I returned to his office after spending two months in the hospital. Over the course of three years of therapy I was rarely late, but since meeting Dwight I'm almost never on time.

"Why are you late?"

"No reason, I'm just late."

"Are you annoyed?" (At the word itself?)

"That you even exist, yes. At the past years of therapy, yes. My attachment to this place, how not of importance it's been. I don't know why I come now."

"Now that you have your favorite buddy," he says coolly, meaning Dwight. He's referencing my mother in the cruelest possible way.

I cringe at the idea that I'm playing cohort to or in any way taking care of Dwight, that I've become Dwight's desire, his toy. But I don't say that.

"Maybe," is all I can come up with.

"You have trouble experiencing attachment to more than one person at a time," he says.

"Yes."

"Like splitting me off."

"Yes."

"You lose," he says.

At the end of the session Dr. Kohl raises his voice: he's as angry as I've ever seen him.

"The opportunity to continue growing is being undermined by identifying yourself with Dwight. I warned you about doing that here."

I'm not listening.

Instead the absolutes of denial and abandon mix edges. Unruly as I feel, bathed in the endorphin-rich blood of being in love, I embrace the novelty of a coupled life. We spend Christmas together with my family at our "camp," a funky summer retreat in the Adirondacks that's been in the family for a hundred years or so. It sits right on the edge of Lake Pleasant, where the loons wake me at dawn, their unearthly cry coming not so much from the lake as from the heavy fog that covers it.

We arrive late and my aunt Sid, coming from Camden, Maine, has brought lobsters. The family—seven at table—have demolished theirs. The remains form a massive redolent heap of crushed claws, tails, legs, pinchers, and vertebrae. Our live lobsters, still blue-gray, are on hold. We join the table, my "new boyfriend" the focus of all eyes. Soon the dappled red crustaceans arrive whole, one to a plate, at which point I realize Dwight, who grew up in Florida, has no idea how to eat lobster. I almost step in to save him the humiliation of trying, but before I can he readily cops to his ignorance and instantly has the whole table in his pocket. Such a charmer.

On Christmas Eve we have furtive sex behind the thin walls separating the second-story bedrooms at camp, afterward exchanging gifts as I break every rule of the house by smoking in bed. I give him a Hamilton watch. It matters to me that he too keeps time.

The next weekend I leave the roommates I've resented for so long and move in with Dwight. It's 01/01/93. There's not much charm in the North End neighborhood where we live, but the place has plenty of windows and a screened-in porch where I contentedly smoke and read my days away. The apartment might be anywhere for all it matters to me. We inherit a long couch distinguished by its emerald-green cushions and ridiculous skirt. It's better than no couch. Empty wine bottles roll across the living room without so much as a nudge. The dressers and bed want half-inch shims.

From the start we'd shared toothbrushes as casually as we joined our debts and assets. Alphabetizing our books side-by-side on the shelf—*Austen scandalized to find herself next to Auster; Brontës confused by Burroughs; Cather sympathetic to Carver; Dickens alienated from DeLillo; Eliot failing to comprehend Ellison; Flaubert positioned in pained admiration of Faulkner; Gorky confused by Godot; Herodotus flummoxed by Hemingway; Ibsen intimidated by Ishiguro; James looking down on Jones; Kipling inspired by King; Lawrence cold to Lowry; Mann irritated by Mailer; Nabokov misreading Naipaul; Orwell pissing on Oates; Poe flummoxed by Pynchon; Rabelais stunned by Rushdie; Shakespeare gazing admiringly on Shakespeare; Tolstoy sympathetic to Thoreau; Updike in thrall over Updike; Verne peering cautiously at Vonnegut; Wharton scooting away from Welsh; and Zola happy to simply be Zola* on a shelf that isn't big enough for the rest of them.

I clinch this broad, risky engagement of styles and types—and the prettiest, most sparkly, magic ring I've ever seen. I've fitted my new, coupled life into a better fiction: 6/11/94. That's the date, of course, we're to be married.

CHAPTER 47

A Bigger, Wilder End

"There's a paradox about love that sells a part of you out."

It's dark in Vermont. Winter cold. Dr. Kohl's words hit a tender spot in spite of the layers I'm wearing. He's warned me from the beginning, cautioning me to take the relationship with Dwight slowly. But I'm engaged and living with Dwight. So much has changed, leaving too much to go back on if I choose to take his advice now. Am I supposed to make a choice between myself, Dr. Kohl, and Dwight? It feels like it—I have no idea how to hold on to all three.

As the haze of my infatuation fades to normal I'm feeling depersonalized again; split in two, with one part of me observing and the other participating. Framed in more positive terms, this might be seen as my conscious remove coming fully to life, once again.

"I'd like to work on not disappearing," I say in February.

"That's what you've been doing here."

"Disappearing from you?"

"Yes . . . "

I'm also splitting during sex, something I didn't use to have a name for but always did. That means it "feels like I'm in my mind, talking to myself inside my head. I go further away during orgasms; sense of lack of control, like with the 11s, a force."

He's still gnawing on sexual abuse.

"Abused children start off as objects," he says. If I'm separate from my body during sex, if I'm splitting body and mind, then I'm missing out on one of the most important elements of the act. Freud observed, "Sexual love is undoubtedly one of the chief things in life, and the union of mental and bodily satisfaction in the enjoyment of love is one of its culminating peaks." But I'm so used to going outside myself, I can't imagine not doing it during sex, just as I can't image not doing it when I go running. Isn't this simply maintaining a critical perspective?

That day he writes a note to himself: "Maybe the splitting has to do with something other than physical-sexual abuse. Her parents were interested in her saying what pleased them rather than how she really felt. Sex is a giving relationship: splits off there also: in giving to someone else what they want." He then adds, "Corollary: if she asks for what she wants, the 'giver' will split off and depersonalize as they give to her so she avoids that at all cost." This analysis has a certain ring of truth to it and yet I'm not convinced it matters, or if it matters I'm not sure I can change. Where my brain goes during sex isn't a problem I need to solve.

He notes in my chart the Zoloft has helped the depression but "Give it a chance for refractoriness, the depth of depression." In other words, he's not convinced by this sudden onset of happiness and now we're finally talking about it.

In April I tell him I've been really depressed. I've been with Dwight for six months.

"Thoughts of burning, suicide?" he asks.

"No," and then I pause. "Thoughts," I say, but "I have no interest. Life is good but I feel very shitty." I've been accepted at NYU and I'm "in love." Still. I can't hold on to joy—sometimes I'm not even sure I know what it feels like. Dwight has noticed I'm not myself, which is refreshing since most people don't notice, or if they do they don't say anything.

"I've been stuck in this my whole life. A few good days but the inevitable starts creeping back in." I'm worried that my withdrawal, anxiety, and sense of dislocation will make me a failure in grad school and infect, possibly spoil, my relationship with Dwight.

"I would be wary of stopping therapy and getting married in proximity. I've warned you about this before and I'm saying it again." He's serious but what can I do? I've reduced my appointments to once a week, a move he calls "leaving early," a way of "acting out" to protect myself from the pain of actually leaving him. He's trying to tell me attaching to Dwight as I have been doing is another way of ducking the real good-bye.

I've shifted my love, taking along as much of Dr. Kohl as I can contain. Maybe it's enough; maybe not.

As the sessions wind down, the impending June separation gets hold of me. Dwight and I are leaving for New York, and my treatment will be over soon. I arrange a visit.

"To bring Dwight in helps me take you with me." I'm working on keeping the two of them alive and present in my mind at the same time. On good days I tell Dr. Kohl, "I see the price I pay for checking out—both in therapy and with Dwight. I feel better," I say, "far less suicidal, happier, more directed. I'm not lonely." I'm not sure if I'm reassuring him or myself.

*   *   *

Leaving 112 Church Street and all the weight it carries holds
an unquestionable logic. My will and resilience can surely stick
long enough to get me out of Vermont, long enough for me to
become someone I don't already know.

Up next: a Ph.D. in New York City for me and a big-city
journalism career for Dwight. We're young and innocent. It'll
all work out. If it's not a perfect future because we have no
plan, it's as close as I've ever come to one. There's no money.
He doesn't have a job waiting in New York other than freelanc-
ing and my father isn't paying for grad school. We'll live on
student loans and sign for a shiny new credit card. Our shared
optimism and the security of mutual solidarity go far. The way
Dwight and I fit together is enough to breed reckless happiness
and varied, unexpected successes.

Just as Dr. Kohl warned, I'm blissfully forgetting where this
new infatuation begins and I end. Freud knew that "at the height
of being in love the boundary between ego and object threatens
to melt away." I've done this before—most notably beginning on
June 26, 1990, when I had my first session with Dr. Kohl. Free
reservoirs of once self-directed energy go to Dwight and to the
existence we're constructing with implausibly uncomplicated
enthusiasm. I've shed my good-girl restraint—the enclosed philosophy of a cautious, controlled existence I've breathed in at 112
Church Street all these years, along with layers of the behavior
designed to hold emotional chaos at bay. I feel caution fray even
as this Dionysian release explicitly rejects big chunks of the work
I've done with Dr. Kohl. I don't care. It's time to go.

I know holding a too-permeable consciousness apart doesn't come easily if at all. What once was Dr. Kohl's now belongs to Dwight. But being alone remains my favorite bad habit. By reading, writing, and spending time in a quiet room I can usually find my center.

On June 17 I can't entirely grasp I have just two sessions left.

"It's purely intellectual that I'm leaving. I'm not feeling it very much."

"You're splitting from the pain of separation from here and your parents." Yes, setting the painful part on a shelf to gather cobwebs while I go on with my life. I'm still really good at doing that.

"I want to be able to miss you." And I do. If I don't miss Dr. Kohl when I go I might not even know I've lost what I wanted to keep.

"You've worked really hard here," he says.

"I don't know if I had a choice."

"That's harder," he says with that sober look of his. He's showing a generosity I've come to rely on. The compliment—for that's what it is—feels so good it holds me to him for days.

June 21, 1993: my final session. He's found me a shrink in New York City and calls her during the session to "pass the baton." I don't speak to her but he tells her about me briefly and gives her my name. I don't plan on going to see her—at least not right away. But I have her number if I need her. He, as usual, has taken care of me.

After the phone call he offers me back the collage I made at the height of my pre-hospital crisis. It's papier-mâché, formed with strips of wedding announcements from the *New York Times*—smiling, perfect couples' faces and names glued together with flour and water. I've stuck a rotted, dried-out cherry with a long-dead worm emerging from its center on the surface next to a spaghetti stick figure of a baby. Abortion: 11/11/88. The whole is decorated with nature's ephemera—bits of flowers, lichen, moss, wood. It's no masterpiece. I've left it with him all this time because when I made it I was so afraid of dying. Giving it to him kept me safe. I wanted to believe I could never kill myself as long as he possessed the collage, so long as he kept that part of me with him.

"I think of the collage as having good parts from here, not cast-off parts of my mutilated self. It has this place in it. It's been well taken care of." I'm choking on the loss, fat tears flowing.

"You'd given up on that, you allowed it to happen here."

But, I say, "I won't have you to take care of me anymore." And with that childish plea the fear takes hold. I ask him to keep the collage—I'm afraid of the practically fluorescent glow of dangerous magic it still exudes.

The clock winds down—just as it has done for three years, ever since the first time the two of us sat together in this serene space whittling away at misshapen pieces. I want to stay forever. As always, it's never enough. But the next patient waits just outside the door and my 55 minutes are played. Rising from the brown leather chair for the last time to pick up my bag and the sweater heaped on top of it proceeds as in a dream. If I were fully present I would never leave—this is the only way out.

In the waiting room his receptionist is busy finishing making a copy of my file. Dr. Kohl offered it to me so I said, "Yes."

"You might want this someday," was all he said as he handed it to me. I feel that I'm taking a thing I don't have a right to. It's a familiar transaction by now—he's given me something I don't yet know I want or need.

I anticipate that at this moment of all others I might finally get the embrace I've yearned for. He doesn't offer it and I lack the courage to ask for it. I wish I were in command of myself enough at least to lean in and plant a deeply affectionate peck on his cheek. We shake hands for the second time ever. Maybe it's just as well.

The anticipatory pleasure of returning to 112 Church Street falls away, his face and voice forfeited with a cool shake of the hand. It's been everything to me. The loss seems impossible. I wander blind down College Street toward Lake Champlain. Unable to find a place to fit my grief, I gravitate toward the water. As I approach, its liquid brilliance reminds me of the February day just four months ago when the solidified gray-blue ice offered itself up, tempting me with its immaculate surface, formed in subzero temperatures without a hint of wind to spoil the thickening crust. I skated that day for six hours nonstop, moving over the frozen water without pause, Roxy Music blasting in my ears as I ventured with careless abandon toward the center of the lake, where the ice grew thinner. I sucked on the fear while reveling in the pleasure of physical exhaustion, a confusion of risky joy and wonder I could practically taste. I'd stolen bliss from the lake that day and it's mine again now, the ecstasy emerging from a pulpy reserve of memory to quiet my overbusy mind.

If I'm lucky and find a little grace I know there might be a bigger, wilder end not even I can guess at. The emotional gloaming that has long defined me refuses to release the day. I can live with it.

Rather than holding on to Dr. Kohl I stash his words: "As long as I'm alive we will know each other." The promise is his final gift to me. The words steady me, clinching a precarious belief in the present. I'm learning to breathe again, this time while wearing and almost liking, the feel of my own disfigured skin.

Acknowledgments

This book would not exist but for the efforts of the four most remarkable women I know. Different as they are, each one of them made *Lights On, Rats Out* possible; the absence of one would have been the loss of all. Elizabeth Gilbert's encouragement, friendship, and faith in my abilities enabled me to begin and continue writing. Sarah Chalfant of the Wylie Agency effortlessly grasped my purpose in the early stages, believed in the book, and guided me to shape the manuscript precisely in the right ways. I also have Sarah to thank for shepherding it into the gifted hands of Elisabeth Schmitz at Grove Atlantic. Elisabeth's tireless dedication to carving out the book's most viable form through many drafts made *Lights On, Rats Out* what it is today. Finally, my current psychiatrist's remarkable intelligence, humor, and perspective kept me going day after day. Her grasp of the book's most essential objective enriched every page.

I'm as grateful to my early readers Jonny Miles, Peter Gil-Sheridan, Erin Hanley, Angela Foster, and the indefatigable Valentina Rice as I am indebted to the individuals who make Grove Atlantic such an extraordinary house. I'd like to thank my copyeditor Lesly Levene and managing editor Julia Berner-Tobin for making me look better than I have a right to, the art and production team for magically making the look and feel of the finished book reflect its spirit and contents, Zachary Pace for his work on permissions, and above all Katie Raissian for her sparkling energy and dedicated work on the manuscript throughout. The people and institutions that provided much-needed solitude and the space to write include David Waldman and his kind staff at Rojo's in Lambertville, NJ, where I spent countless hours; the remarkable duo Harold Varmus and Constance Casey for more than once offering me (and my dog) their cozy cottage; my almost-cousin Scott Kraus for making me so welcome at "camp"; and everyone at the Ucross Foundation who made my stay there so memorable and productive. My two children sustained me and gave me the greatest joy throughout the process of writing this book. Finally, I am indebted to my husband, Dwight. Our instantaneous connection has only strengthened over the years. It is unbreakable. My love and gratitude are infinite.